PELICAN BOOKS

ENGLAND IN THE
SEVENTEENTH CENTURY

Maurice Ashley is the author of many books on
seventeenth-century English and European history.
Part of his life has been spent as a serious journalist
and part as a full-time historian. From 1958 until
1967 he was editor of the *Listener* and from 1967 to
1969 he was a Research Fellow at Loughborough
University of Technology. Educated at St Paul's
School, London, and New College, Oxford, where
he was a Scholar, he took a First Class in modern
history. While acting as historical research assistant
to Sir Winston Churchill, when he was engaged in
his *Life and Times of Marlborough*, Mr Ashley also
obtained his D.Phil. at Oxford for a thesis on
*Financial and Commercial Policy Under the Cromwellian
Protectorate*, reprinted with a new introduction in
1962. Before the war he was on the editorial staff,
first of the *Manchester Guardian* and then of *The
Times*. He is president of the Cromwell Association
in succession to the late Isaac Foot. During the
war he enlisted as a private in the Grenadier
Guards and ended as a major in the Intelligence
Corps. His books include *The Glorious Revolution of
1688*, *Life in Stuart England*, *Great Britain to 1688*,
The Greatness of Oliver Cromwell, *Cromwell's Generals*;
short studies of *Marlborough*, *Louis XIV and the
Greatness of France*, and *Oliver Cromwell and the Puritan
Revolution*; *The Golden Century: Europe 1598–1715* and
Charles II: the Man and the Statesman.

MAURICE ASHLEY

ENGLAND IN THE SEVENTEENTH CENTURY

PENGUIN BOOKS

Penguin Books Ltd, Harmondsworth, Middlesex, England
Penguin Books Inc., 7110 Ambassador Road, Baltimore, Maryland 21207, U.S.A.
Penguin Books Australia Ltd, Ringwood, Victoria, Australia

—

First published 1952
Second edition 1954
Reprinted 1956
Reprinted with revisions 1958, 1960
Third edition 1961
Reprinted 1962, 1963, 1965, 1966
Reprinted with revisions 1967
Reprinted 1968, 1970, 1971, 1972
Reprinted with revisions 1973

—

Copyright © Maurice Ashley, 1952, 1954, 1961, 1967

—

Made and printed in Great Britain
by Cox & Wyman Ltd,
London, Reading and Fakenham
Set in Monotype Baskerville

Introduction to Edition of 1973

This book was first published twenty years ago, but I have tried in revising it to keep it up to date in the light of modern knowledge. The tendency today is to lay stress upon socio-logical and economic factors in British history and to re-habilitate the underdog. No doubt if I were writing the book again, my presentation would be somewhat different, though I still believe in the value of chronological history. As it is, I have for this edition inserted at various points some of the very latest theories and I have carried the bibliography up to 1972.

Since my retirement from the British Broadcasting Corporation six years ago I have devoted most of my time to reading and writing about British history. Three of my books that have been published are *The Glorious Revolution of 1688* (revised for Panther in 1968); *Charles II: the Man and the Statesman* (1971); and *Cromwell and His World* (1972). These are books based on careful research and thus I am aware of the latest discoveries about seventeenth-century history, even though the output of books and articles on the subject is formidable. I should like to take this opportunity to express my gratitude to Professor Austin Woolrych and to Professor Ivan Roots for encouraging me to continue writing. I am also grateful to the doyen of English seventeenth-century historians, Sir George Clark, who was my supervisor at Oxford, and who was good enough recently to read and praise my book on Charles II.

In the first edition of this book I offered grateful thanks to my old teachers; now that I am getting old myself, I would like to pay admiring tribute to those younger scholars who have done so much lately to illuminate this fascinating century.

MAURICE ASHLEY

RUISLIP, JANUARY, 1973

CONTENTS

CHAPTER I

Prologue: The Road to England

KING JAMES VI of Scotland, whom one of his Presbyterian subjects had addressed as 'God's Silly Vassal' and a contemporary French statesman was to call 'the wisest fool in Christendom', left Edinburgh on 5 April 1603 for Westminster, to be crowned King of England in succession to Queen Elizabeth I. He had long been eager for this fine heritage – so eager that when his mother, the attractive but foolish Mary Stuart, Queen of Scots, exiled in a foreign land, had been faced with execution at the prayer of the English parliament, he had contented himself with restrained protests. After all he had owed nothing to his mother but his existence. She had connived at, or at any rate condoned, the murder of his father, Lord Darnley, and a few months after the crime, when James was just over a year old, had abdicated her throne; next year she fled her country. Since 1568, James had writhed under the tutelage of a turbulent nobility and militant Scottish clergy. At last, however, his course was set fair. He had in the end been acknowledged by Queen Elizabeth as her heir; 'Who should that be', she had murmured on her death-bed, 'but our cousin of Scotland?' Her Secretary of State, Robert Cecil, had astutely and secretly paved the way for him. The English peers and Privy Council had approved his claim to the throne, though it did not accord with the testament of Queen Elizabeth's father, King Henry VIII, who had been empowered by parliament to bestow the succession as he thought fit. Moreover the mass of James's new English subjects were satisfied that an authentic Protestant, descended directly from the elder daughter of the first Tudor ruler, should start a line of Stuart kings. 'If ever there was an act in which the nation was unanimous,' wrote a great historian, 'it was the

9

welcome with which the accession of the new sovereign was greeted.'

And King James himself was more than delighted that he had finally realized all his dreams. Now that he and his retinue had crossed the border, he need no longer fear the grip of the tough Scottish chieftains and elders who had long humiliated him even to the extent of kidnapping him as a boy and keeping him in captivity. In England a man might be king indeed. Was he perhaps not Lord Darnley's son? Might his title be questioned? Had he been treated in Scotland as a figurehead, a monarch who had to fight for the realities of power with all the cunning of an Italian princeling? All that did not seem to matter now. For he was the proclaimed – and would soon be the anointed – heir of the Tudor rulers who had defied Popes and Emperors and singed the beard of the King of Spain. By way of compensating himself for any uncertainty there might be about his right to succeed, he would draw attention to the absolute power of monarchs that flows from 'divine right', the doctrine that God alone makes and God alone breaks kings – even though he knew enough about men and affairs not to press absurd claims too far. When he reached London, fortified by the experience gained in the less congenial Lowlands, he could begin afresh as a ruler and a statesman.

The crowds of noblemen, gentlemen, and common people who flocked the roads to greet his progress south put him in good heart. He bestowed favours on all who entertained him, conferred numerous knighthoods, as later he was to create many peers, and once gave expression to the fires that burned within him when he commanded a thief to be hanged forthwith without trial. After he had moved down through the poorer and less populous northern counties, still not a placid nor wholly civilized portion of his new realm, his journey became lit with richer and warmer hues. Just before he came within reach of his goal, he spent two nights at the splendid mansion of Hinchingbrooke in Huntingdon, then owned by a gentleman named Sir Oliver Cromwell, whose four-year-old nephew and namesake was later to figure in the Stuart story. Loaded with Cromwell's gifts and with addresses from the University of Cambridge, King James now took the road to London. That the streets of the English capital were paved with gold, as James appears to have expected, might be doubtful – though assuredly it was already one of the largest and wealthiest cities in the world; what was certain then was that it was lined with plague. In the first of three terrible visitations of the bubonic plague that darkened the history of London in the seventeenth century, one in every ten perished. That spring the nights were disturbed by the groans of dying men, while bodies were smuggled out of houses to be buried in nameless graves. The new King was therefore advised to avoid the City on his way to Whitehall. But it would have taken more than the bubonic plague to put a damper on his spirits. He was rich, he was powerful, indeed he was absolute. How could he foresee that he would be the last English ruler to command the authority attained by King Henry VIII and Queen Elizabeth I? He might conceivably have recognized that the House of Commons, now filled with vigorous and ambitious country gentry, growing conscious of their political strength, would not tolerate from him the scoldings they had reluctantly taken from the old Queen, and would assert many new rights. But he could scarcely imagine that his son would follow his mother to the scaffold or that a little boy, who had perhaps caught a glimpse of him hunting around Hinchingbrooke, would become the hammer of the Stuarts. King James looked upon the promised land and found it good.

CHAPTER II

The Classes and the Masses

THE population of England and Wales at the beginning of the seventeenth century was over four million: by the end of the century it had risen to some five and a quarter million. London, a term usually taken to embrace the City proper and a number of suburbs lying outside the City walls, and also Westminster, had a population of more than 200,000 at the opening of the century; by the end of the century it increased to 400,000 – thus growing in numbers more than in proportion to the increase in population as a whole. Furthermore it has been estimated that towards the end of the century a million people, or one-fifth of the entire population, dwelt in the Thames valley or the immediate neighbourhood; Middlesex and Surrey were among the richest English counties, while the poorest were to be found in the north of England, where robbers and highwaymen abounded and travellers needed guides. Many contemporaries were perturbed at the growth of London and compared the country to a man suffering from the rickets with his head too big for his body. Certainly it was the supreme English town and one of the most impressive cities in Europe, especially after it had been rebuilt by Sir Christopher Wren towards the end of the century and King Louis XIV had diminished the prestige of Paris by removing his Court and Government to Versailles.

The rising importance of parliament enhanced the popularity of London; it was the home of busy tradesmen and merchants, of poets and painters, of beautiful women and witty and intelligent men. It was by far the largest port in the country and provided much employment; at the same time it contained abject poverty and disease and there were many slums. Though it was a gay city, above all when decorated by the full pageantry of the Court, it was also incredibly dirty and smelly. Hackney and Stepney (which contained many French Protestant refugees) were overcrowded and insanitary, while modern suburbs, such as Kensington and Hampstead, were still country villages. When the frequent plagues or other reasons compelled the government and parliament to leave London, they usually met at Oxford, always a rallying point for Church and King, whereas Cambridge became the haunt of Puritans, Broad Churchmen, and Cromwellians.

At the opening of the century, Norwich with nearly 30,000 inhabitants, Bristol, the second largest port, with 20,000, York, and Newcastle upon Tyne were the most populous towns after London. Manchester and Birmingham were obscure villages. Thomas Wilson, writing on 'the State of England' in 1600, asserted that there were twenty-five cities and 641 'great towns' in England and Wales. But 'the great towns' were, in modern terms, nothing more than villages: they might have contained only 1,000 inhabitants. Big towns are the product of concentrated industries and – with a few exceptions – industry was still organized largely on a loose domestic basis, work being commissioned by middlemen, who bought the raw materials and disposed of the finished goods. Many industrial workers would have a cottage and a little land, perhaps as much as six acres: the spinning wheels and looms on which, for example, Yorkshire kerseys, Lancashire fustians, and Norfolk worsteds were manufactured would be found in the operatives' own homes, while yeomen with smallholdings might also engage in industry as a a part-time occupation. Most work was performed by small family units: apprentices lived and fed with their masters. No real factory system yet existed.

The manufacture of woollen cloth, which had begun much earlier, remained the principal English industry throughout the seventeenth century and the most valuable source of exports. Centred in Yorkshire, where Leeds was already a prosperous town famous for its strong ale, in East

Anglia, where Norwich was the most thriving city, and in the West Country, celebrated for its broadcloths, the industry's finished products were usually dispatched for sale through agents at Blackwell Hall in Basinghall Street where the big London buyers gathered. But during the century the cloth trade was subject to fluctuations. First came the disastrous attempt by Sir William Cockayne's company to dye and finish all cloth for export, buttressed by a royal proclamation of 1614 forbidding the export of unfinished cloth. Secondly, the industry was disorganized by the civil wars, especially in Yorkshire. Thirdly, at the end of the century it was meeting effective foreign competition, notably in Holland. Between the accession of James I and that of Charles II civil war, pestilence, and international politics all damaged the industry, and even after the Restoration progress was irregular, the industry recovering but slowly from the troubles it had encountered in the previous thirty years. Nor had the Lancashire cotton industry yet developed sufficiently to reinforce the textile trade, although cotton was mixed with wool to produce fustians, which provided clothing for the poor, and with linen for bed-clothes and bolsters. Calico printing only started at the end of the century.

The industry to record the most spectacular advance in the seventeenth century was coal mining. Until the sixteenth century 'coal was hardly ever burned either in the family hearth or in the kitchen at distances more than a mile or two from the outcrops' and then 'only by the poor who could not afford to buy wood'. (Nef.) But by the beginning of the seventeenth century it had become a national asset. Seven times as much coal was imported into London (chiefly by sea from Newcastle upon Tyne) in 1605 as in 1580, and the estimated annual production increased fourteen-fold between the middle of the sixteenth and the end of the seventeenth century. The coal industry was one of the earliest fields of modern capitalist enterprise, since the production of coal could not be organized on a commission basis and the expense of sinking mining shafts and moving coal from the pits to market was so considerable that it could not be met except by means of large investment. Miners had to be employed together in a big group. They led hard, rough lives, for theirs was a badly-paid occupation and governed by harsh regulations. Apart from the coal industry, iron mining and foreign trade, now being financed by a joint-stock method, were the only important capitalist businesses; and it is no coincidence that merchants and ironmasters were among the biggest investors in the rising coal trade.

One of the reasons for the rapid growth of the coal industry in the seventeenth century was a growing scarcity of timber. Although there were still thick forest in various parts of the country, such as the New Forest and Sherwood, so that England could still be called a 'shaggy land', the problem of moving timber was severe and often insuperable. In the reign of James I 'from every county came the same lament of deforestation'. This was owing to an increased demand for wood and its consequent high price. In London people began to burn coal instead of wood and by 1618 two hundred sweeps earned their livings in the capital. Other expanding industries included the manufacture of salt – the output of which had more than doubled since the previous century – and of glass, which was carried on particularly in London, Stourbridge, and Newcastle. Shipbuilding was another industry which thrived during the century. Owing to the coal trade, shipbuilding, and glass manufacture, by the end of the century Newcastle, 'a noble town tho' in a bottom', as a lady traveller remarked, almost rivalled Bristol as the second busiest English port.

Although the growth of industries was certainly one of the most striking aspects of English history in the seventeenth century, agriculture, including sheep farming, was still the most usual occupation of Englishmen. About 9,000,000 acres were devoted to arable. Twice as much barley was grown as wheat. Barley went to the making of beer, of which the consumption was enormous. The call for wool both to make clothing and for smuggling abroad was large, though it declined as the century advanced. There was during the reign of James I, as during the Tudor period, a volume of complaints about arable land being enclosed for the purpose of grazing sheep, but these complaints were exaggerated. Since the early sixteenth century enclosure for one purpose or another had gone steadily forward, sometimes, it is true, to make more room for sheep – which were valued as much for their meat as their wool – but more often to improve the standard of agriculture by getting rid of the inefficient system of cultivation in which the villagers' strips were mixed together in 'open fields'. King James I himself maintained that more land was ploughed up from the waste during his reign than was converted from arable into pasture. Though King Charles I levied heavy fines on landowners for carrying out enclosures, he did this mainly to help his finances; there was little restriction on enclosure under Cromwell, and in the reign of Charles II all the writers who understood the subject began to urge that more enclosure should be permitted, not less. But progress was slow. Much of the midlands was still unenclosed by the end of the century. The biggest enclosure movement in the seventeenth century arose out of the draining of the Great Fens, covering six counties from Lincoln to Cambridge, which provoked violent protests from the local population who were accustomed to extracting a meagre living from keeping geese, hunting wild fowl, and catching pike.

In the seventeenth century it was possible to define men according to the social rank or 'degree'. Men of high degree were expected to carry out duties according to their calling and not to behave themselves in a way unsuited to their rank. The College of Arms could explain who was a peer, a knight, a baronet, an esquire, or a gentleman. Men were generally born into these ranks but they were purchasable. One could buy a peerage, as did the grandfather of Sir Thomas Fairfax, the parliamentary commander-in-chief. Knighthoods were pressed on reluctant gentry who frequently declined or evaded the honour, preferring to pay a fine instead. For financial reasons James I created peerages with enthusiasm and the numbers of the lay peerage doubled in the first quarter of the century. Baronetcies were invented in 1611 to fill the gap between the peers and the knights. As to gentlemen, they were said to be cheap in England. This 'inflation of honours' lowered the average value of the highest ranks; while peers were often immensely rich men, judged by modern standards, it has been estimated that their holdings of property per head decreased in comparison with Elizabethan times. And all of them had costly obligations.

Once one abandons these technical social definitions it becomes harder to draw precise distinctions between the so-called 'upper' and 'lower' gentry, who are the invention of the modern historian, the merchants or financiers, the King's servants, the professional classes like doctors, the so-called 'middle classes', the yeomen, and so on. There was certainly a good deal of movement between economic classes. Merchants intermarried with old-established country gentry and sometimes restored declining landed fortunes by doing so. A successful yeoman would sometimes marry 'above him'. Civil servants and professional men would invest their savings in land – indeed, apart from shares in oversea adventures and a little industry there was not much else to invest in – and whereas some landlords lived entirely on rents and might properly be described as enjoying unearned incomes, others, especially at the beginning of the century, when wool was in heavy demand for the cloth industry, enhanced their fortunes out of the calculated profits from pastureland or at times out of horticulture for the food markets in the towns.

Provided these qualifications are kept in mind, it may be said that the people of seventeenth-century England could roughly be grouped into four main classes. At the top were the peers. Gregory King, who supplied us with some useful, if not completely credible, statistics relating to the population of England and Wales in 1688, estimated that the number of lords spiritual and temporal and their families in those days was about seven thousand. Some noblemen belonged to ancient families, many dated from the Reformation, some were gilded favourites like the first Duke of Buckingham, others brilliant upstarts like the merchant, Lionel Cranfield, who began life as a London apprentice and ended it as the Earl of Middlesex. Many of these peers were extremely wealthy if their servants were counted or if their expenditure were translated into present equivalents, for in terms of wages the pound was worth perhaps twenty times what it is today. The average capital value of forty-one peers' estates in the middle of the century has been estimated at over £30,000. If Lord Berkeley, who was Lord Lieutenant of Gloucestershire in the reign of James I, visited London he would be accompanied by 150 servants. His expenditure exceeded his income by £1,500 a year. When the Earl of Bedford took his sumptuous retinue to the Tower of London to greet the returned Charles II he spent over £1,000 on his display of duty.

After the nobility came the gentry. A substantial squire would have an annual rent roll of £1,000 or more a year and a smaller squire £800 or less. The poorest members of the House of Commons had incomes of £500 a year. One well-to-do knight had twenty-four servants and spent £500 a year on his housekeeping alone. One may discover in the letters and diaries of the time a difference of opinion about the proper life of a seventeenth-century gentleman. For example, Nicholas Assheton, a squire who lived during the reign of James I in an E-shaped manor in Lancashire and passed his time hunting foxes and stags, recorded as a typical day in his diary: 'Ate, drank wine, and was merry, and to the field again.' Viscount Conway observed: 'We eat, and drink and rise up to play and this is to live like a gentleman, for what is a gentleman but his pleasure?' But Sir Henry Slingsby, who was M.P. for Knaresborough in 1640 and active in local affairs, was of the opinion that 'idleness was the nurse of all evil'. Sir George Reresby, who, because his wife was a Roman Catholic, kept out of all public affairs, devoted much of his time to his estates, bred horses, and left exact accounts when he died. As an instance of the still busier kind of gentleman we may notice Sir Robert Harley (grandfather of a future Tory Lord Treasurer) who conscientiously functioned as a Justice of the Peace, managed his own estates, organized fairs, and as a Puritan commissioner distinguished himself by destroying the stained glass in Westminster Abbey and St Margaret's Church and burning embroidery used on the altar at Canterbury Cathedral.

The old English gentry were powerfully reinforced in the late sixteenth and early seventeenth centuries by an influx from professional and mercantile classes. Lawyers, government officials, and successful merchants bought land not only to improve their social standing but also to increase their incomes. Writing in 1600, Thomas Wilson observed:

Gentlemen ... are now for the most part grown to be good husbands and know well how to improve their lands and to the uttermost as the farmer or countryman, so that they take their farms into their hands as leases expire and either till themselves or else let them to those that will give most; whereby the yeomanry of England is decayed and become servants to gentlemen which were wont to be the glory of the country and good neighbourhood and hospitality.

This broadening of the squirearchy was a notable feature of English society in the years before the first civil war – even if its exact causes and repercussions are matters of dispute. It came about because lands formerly belonging to the Church or Crown were sold in large quantities after the Reformation. Again many of Cromwell's officers were able to buy land at low prices during the civil wars and a few of them managed to cling on to them long after Cromwell was dead. The opportunities offered by the civil war converted money-lenders like Humphrey Shalcrosse or doubtful attorneys like John Wildman into respectable country gentlemen before the century was over. James

Harrington, one of the outstanding political philosophers of the century, commented on the shift of property from the Church, the Crown, and the semi-feudal landlords to the squires at the time of the Restoration of King Charles II, and Mr H. J. Habbakuk has written that 'this notion of the rise of the squirearchy has become the organizing conception of English social history between the Dissolution of the Monasteries and 1640'. Professor J. H. Hexter has justly observed that the rise of the gentry is 'not a hypothesis to be verified; it is a simple fact'.

Some contemporaries and later scholars suggested that the consequence of the broadening of the squirearchy was that land was now managed in a more business-like way than before. We have noticed Thomas Wilson's views. Instances may certainly be cited of individual 'improving' landlords. Lord Brudenell, for example, doubled his income from land in the first half of the century, while the Ishams, a Northamptonshire family, trebled theirs. The Spencers in the same county made as much as £8,000 a year, chiefly out of sheep farming. On the other hand, some peers – Lord Fitzwilliam, for example – and some gentry, such as the Trenshams, ruined themselves by personal extravagances. Those at Court or in office were expected to keep up their 'port' or social position and did not always receive, as some had done in Elizabethan times, help from the Crown in doing so. So there could usually be found some peers or gentry on the decline, as well as many rising peers and gentry.

During most of the century the land-owning class was undertaxed. This was scarcely surprising since the bulk of the House of Commons, which imposed taxation, consisted of gentry. Moreover the Commons had in the reign of Elizabeth I and James I grown in strength, numbers, and influence, precisely because the country gentleman and his cousin, the lawyer, set out to capture the House, which had become the centre of influence, fashion, and education. When in 1626 Sir George Chudleigh nominated his son to a Cornish borough seat in his place, he said: 'I should gladly now ... give my son a little breeding there'. If the county seats were almost hereditary properties of established families, the boroughs were becoming the happy hunting ground of ambitious and rising gentry.

Did the class below the gentry – the yeomen – also benefit from the active land market and broadening economic opportunities at the beginning of the seventeenth century? Let us first consider who the yeomen were. Bacon described them as 'middle people of a condition between gentlemen and cottagers or peasants'.

A modern historian has divided the yeomen into two groups, those of ancient lineage sprung from old families of free tenants and those who rose by their own exertions from a lower estate. They might be freeholders, who owned land worth forty shillings or more, copyholders with prescribed obligations to their landlords, or leaseholders with extremely long leases. All of them in any case earned their living from the land. In the legal documents of the time they were clearly differentiated from 'gentlemen' (for example, fines imposed on them for evading jury service would be on a lower scale than similar fines imposed on knights and squires) and also from butchers, bakers, and the like who depended for their incomes on services given to other members of the community. On the whole, yeomen were pretty prosperous at the time. Even those who were leaseholders, though they might have to pay increased rents to their landlords on the renewal of their leases, would also have obtained bigger returns for their produce at any rate during the reign of James I when prices were continuing to move upwards. Some yeomen undoubtedly declined in status at the beginning of the century, as Wilson observed, but the majority did well enough. If, as some contemporaries maintained, the yeoman belonged to a disappearing class, it might well have been because he was becoming a gentleman rather than because he was becoming a pauper. The English yeoman farmer worked hard at his job, took an active part in local affairs, manned the militia, and was politically conscious. Jealous of the gentry, he fought the

Royalists in the civil wars. He 'thinks nothing to be vices but pride and ill-husbandry,' wrote one of them. Vigorous, tough, and self-respecting, he put small store on outward appearances, but was sometimes a keen reader, an attendant at religious exercises, and a good and hospitable neighbour. It is no mere sentimentality to think of him as the backbone of England.

After the nobility and gentry, the professional and merchant classes (Gregory King thought that 64,000 merchants were trading in 1688), and the yeomen and tenant farmers (that is 'tenants at will') came the largest class of all, the common people, perhaps three-quarters of the entire population. Little is known of them for they did not publish autobiographies and few writers thought them worthy of mention. Leaders of democratic movements in the mid-century, men like John Lilburne, John Wildman, and Gerrard Winstanley, who wrote copiously and agitated violently, usually belonged to the merchant class: Winstanley was a cloth merchant, Lilburne and Wildman shrewd business men. In their writings can be read some of the grievances of the common people, particularly against the slow working of the law and against having to pay tithes to the Church. But perhaps the nearest we come to them as human beings is in the diary of Roger Lowe, a shop assistant in a small Lancashire town who was unique only in his ability to read and write and in the fact that his diary for the years 1665–7 has survived the centuries. He mixed with farm labourers and apprentices in taverns, courted more than one village lass, rarely resisted temptation, and never failed to express regret when he gave way to it. 'I must not spend 1d,' he wrote on one occasion, 'but yet I did.' Or again: 'When I came home I was very pensive and sad in consideration of my poverty, and I sung the 24th Psalm, and after I was very hearty.' The spending of a penny or twopence was always an affair of note to him, he suffered from sickness, headaches, and worry, he was delighted with a gift of plums or with a merry evening in the ale-house, and he constantly reflected on how poor he was and on the bright prospects that awaited the virtuous on the other side of the grave.

Indeed though the rich were often extremely rich (a landowner was not accounted really wealthy with less than £30,000 in property) the poor were always very poor. The steady rise in prices since the beginning of the sixteenth century had fallen heavily on those who depended on a day wage, more especially as wages were fixed and, at least in theory, held down by law. The Statute of Artificers of 1563 enabled justices of the peace to fix wages according to the needs and conditions in different parts of the country. Employers who paid or employees who received higher wages than those prescribed by the justices could be sentenced to terms of imprisonment. Nevertheless the laws of supply and demand had a way of overcoming legal enactments. Such evidence as exists suggests that in many cases the justices of the peace varied wage assessments not in accordance with changes in the cost of living but in accordance with the plenty or scarcity of labour at the time. The precise extent to which wages and prices rose – and therefore the level of real wages in the seventeenth century – has not yet been established. It is generally accepted that prices increased about sixfold between 1500 and 1640 and that money wages rose much less.

The two classes into which Gregory King divided the common people – 'labouring people and outservants' and 'cottagers and paupers' – must have found it desperately hard to make both ends meet. Wages varied between about 7d and 1s a day (without food), less for agricultural labourers and unskilled workers, more for the skilled; the highest paid masons in the country earned as much as 2s 6d a day (without food). Foot soldiers were paid 8d a day under Cromwell. Of course it is true, as has often been pointed out, that the cottagers at any rate were able to grow most of their own food; accommodation, food, and fuel were sometimes provided by employers, and villagers could use the wasteland or common village land to graze their animals if their landlords did not filch it from them. Also the whole family, including small children, would work. And whatever they might have lacked in the way of fuel, clothing, or housing, it seems that those in employment usually ate well. A foreign observer noted: 'These English have their houses made of sticks and dirt, but they fare commonly as well as the King.' They might not get red meat and white bread, but as a rule they had white meat and black bread with ale or cider to wash it down. But potatoes, the staple diet of the poor in later times, were then little known or used.

Recent research suggests that in the first half of the century about 8 per cent of the population 'lived below the line of poverty as then most harshly defined' (W. K. Jordan) while in times of depression – and there were depressions in the sixteen-twenties, in the early sixteen-forties, and in 1659, and later – this percentage might rise to 20 per cent of the entire population. According to Gregory King, as many as a million persons were in occasional receipt of alms. The Elizabethan poor-law system, whereby each parish was responsible for its own poor, tended to create vagabonds and beggars, while efforts to manufacture work for the unemployed seldom succeeded.

Out of money expended by private charity in the first half of the seventeenth century (secular charitable institutions grew apace after the dissolution of the monasteries) as much as one-third was devoted to helping the poor, many of whom were concentrated in London and the other big towns and were constantly harassed by epidemics, wretched housing and hygiene, and by unwanted children and by industrial failures or economic setbacks. While the Puritans disapproved of deliberate idleness and professional beggary as sinful, they recognized that a really grave problem existed menacing the social order and they even proclaimed that God was 'a poor man's God' who imposed strict charitable obligations upon the rich.

During the Interregnum in the middle of the seventeenth century, once the civil wars were over, there was a marked revival of economic prosperity; restrictions on trade and labour were loosened, and more consideration was shown towards the poor. But after the restoration of King Charles II and the world depression of 1659 there was a setback. The price boom ended; although real wages were relatively steady, chronic unemployment was rife; the excise was a burden on the poorer classes; and it has been estimated that the total of the poor rate and private charity hardly yielded £1 per head a year.

Thus between the peers of the realm, whose annual incomes may have averaged £5,000 a year, and the poor and unemployed, seasonal or other, dependent on private charity or public poor relief to save them from starvation, a great gap existed. Though the statistics of the age may be fragmentary, modern historical research has established this beyond any reasonable doubt. Why then was there no social revolution? Why no articulate discontent? The answer is that such discontent did play its part in the Puritan revolution and its aftermath and in Monmouth's rebellion of 1685 and in the writing of political extremists like the Levellers and Diggers. But the hungry man is rarely an agitator. And one thing is certain. If one puts the most optimistic interpretation on the known facts about the economic position of the common people, the mass of ordinary Englishmen can scarcely have lived merrily.

CHAPTER III

Climates of Opinion

As King James I wended his way from Edinburgh to London in 1603, he was met by a group of Puritan clergy who presented him with a petition in which he was asked to redress various abuses in the Church of England. This petition was called the Millenary Petition because a thousand ministers of the Church were supposed to have subscribed to it. However, there is no reason to believe that a thousand signatures were in fact attached, nor is it certain that so many clergy accepted all the opinions expressed in it. For the Puritans in 1603 represented only a large, able, and noisy minority within the Church – a minority that enlisted much support from the laity including many squires, especially in the eastern counties, the Midlands and South, and a large number of merchants and weavers. The petitioners asked that certain ceremonies, such as the cross in baptism and the ring in marriage, should be left out of the church services, that only educated men competent to preach should henceforward be made ministers, that bishops should not be allowed to be 'pluralists', holding benefices which they did not administer, and that in the exercise of church discipline men should not be excommunicated by minor officials 'for trifles and twelve-penny matters'. Clearly, except for the first request, which belongs to the realm of dogma, the petitioners had an arguable case. If what they said was true, something was radically wrong with the organized religious life of England and King James felt it was right that the petition should at once be considered. True, he did not much care for Puritans as such for he knew they shared the political theories of the Scottish Presbyterians who had bullied him unmercifully and driven his mother to her doom. But, on the other hand, neither was he a Roman Catholic.

He owed his throne to his Protestantism and he had no intention of upsetting the Elizabethan settlement and restoring England to allegiance to the Pope. For reasons of State he had flirted with the English Roman Catholics before the death of Queen Elizabeth, but as soon as he saw how strong his new position was, he said: 'Na, Na, we'll not need the Papists now.' How stood the Church and what was the condition of the English Puritans and Roman Catholics when King James I was enthroned?

The Elizabethan church settlement had been a cautious compromise in which Calvinist and Catholic elements were blended. As Lytton Strachey wrote, the Church then walked along a tight-rope and in a sense has been walking along it ever since. The Queen had been made the Supreme Governor (but not the Head) of the Church, an Act of Uniformity had been passed, a Common Prayer Book introduced, and Thirty-Nine Articles drawn up which all clergy had to accept. The settlement had been carried out with the help of a number of bishops who had been exiled in the reign of the Roman Catholic Queen Mary I and had sat at the feet of John Calvin in Geneva. John Calvin taught the terrible doctrine of predestination: either an individual on this earth was chosen to be saved by grace and dwelt forever 'in the Great Taskmaster's eye' or he was incurably reprobate – hardened in sin; neither faith nor good conduct could lift a man into the ranks of the elect, if he had not been elected. Calvin laid it down therefore that the Church should be governed by assemblies, presbyters or elders, and deacons, constituting the elect, with authority to order the doings of the reprobate. The doctrine of predestination – or at least election by grace – had been propounded at times by eminent members of the Church of Rome, notably by St Augustine and in the seventeenth century by a group known as the Jansenists in France. But the alternative doctrine of 'free will' which permitted a Christian to be saved by his faith and works as well as by grace was the more usual Catholic doctrine. The Thirty-Nine Articles were so framed as to enable members of the Church of England to believe in either predestination or free will as they thought fit. A similar ambiguity attached to the exact significance of the sacrament in the Communion Service. However, according to one leading authority, at the outset of Queen Elizabeth's reign 'the Calvinistic system had penetrated with more or less completeness into the minds of the great majority of English Protestants'.

Still the Reformation had been fundamentally political and doctrinal changes came slowly. Ample evidence exists that in many parts of the country services continued much as before the Reformation. The ordinary parishioner was conservative; the prayer book was catholic in tone and accorded with his wishes. When in the reign of Queen Elizabeth it was proposed to alter the kind of bread given at Communion the Archbishop of Canterbury warned the monarch that public opinion would not stand it. The parish priest tried to meet the wishes of his flock without angering the authorities above him. He was as ill paid as most of the common people were – his stipend ranging between about £8 and £10 a year – and if he were told to administer the Communion in both kinds instead of holding Masses or to read the prayers in English instead of Latin he was ready to do so. Unless he were an educated man with scruples he was not prepared to lose his job. And fewer than half of the clergy were educated men. When King James came to the throne, only 454 out of 1,065 clergy in the Province of York were licensed preachers and only 3,352 out of 8,179 in the Province of Canterbury. Some of course had taken degrees at the universities, but even that was not a clear proof of learning as many students attended lectures, read little, and obtained their degrees without passing examinations. Under the circumstances there could be little common practice in the churches, sermons were unusual, and the clergy met their poverty as best they could. Some vicars kept their cattle in the churchyards. Others neglected their duties in favour of farming. The Rector of Normanton used not to hold the Sunday service 'because he was playing at the tables with the schoolmaster of Hambleton'. Archbishop

Whitgift, who was at Canterbury at the beginning of King James's reign, admitted that there were not 600 benefices out of the 9,000 in England and Wales where the stipends were sufficient for the support of a learned man. Many of the tithes, taxes meant to support the Church, had been expropriated by laymen who paid the vicars a pittance; in other cases the tithes had been commuted so that the rector suffered a heavy loss in income from the general fall in the value of money. If most of the clergy were poor and ignorant, they received little assistance from their parish officers, who in many cases could neither read nor write, or from their congregations, who were frequently apathetic.

At the other end of the scale stood the bishops. They too found it impossible to keep up their positions on their ordinary incomes, for just as tithes had been appropriated by laymen or stipends reduced by greedy patrons, so the Queen and her courtiers had battened upon episcopal properties. Queen Elizabeth I had treated her bishops as useful officers of state and had struck hard bargains with them whenever she had made new appointments; they had responded by seizing other paid posts to augment the income of their sees. Thus while some efforts had been made to check the evil, nearly all the bishops were 'pluralists'. The Bishop of St Asaph's, for example, had held sixteen livings. When Richard Bancroft became Bishop of London, he resigned eight rectories and prebends. Although the property and incomes of bishops were reduced by the Queen and her courtiers and the upkeep of many episcopal palaces and properties was very costly, the bishops could hardly be defended for the way in which they in their turn sold livings, leased episcopal lands to their families, and ravished their properties, for example by cutting down all the timber. Moreover while nearly all of them were earnest and hard-working men, the importance of their duties as administrators and politicians often seemed to overshadow the example they set as men of God. Thus, when the Puritans attacked the bishops and demanded a preaching ministry, they had fuel for their fire.

At the beginning of the seventeenth century there was no such thing as a Puritan 'party'. There were Presbyterians or Disciplinarians who had drunk deeply at the fountain of Geneva and who in the early years of Queen Elizabeth's reign had actually created a shadow Presbyterian organization within the orbit of the Church of England. Puritan-minded clergy were wont to take part in 'prophesyings' or diocesan meetings at which moral and ecclesiastical problems were discussed; 'classes' or secret synods were set up in a number of sees and some ministers had insisted on being elected by their local congregations rather than being installed by their bishops. The Presbyterian leader was Thomas Cartwright, Lady Margaret Professor of Divinity at Cambridge, who had discovered that the Anglican Church did not at all accord with the principles of the primitive Christian Church and urged that bishops should be deprived of their disciplinary powers and stick to preaching. In the last fifteen years of Queen Elizabeth's reign the Presbyterians had suffered a setback, but they had received strong support in the House of Commons and were driven underground rather than suppressed. Secondly, there were the followers of Robert Browne, another Cambridge man, who presided over a 'congregational' church at Norwich and after being imprisoned thirty-two times fled to Middelburg in Holland. He, in contrast with the Presbyterians, who believed that the State should enforce and uphold their own favoured form of church organization, maintained that the civil magistrates should have no power at all in religious matters, that the ministry should rely on free-will offerings, and that in each parish the pastor must be chosen by his own parishioners. Two other Puritan thinkers, Greenwood and Barrow, who perished on the scaffold for sedition, had also advocated independent and self-governing churches. Another rising Puritan sect were the Baptists or 'Anabaptists'. The first English Baptist, John Smythe, yet another Cambridge man, who baptized himself and considered that all Christians should be rebaptized after accepting voluntary membership of a church, founded

the first English Baptist church in Amsterdam in 1609, followed by a London church in 1611. These 'general Baptists' did not, however, like the Presbyterians and Congregationalists, accept the doctrine of predestination, although
another sect, 'the particular Baptists', which was founded
later in 1633, acquiesced in the Calvinistic tenets. Among
other sects which trace their beginnings back to the first half
of the seventeenth century were the Family of Love and the
Seekers. The Family of Love believed that the resurrection
of the dead was fulfilled in them. The Seekers maintained
that since 'Antichrist' had ruled over the Church so long,
no true Church existed anywhere in the world. Led by Dr
John Everard, one of the most vital preachers in London in
King James I's reign, they insisted that the Truth could only
come from within: they therefore left 'all visible Churches
and societies and wandered up and down as sheep without
a shepherd and as doves without their mates, seeking their
Beloved' (William Penn). The Seekers were the forerunners
of the Society of Friends or 'Quakers' founded by George
Fox in the sixteen-forties.

Probably none of these Puritan sects was numerically
strong in the first years of the seventeenth century. The
Brownists, for example, did not number more than 500 persons and the active Puritans as a whole did not themselves
claim more than 750 adherents among the parish clergy in
the Church of England in 1603. On the other hand, many
of the most effective preachers within the Church were Puritan in sympathy and it was for this reason that Queen Elizabeth had discouraged preaching as subversive of her government. What had these Puritans in common? In the first
place, they believed in the right of the individual Christian
to interpret the Scriptures – 'God's Covenant' – for himself
by spiritual illumination – a practice which was assisted by
such English translations of the Bible as that of William
Tyndale. Secondly, they were opposed to a mystical interpretation of the Communion service. Thirdly, they disliked
the institution of episcopacy since it implied that bishops
ruled by divine right – although some Puritans were

prepared to consent to an emasculated bishopric simply as a convenient instrument of government. Finally, they condemned all the old Catholic ceremonies as being idolatrous. Thus the first grievance voiced in the Millenary Petition was more radical than it appeared on the surface because in condemning such ceremonies as the ring in marriage the Puritans were in fact attacking the Book of Common Prayer and the whole machinery of church discipline that lay behind it. In sum, all Puritans were against any priest or ceremony being interposed between the Christian soul and its Maker. These doctrines were preached in a spirit of evangelical revivalism which is common enough in the history of all Churches, but the strict and censorious behaviour of those who were struck by it often caused their practitioners to be mocked. The saintly Richard Baxter related how his father 'was reviled for reading Scripture when the rest were dancing on the Lord's Day, and for praying (by a form out of the Common Prayer Book) in his house and for reproving drunkards and swearers, and for talking sometimes a few words of Scripture and the life to come, he was reviled commonly by the name of Puritan, precisian, and hypocrite.' Thus even if the Puritans did not constitute a united and definable party when King James I came to the throne they had a common attitude of mind and stood out from the ordinary run of English Christians.

If the Puritans were an active but disunited Protestant minority when James became king, the Roman Catholics could claim to be fairly numerous but lacking in power or influence. One authority has estimated that there were 500 Catholic priests and perhaps a million Catholic laity in the country when Queen Elizabeth died (though this latter figure is certainly excessive). Although Catholic priests who acknowledged the supremacy of the Pope were liable to the penalties of high treason, they celebrated the Mass in many parts of England and Wales; on the Continent colleges existed where young Englishmen were trained to reconvert their countrymen to the true faith and since no English Roman Catholic was supposed to travel more than five miles from his home, a secret route was established for smuggling them in and out of the island. Among the laity were to be found both practising and secret Roman Catholics. As with the Calvinists, the influence of a local peer or lord of the manor might be decisive. Roman Catholicism was especially strong in the North of England and it was the persistence of the Roman Catholic tradition in these parts which explains much in the civil wars of the seventeenth and early eighteenth centuries.

The death of Queen Elizabeth I inspired hope in many Roman Catholic breasts. Priests hurried from abroad along the secret route and their numbers probably doubled in the first ten years of King James's reign. Some leading Catholic laymen entered into direct negotiations with the King, while Scottish Catholics fancied that his throne could only be maintained with the help of the Pope. But other Roman Catholics were less patient and plotted either to kidnap the King after the Scottish manner or even to murder him and his counsellors and enforce Catholic rule. Once these plots came to light and were foiled they inevitably diminished the chances of tolerances for Roman Catholics to whom the King was not ill disposed and to whom his Queen belonged.

Such was the disposition of the Christian land at the beginning of the seventeenth century. Beneath the umbrella of the one official Church sheltered avowed Puritans and concealed Roman Catholics. In addition, in areas where they commanded the sympathy of the local government secret conventicles gathered or Masses were celebrated; but the bulk of the population did what it was told by authority and partook of services read from the Common Prayer Book. Elizabethan severity combined with the all-embracing character of the Thirty-Nine Articles had imposed greater uniformity on the Church in the closing years of the sixteenth century than many might have thought possible after the previous upheavals. Moreover the teachings of the 'Judicious' Hooker in his *Ecclesiastical Polity*, which praised the virtues of compromise as exemplified in the Elizabethan settlement, and of Bishop Lancelot Andrewes, who sought to reconcile Catholic ceremonies with Protestant beliefs, convinced many that the practices of the Church of England were defensible. Justification was found for them not in Catholic history but in the early conduct of the Primitive Church, and they were given a reasonable and persuasive shape in the writings of men like John Donne and George Herbert. Indeed a Church of England faith can be seen in the making from Hooker and Andrewes to Jeremy Taylor and Stillingfleet, a faith for which Laud and Charles I were to die. The inquisitorial morality favoured by the Puritans did not suit the taste of the age of Shakespeare and since separatism had not yet made much headway, the idea that Church and State had to be one society was not yet seriously challenged. If the choice had to be between King and Pope as head of the Church the majority of Englishmen preferred the King, and especially those who enjoyed the fruits of the dissolution of the monasteries and the alienation of church lands.

Such was the climate of opinion among Christians. But a new wind was blowing. The theories of such foreign pundits as Copernicus and Giordano Bruno (who was burnt at the stake), Tycho Brahé, Kepler, and later Galileo about the nature of the universe, which assigned to the earth a more modest place, began to disturb thinking men and to cast doubt upon the literal truth of the Holy Testaments. And not only the teachings of the Bible but the concepts of the Greek philosopher, Aristotle, which had been embodied in the world outlook of the medieval Church by St Thomas Aquinas, and others, were shaken. 'Galileo did not refute the Angelic Doctor; he took no notice of him.' (Basil Willey.) Sir Francis Bacon, the statesman-philosopher, who became Solicitor-General early in the new reign, rejected the scholastic tradition and argued that abstract speculation (or deductive reasoning) should be given up in favour of the observation of nature (or induction). Urging the need for experiment, he 'rang the bell that called the wits together'. He did not of course apply scientific methods to the study of the Bible, but contented himself with observing that 'sacred theology must be drawn from the word and works of God, not from the light of nature or the dictates of reason'. It has been said that Bacon pleaded for science in an age of religion, while Sir Thomas Browne, whose famous book *Religio Medici* was begun in the next reign, pleaded for religion in an age of science. That is the measure of the change in the climate of opinion which the century was to witness. Browne's attitude to religion was, however, similar to that of Bacon in that he assigned the Scriptures to the region of faith which was held to be immune from the questionings of reason. 'The thing is certain,' he asserted of Christianity, 'because it is impossible.' But in spite of Bacon's and Browne's somewhat paradoxical solution to the contradictions of science and religion 'reason' kept jostling the minds of seventeenth-century thinkers. G. K. Chesterton once rightly wrote that a Puritan was a man whose mind was never at rest, and the finer types of Puritan, such as John Milton (who in his youth had been profoundly influenced by Bacon), could not, as they mulled over the pages of the Book of Life, free themselves from puzzlement or ignore startling possibilities. Milton, like Browne, interpreted the allegories of the Old Testament in a novel way, while among other things he refused the Son equal status with the Father, denied that God created the universe out of nothing, and held that at death 'all of me shall die' to be revived only at the Last Judgement.

As the century wore on (as we shall show in a later chapter) even those who were professional theologians and officers of the Church parted under the impact of scientific and mathematical arguments from the literal interpretation of the Bible and from customary scholastic methods of argument and preferred to defend their faith by light of the candle of reason. And before the first half of the century ended Thomas Hobbes was to expound a mechanical and materialist explanation of life. On the other hand, Lord Herbert of Cherbury, who wrote in the reign of King Charles I and was the friend of Ben Jonson and John Donne, tried to invent a religious creed that would be acceptable not merely to all Christians but to all men. And a group of thinkers at Cambridge, following Plato or his disciple Plotinus instead of Aristotle, started to substitute a rational but spiritual conception of Christianity for the idea that God was just a superior kind of man.

But all that lay in the future. For the moment men did not throw doubt on the fundamental creeds of Christianity, but were concerned with theological disputations, with arguments over the proper organization for the Church, and, above all, questions of moral behaviour.

In the literature written or published during the first half of the seventeenth century can be traced not only a conflict between, or an attempt to reconcile, religion and science, but also a clash between religion and passion or sensuality. Much fine literature deals of course with such conflicts, though the conflict may not be a subjective one gnawing at the author's heart but only an objective one, the theme of his story-telling. It is sometimes forgotten that the outstanding Jacobean poet and dramatist was William Shakespeare – who overshadowed his contemporaries and successors, Webster, Massinger, Beaumont, Fletcher, Ben Jonson, and John Ford. All his famous tragedies were first published in the reign of King James I and several other plays were either given for the first time or again acted at Court. (It has been estimated that Shakespeare received about £170 for the plays he wrote in King James's reign; happily he had other means of livelihood.) In Shakespeare one detects no subjective religious perplexities, though some have observed in *Hamlet* a conflict between love and duty and in his last play, *The Tempest*, Prospero expounds moral precepts of varying value. Few people have accused Shakespeare of being a Puritan, though several have claimed him as a Catholic. If one were to judge by some of the more striking phrases put into the mouth of his characters, such as

> As flies to wanton boys are we to the gods;
> They kill us for their sport

he might be classed as an agnostic. But we are warned that 'speeches such as these cannot be displaced from their context and read as the poet's own comments upon life and the significance of the story'. (Grierson.) Since we know so little about Shakespeare's own life, the most that we can say is that he does not appear to have been a deeply religious man and we may venture to suppose that he was not unaffected by those scientific and geographical discoveries in his time that were beginning to shrink the majesty of the Christian universe.

Another great poet who, though he died in 1600, had considerable influence during King James's reign and followers in Michael Drayton, Fulke Greville, and George Wither was Edmund Spenser. His famous if difficult epic, *The Faerie Queene* reveals at many points a conflict between religion and sensuality. Himself a Puritan, taught by Cartwright at Cambridge, he left miracles out of his allegory and found it impossible to reconcile medieval chivalry with Puritan restraints. The most successful of the Puritan writers was not Spenser but John Bunyan and John Milton, though Milton was not guiltless of unorthodoxy in Calvinist terms.

Another poet who comes near to being the greatest of all in the century (a bold statement of an age that embraced Shakespeare, Milton, Dryden, and Pope), John Donne, was conscious both of the conflict between science and religion and also of the conflict between religion and sensuality. He began life as a gay spark about town, 'a great visitor of ladies, a great frequenter of plays', and wrote satires and love songs. An early poem reflected the impact of the scientists:

> The new philosophy calls all in doubt,
> The element of fire is quite put out;
> The sun is lost and the earth, and no man's wit
> Can well direct him where to look for it.
> And freely men confess that this world's spent,
> When in the planets and the firmament
> They seek so many new; they see that this
> Is crumbled out again to his atomies.

Later Donne took holy orders, hid away the indiscreet verses of his carefree youth, and inspired by Bishop Lancelot Andrewes became a great Christian poet and pulpit orator. But ever in his beautiful verse and his sermons is an awareness of the mighty riddles of human life. He was an intellectual and a realist, unlike Spenser and Milton who exerted profound influence over later English poetry.

The seventeenth century is so rich in literature that one could not possibly list all its poets, playwrights, and prose writers. The Church of England could boast Donne, George Herbert, Henry Vaughan, and Jeremy Taylor; the Puritans Milton, Bunyan and – if they liked – Sir Walter Ralegh; the Roman Catholics Richard Crashaw, John Dryden, and perhaps Alexander Pope; the materialists, Thomas Hobbes and the second Duke of Buckingham. The fashionable pulpits were filled by impressive orators, the Court of King James I and King Charles I with witty or sensational dramatists and talented poets. And for all the religious fervour felt and expressed during the first half of the century, a questioning spirit was in the air. The Reformation was the Mother of Dissent. Scholasticism was dying. And once separatist ideas were put forward, nonconformity and therefore free thinking were quickly to follow. The civil wars appeared to act like a philosopher's stone changing the elements of which life was composed so that in the reign of King Charles II political thought and religious and philosophical ideas were freer and more varied than they had ever been before in the history of England. But this variety and freeing of thought, with the clashes and conflicts that it brought, may already be detected in some of the writings of the first half of the century.

Yet in the dawn of a scientific and mathematical century was also evil. On the face of it, it seems extraordinary that with the beginnings of modern science should coincide a growth in the belief in witchcraft not among ignorant peasants but among educated men. But the reason is not hard to understand. The Calvinists emphasized the reality of Satan and the verbal accuracy of the Bible. Who were witches but the handmaids of Satan and was it not written in Exodus: 'Thou shalt not suffer a witch to live'? John Calvin himself was conspicuous in organizing the killing of witches and many of his English disciples, including even

Richard Baxter, accepted their existence. One reason for Puritan faith in witches was that they were associated with Roman Catholic practices and traditions as 'women, which be commonly old ... poor, sullen, superstitious and Papists'. But belief in witchcraft was not limited to Puritans. For Sir Thomas Browne witches were proof of the mysteries of science. 'For my part,' he wrote, 'I have ever believed and do now know that there are witches.' The leader of the Jews who were allowed back into England by Cromwell wrote a book on witchcraft, while King James I himself produced a book called *Daemonologie* in 1597, based on seven years' research. In 1604 an act increasing the penalties against witches was passed by the English Parliament and under it a great many witches were condemned and burnt in the first twelve years of the reign. However, King James began to have qualms when in 1621 a thirteen-year-old boy confessed that all his evidence against witches had been false and that he had received instructions to simulate the symptoms of the bewitched. Another witch scare occurred during the civil war, but witch mania died during the reign of King Charles II and the last execution for witchcraft probably took place at Exeter in 1685.

His conversion from witchcraft is but one example of King James I's innate intelligence. Intellectually shrewd, though, like most clever men, sometimes led astray by an ingenious theory, he was a lover of peace and naturally inclined to tolerance. It was his wish, when he came to the throne, to impose peace and unity on the Church. Plots engineered against him by the wilder Roman Catholics frustrated his good intentions. One plot, known as 'the Bye Plot', to kidnap him was presided over by a secular priest but betrayed by the Jesuits, another known as 'the Main Plot', in which the leader was said to be a Roman Catholic layman, Lord Cobham, aimed at placing King James I's cousin Arabella on the throne with the aid of Spanish arms. The second plot was discovered by questioning prisoners taken in connexion with 'the Bye Plot'. Grateful perhaps for the Jesuits' betrayal of these plots and assured that the

bulk of the Roman Catholic laity was loyal, King James
agreed to meet one of the chief Roman Catholic grievances
by ceasing to levy the fine of £20 a month on Roman Catholic gentlemen who failed to attend church; but as Roman
Catholic priests were shown to have been concerned in the
conspiracies against him, he ordered them all to quit the
kingdom. As to the Puritans, he summoned an immediate
conference to consider the requests made in their Millenary
Petition and wrote to the universities asking them to help
to supply capable preachers and to restore tithes alienated
from the Church: he also promised to do this himself.

After a delay caused by the plague a conference between
representatives of the bishops and the Puritans opened at
Hampton Court Palace in January 1604 under the chairman-
ship of the King, who had an open mind about the need for
Church reform. He was, it has been said 'readier than the
bishops to acknowledge that the abuses in the Church were
serious matters demanding immediate remedies' (M. H.
Curtis). On the last day of the conference the King agreed
to changes in the Book of Common Prayer (such as the
abolition of the administration of private baptism by laymen
and women), a reduction in the powers of the bishops in
degrading and depriving ministers, and steps to encourage
more preaching in the parishes. The conference could therefore hardly be called a failure, though the bishops were not
pleased and did their best to sabotage its decisions. It was
over the tricky question of church discipline that difficulties
arose. One of the Puritan representatives indiscreetly suggested that 'prophesyings', that is to say diocesan meetings
of the clergy, should be revived and if any disputed matters
should arise out of them they should be referred to the
bishop and a group of 'presbyters'. King James then said
angrily that they were aiming at a Scottish Presbytery which
'agreeth as well with the monarchy as God and the Devil'.
He maintained the maxim 'No bishop, no king' and feared
that a presbyterian system would open the road to clerical-
ism and democracy. Soon after the conference the aged
Archbishop Whitgift died and was succeeded by the pas-

sionate and energetic Bancroft who had abused the Puritans at Hampton Court. He at once demanded that all ministers should conform to the use of the Prayer Book and subscribe to each of the Thirty-Nine Articles. A number of ministers who refused to do so, perhaps fewer than one hundred, were thrown out of their livings.

One happy result of the Hampton Court conference was that the King authorized a new translation of the Bible. This was finished by 1611 and was recognized to be a magnificent work of English prose, though the language was a century out of date 'and was drained of those brisk personal touches which were typical of the natural, native prose of England'. (C. V. Wedgwood.) Its publication undoubtedly gave a further impulse to the Bible-reading Puritan movement. About the same time that the Authorized Version appeared, Sir Walter Ralegh, naval hero of Queen Elizabeth's reign (and a financial adventurer), published his *History of the World*, written by him in the Tower of London where he had been imprisoned for plotting against the King. In the *History of the World* he wrote 'Let us build upon the Scriptures themselves and after that upon reason and nature.' This advice was pleasing to the reading public of his day, and his large and at times brilliant folio soon became a best-seller, devoured, among others, by Oliver Cromwell who instructed his son to read it too. Thus the Puritan movement had literary backing and this was soon strengthened by a whole battery of pamphlets, written by William Prynne, Henry Burton, John Lilburne, and dozens of others in the lively and aggressive prose style that marks their age. Meanwhile King James's well-intended efforts to obtain a religious settlement did not even paper over the cracks in the Church of England. Henceforward the struggle between the bishops, led first by Archbishop Richard Bancroft and later by William Laud, supported by the first two Stuart Kings, on the one side, and a growing Puritan movement, sustained by the majority in the House of Commons, on the other, was to be one of the most powerful factors in seventeenth-century history.

CHAPTER IV

The Reign of King James I
1603–25

IN the first two chapters we have shown that at the opening
of the seventeenth century the English 'gentry', that is the
class immediately below the peers, was being reinforced and
transformed by professional men, merchants, industrialists,
and successful yeomen, and that many among this class
were of an aggressively Puritan outlook. Such people formed
the mainstay of the House of Commons which had already
waxed in importance under the Tudor monarchs. Membership of the House was no longer regarded by the country
squires as a burden to be escaped but as a political duty
affording a convenient door into high society. Some of the
privileges and much of the procedure of the House had been
firmly established in the reign of Queen Elizabeth and it
was the cherished, and almost unquestioned, right of its
members to vote taxes, to make laws, and, within limits, to
discuss grievances. But Queen Elizabeth had repulsed all
attempts by the Commons to interfere in foreign policy or
questions of religion – the preserves of the Crown. And it
was therefore not surprising that King James I, coming
from Scotland, where he had been little more than a feudal
chieftain, to England, where he knew the royal prerogatives
to be far-reaching, should at first have underestimated the
strength of this rising political body and spoken in a lavish
way about the rights of kingship.

   Historians, writing in our own times when the House of
Commons has become the terminus of political ambition,
have sometimes pictured King James I as trying to put back
the clock by resisting the wishes of the Lower House. The
reason why they have done so is no doubt because that was
how early seventeenth-century members of parliament

themselves painted the picture: they stated that their claims
to wider powers were founded on historic precedents. But
that is to see events upside down. Up till the seventeenth
century the Commons had in fact taken only a limited part
in government. They had met irregularly and their rights
had been narrowly defined. It was only in the course of
Queen Elizabeth's reign that they had become more forceful
and inquisitive as the middle classes started to feel their political strength. In the reign of King James I members of
the Commons frankly admitted that out of respect for the
age and sex of their late sovereign they had not pushed their
constitutional demands as far as they might have done.
Now, however, the conditions were changing, the prerogative itself came under fire, and the history of the seventeenth
century saw a contest between Parliament and the King
for predominance in the State. In the middle of the century
the two sides took the sword and fought it out, and by the
end of the Stuart period Crown and Parliament had almost
ceased to be rivals and again become partners, but with
their relative positions reversed from what they had been
under the Tudors.

King James I was a clever and learned man – far from the
slobbering pedant he has sometimes been made out. His
defects were vanity and a softness in his nature, shown by
his habit of lecturing people at one moment and giving way
to them at another, and a liking for worthless favourites.
'He could criticize a theory, but he could not judge a man.'
(Holdsworth.) It was hard for him to realize that because
he had a weaker character than that of Queen Elizabeth
and because, unlike her, he had a large family and extrava-
gant tastes, he could not hope to hold Parliament in check
quite as she had done. Queen Elizabeth had died some
£400,000 in debt and had been able to keep her head above
water only by selling Crown lands. King James was therefore obliged to ask the Commons for money. But soon after
he came to the throne he wisely concluded peace with Spain,
ending a war that had lasted nearly twenty years; and the
Commons did not expect to have to vote taxes except in

times of war. Therefore the 'power of the purse' became an effective bargaining counter with the monarchy. Finally – and this was an error of judgement on his part – the King did not seek effective representatives of his interests in the Lower House such as Queen Elizabeth had commanded to direct and influence its debates. So the Commons, instead of working along with the King's Government in its not unreasonable policy, which was to maintain peace by avoiding foreign entanglements, to impose unity on the Church, and to arrange a legislative union between England and Scotland, began to put forward policies of their own and, by-passing the Privy Councillors and the Speaker, to win the initiative in legislation. They insisted on their right to give advice on foreign affairs and on the need to purify the Church, and they demanded that the King should abolish various traditional means by which the Crown raised money, such as 'purveyance' (the right to requisition goods and services for the royal use), wardship (the right of the Crown to administer the lands of minors), and the sale of patents or monopolies to parties that were prepared to pay for them. These clashes over policy continued throughout the reign.

King James sometimes made foolish or irritating remarks in his speeches to Parliament, but he can scarcely be blamed for believing that he governed by 'divine right' or that he had inherited 'prerogative powers' that could not be questioned. In the seventeenth century every authority claimed that it ruled by divine right, while the royal prerogatives were amply founded on precedents. The monarch had always taken whatever action he thought right when necessary for the safety of the State. If, for example, the country were threatened with invasion, the King could call on loyal subjects to give military and financial aid without parliamentary sanction. If insurrection were likely, the King could order the arrest of men he considered to be dangerous without the customary processes of law. Indeed such reserve powers rest with the executive in every nation at any time. When the seventeenth century opened, broad discretionary and emergency powers unquestionably belonged to the Crown and were later confirmed by test cases in the courts. The only danger was lest the medicine of the constitution should become its daily food. King James I and his advisers had the good sense not to press too hard nor too far. In the struggle that lay ahead it was Parliament, not the King, that threw out the challenge and demanded that the sovereign should submit to a modification of his traditional rights. Thus since the King was incapable of living within his income out of the royal revenues, he was always on the defensive against a growing opposition and the letter of the law retreated slowly before the spirit of the age.

And yet the spirit of the age, as seen by its revolutionaries, was conservative. The parliamentary leaders did not regard themselves as militant reformers but in a romantic haze as repairers of an ancient (but imaginary) political fabric, in existence even before the Conquest, that had been damaged by abuses. The first Stuart Kings for their part thought of themselves as progressive, enlightened rulers, 'nursing fathers' to their country. It was John Pym, the Uncrowned King of the Commons, who maintained that 'the form of government in any state cannot be altered without apparent danger of ruin to that state' and his friend, Sir John Eliot, who confessed that religion was a means of securing obedience to the powers that be.

Antagonism between King and Parliament soon revealed itself when the first parliament of the reign met in London after God had 'lightened his hand and relented the violence of his devouring angel against the poor people of the City'. The Commons at once thought it necessary to affirm their privileges. In the first place one of their members, Sir Thomas Shirley, had been cast into the Fleet prison for debt and it was not until they persuaded the King to confirm the justice of their demand for his release that the Warden of the Fleet consented to free him. Secondly, an outlaw, Sir Francis Goodwin, had been elected M.P. for Buckinghamshire: the Court of Chancery had declared that the return was void; and when the Commons decided that he was properly elected and ought to take his seat, the King countermanded their order. In this case the monarch was in the end obliged to give way, though Goodwin in fact never took his seat. So indignant were the Commons about these two episodes that they drew up and printed in their journal an 'Apology' affirming their ancient rights which they identified with the liberties of all the King's subjects. In this 'Apology' was embodied the notion, so dear to later historians, that the privileges of Parliament had been attacked by a foreign king. 'The prerogatives of princes may easily, and do daily grow,' the 'Apology' observed, 'the privileges of the subject are for the most part at an everlasting stand.' On the other hand, the King did not sweeten his relations with the Commons when in proroguing Parliament in 1604, he made a sarcastic speech referring to the Commons as 'my masters of the Lower House'.

Still, whatever the preliminary brushes amounted to, it could scarcely be maintained that under the cautious guidance of Sir Robert Cecil, the Secretary of State whom King James had inherited from Queen Elizabeth and was later to make Lord Treasurer and create Earl of Salisbury, the new ruler was acting despotically. He set out to fulfil his declared policy as a prince of peace. The treaty of peace with Spain was concluded without betraying the cause of England's late allies, the United Netherlands, which were now fully able to defend themselves; the King promoted plans for a legislative union between England and Scotland, which fell through owing to English jealousy of the Scots; and he hoped that by expelling the Puritan ministers who refused to bow the knee to Church discipline and by allowing thousands of Roman Catholics to be fined for 'recusancy', he would impose unity within the Church.

Just before Parliament met again in the autumn of 1605 a shocking episode came to light. A number of Roman Catholic conspirators, directed by the persuasive Robert Catesby, with the active and selfless assistance of a soldier of fortune named Guido Fawkes, planned to blow up the King and both Houses by means of barrels of gunpowder stored in a Westminster cellar. Some of the conspirators, who were in any case too numerous to preserve their secrets, were understandably reluctant that the Catholic peers in the House of Lords should be blown to pieces in this Catholic endeavour and dispatched a warning. A peer who received an anonymous letter at once informed the Government and a search party unearthed the gunpowder beneath a pile of coals and wood in the presence of Guido Fawkes who intended to apply the torch. At least that was the official story. The discovery of the plot meant a renewal and increase of penalties against English Roman Catholics, the introduction of a day of thanksgiving which was officially celebrated for 250 years, and an amicable interlude in the contest between the King and his Parliament. The Commons granted the King subsidies and the session ended in May, 1606, in general good humour.

The following four years, however, were consumed in financial discussions and debates. Salisbury was anxious that in return for the surrender by the Crown of its right to such established resources as 'purveyance', wardships, and the like, the Commons should vote a large sum to pay off the royal debts. Hard bargaining continued for several years, but eventually the negotiations for the 'Great Contract' broke down, partly because the Commons demanded so much in the way of concessions and offered so little in the way of money, partly because the King tired of the whole business and thought that he had nothing much to gain from it. An important constitutional case in 1606 strengthened the royal financial position. A merchant named John Bate had refused to pay the 'poundage' or import duty that had been levied purely by executive action on currants brought in from Venice. But the Court of Exchequer ruled that since the King had the right to regulate foreign trade such 'impositions' came within the scope of his prerogative. Salisbury was delighted with this decision and proceeded to publish a new book of rates in 1608 which was expected to yield an additional £70,000 to the Crown. The Commons were most indignant, refused to vote further taxation, and complained about the prodigal way in which the King was spending money on his Scottish favourites. Their tempers were not improved when they learned that a certain Dr Cowell, who was Professor of Civil Law at Cambridge, had published a book affirming that the King was 'above the law by his absolute power' and that the right of the Commons to vote taxes only existed by royal favour. King James took the wind out of the sails of the Commons by repudiating these extreme doctrines as denying the 'marriage between the prerogative and the common law', but in February 1611, upset by the sharp criticisms of his personal conduct offered in the Commons, he defiantly dissolved his first Parliament.

Thus ended the opening phase of the reign. In November 1610 Archbishop Bancroft, who had carried out an ecclesiastical policy in harmony with the King's wishes, died and was somewhat surprisingly succeeded by George Abbot who had been Bishop of London and sympathized with the Puritan doctrines while ignoring their implications; in May 1612 Salisbury died and the Treasury was put into commission; and in November of the same year King James's eldest son, Prince Henry, a more promising youth than his stuttering brother Charles, perished of fever, though his mother, the Queen, begged Sir Walter Ralegh, then a prisoner of state in the Tower, to prescribe a last-moment medicine. In February 1613 King James's daughter, Princess Elizabeth, was married to Frederick, the Elector Palatine in Germany, and thus became a tragic heroine. At the same time her father joined a Protestant Union of European princes.

The middle of King James I's reign was distinguished chiefly by struggles between personalities, often more extraordinary than they were edifying. Approached from a modern point of view, the King's subservience to his favourites might appear so pathetic and degrading as to raise doubts about his sanity. It is fair, however, to bear in mind that nearly every monarch in English history has had favourites, either men or women: the late Queen Elizabeth, for example, had behaved foolishly over both Leicester and Essex; what one needs to consider is how far the influence of such popinjays affected the course of history. King James's first favourite was Robert Carr, a Scotsman whom he made Viscount Rochester and afterwards Earl of Somerset. Somerset's weakness was his wife, born Frances Howard. Frances had been married at the age of thirteen to the Earl of Essex (son and heir of Queen Elizabeth's unfortunate favourite) who was fourteen at the time. The formalities of marriage having been completed, the two children were separated and when, after an absence of nearly three years on the Continent, young Essex returned to claim his bride and the felicities that accompany marriage he found that Frances had fallen in love with Robert Carr. She therefore refused her husband conjugal rights and later demanded that her marriage should be declared null and void. The King proved eager to promote her desire and appointed a commission of bishops and others to try the case. It was a delicate matter to handle since Essex was unwilling to admit that the nullity was any fault of his. Moreover the Archbishop of Canterbury, Abbot, was dubious about the whole business; and although Lancelot Andrewes, the saintly Bishop of Ely, was willing to accept the evidence, other commissioners were more squeamish or more suspicious. Two Bishops who were susceptible to the King's wishes had to be added to the Commission and in the end Frances Howard had her way and was married to her lover. All her relatives were delighted, for many of them enjoyed, or were soon to acquire, posts of influence and value. One Howard was Lord High Admiral, another was Lord Privy Seal, a third, Thomas Howard, Earl of Suffolk, father of the newly wed, was now to have Salisbury's place as Lord Treasurer. Had the young lady's passions been quenched at that point, all might have been well for her and her relations. But she took a violent dislike to a friend of her husband's, Sir Thomas Overbury, who had apparently advised against the marriage. The King had Overbury imprisoned in the Tower of London for refusing to accept a diplomatic appointment abroad. Frances was then said to have plotted Overbury's murder and to have bribed a warder to poison him. But he may have been killed by the incompetence of his doctors. Later the plot was discovered. Meanwhile Somerset himself, now the richest man in England, holding the post of Lord Chamberlain and forming the gilded bottleneck of the Court, began to be concerned about his universal unpopularity. He therefore decided, so one story runs, to bring a handsome youth named George Villiers to the King's attention, arguing that if the King were known to have English favourites, as well as a Scottish favourite, those who disliked him mainly because he was a Scot might be mollified. Unfortunately for him, matters worked out badly. The King was much attracted by Villiers and though he defended himself, when Somerset upbraided him, in a most peculiar letter, the Scotsman began to lose favour. When the full story of the Overbury affair came out, his fate and that of his wife were sealed. Though they were not put to death, as were Overbury's alleged murderers, they were deprived of all their offices and placed in honourable confinement for their crimes. Somerset died in obscurity and Villiers, later made Earl of Buckingham, took his place. The fall of Somerset entailed the fall of the Howards. Buckingham obtained the post of Lord High Admiral and, after Suffolk had been dismissed and then punished for taking bribes, the Treasury was once more put in commission. But the difference between Buckingham and Somerset was that not only did Buckingham rule the Court so that all approaches to the King for personal favours and offices had to be negotiated through him, but he also himself aspired to be an active commander, diplomatist, and statesman – roles for which he lacked the capacity. The King, however, was loyal to him to the end and instructed his heir, Prince Charles, ever to uphold Buckingham and his family. Charles was to follow his father's bad advice. And in so far as one man caused the disasters that befell the Stuart monarchy in the middle of the century, that man was Buckingham.

So much for the favourites. They were a main item in the

royal extravagance. In 1614 the King summoned a fresh parliament, designed to be a 'parliament of love', in the hope of persuading it to vote him money. Some attempt was made to obtain a House of Commons more friendly to the King than its predecessor. But the new House, far from voting the King money, protested against 'undertakers' and attacked 'impositions'. The King therefore dissolved Parliament in the same year, and it is known to history as the 'Addled Parliament'. He tried to fill the financial gap by inviting towns and individuals to lend him money of their own free will, though without notable success. Indeed, not unnaturally opposition to such exactions, known as 'benevolences', developed among the gentry, while merchants had already been alienated by industrial and commercial monopolies conferred on courtiers and by the impositions. A Somersetshire clergyman named Peacham, who was alleged to have written a sermon treating of the grievances of the subject, was put into the Tower and after torture the Court decided to charge him with treason. The Peacham case proved to be a trial of strength between Francis Bacon, the Attorney-General, who was afterwards promoted Lord Chancellor, and Sir Edward Coke, the Lord Chief Justice. The Bacon–Coke struggle coincided with that between Somerset and Buckingham. But Bacon and Coke were men of far higher calibre. Bacon honestly believed that good government consisted in maintaining the royal prerogatives intact and thought that the judges should be 'lions under the throne'. Coke, on the other hand, wanted to erect the Common Law into an institution of even greater moment than parliament and saw the high court judges as mediators, holding the balance between the King and his subjects. Coke, therefore, refused to agree to the King's request that in the Peacham case he should give his advice independently instead of along with his fellow judges. In the end the King dismissed the Lord Chief Justice in November 1616, but Coke had vindicated the independence of the judiciary. Bacon proved, on the whole, a wise adviser to the King, but although he kept on good terms with Buckingham, he never wielded real power and finally he fell in the same way as many other leading figures in the period, because he was accused of accepting bribes. Lionel Cranfield, Earl of Middlesex, the genius who for a time succeeded in putting the royal finances in order, also lost his office in much the same way. It is hard to say how far Bacon and Middlesex – and Suffolk, too – were guilty of heinous offences judged by the standards of their own day. Gratuities and presents were a recognized part of the payment of many of the King's servants. With the disgrace of Bacon and Middlesex the King lost two remarkable servants, men who under other circumstances would have served the State with distinction. But he threw his protective cloak over Buckingham – and Buckingham survived.

From such fascinating matters as nullity cases and murders in the Tower the King was compelled to turn to foreign affairs, when the Thirty Years War between Protestants and Catholics broke out in Germany in 1618. Hitherto his foreign policy had been determined by his anxiety to keep the peace and to improve his somewhat rocky finances. In 1616 he surrendered three Dutch 'cautionary towns', which had been in English hands since the reign of Queen Elizabeth as pledges for the debts contracted by the United Netherlands to the English Crown, and received in return £215,000 cash down. Next, chiefly because he had hopes of a large dowry, he devoted his attention to planning a marriage between his eldest surviving son, Prince Charles, and the Spanish Infanta. In any case an understanding with Spain, still reckoned the strongest state in Europe, was an essential part of his programme and was astutely promoted by the Spanish ambassador, Gondomar, whose Government wanted at all costs to keep the English out of European affairs. To please the Spaniards, Sir Walter Ralegh, who had been released from the Tower in 1617 and allowed to sail across the Atlantic in search of a mythical gold mine in Guiana, was put to death on a charge of treason dating from fourteen years earlier. If he had found his gold mine and so supplemented the royal wealth, his life would no doubt have been spared; he had gambled for high stakes and paid for his failure on the scaffold. But the pro-Spanish policy was threatened when in August 1619 King James's son-in-law, Prince Frederick, the Elector Palatine, rather unwisely accepted the throne of Protestant Bohemia which was considered the sovereign possession of the Habsburg Emperor Ferdinand. The Spanish Habsburgs joined the Imperialists and the Roman Catholic princes of Germany in a campaign to drive the Elector from the new throne he had been persuaded to occupy. In October 1620 the Elector was decisively beaten in the battle of the White Mountain and he and his wife, 'the Winter Queen', were driven into exile. The outcry of the English Protestants at his fate as victim of a papist coalition was loud and bitter. King James still hoped that if the Spanish marriage could be concluded, the Spanish Habsburgs would withdraw their support from their German relatives and permit his son-in-law to be restored at least to his hereditary possessions. The King tried to collect further 'benevolences' to pay for his foreign policy, but in January 1621 was compelled to seek aid from a new parliament. His ministers considered that he would need an army of 30,000 men to help the Elector Frederick to recover the Palatinate and that its cost would be some £900,000 a year – laughable figures by modern standards, but then considerable. The House of Commons took the view that the best method of counter-attacking the Roman Catholics in Europe was not to ally with but to assault Spain and by confiscating her treasure fleets to make the war self-supporting as in the palmy days of Queen Elizabeth. Therefore, after making a smallish grant, the new House, now led by John Pym and Sir Edward Coke, the former Lord Chief Justice, returned with a keen appetite to the discussion of their grievances. Bacon was condemned by the House of Lords and the Commons impeached Sir Giles Mompesson, a relative of the Earl of Buckingham, for exploiting 'patents' or monopolies. The King intervened only when the Houses of Parliament assumed the right to whip, pillory, and fine an aged Roman Catholic barrister named Floyd who was merely accused of speaking scornfully of the Elector Frederick and his wife. When, in November 1621, the members of the House rose one after another and urged the King to head a Protestant alliance in an offensive against Spain and condemned the Spanish marriage negotiations King James could stand no more. He wrote a sharp letter to the Speaker instructing the Commons not to interfere in the mysteries of state. The Commons then entered a protestation in their journal, but the King dissolved Parliament, tore the protestation from the book, and ordered the arrest of Coke and two other members of parliament and the confinement of Pym to his London house. Thus he refused to recognize 'freedom of speech' in the Commons, and even if they denied him the sinews of war, he would not, under their pressure, change his foreign policy.

In pursuit of that policy Prince Charles and Buckingham visited Spain *incognito* in 1623. But though both the King and his son were prepared to go to ridiculous lengths to meet the Spanish King's terms, the Pope was dubious and the shuddering Infanta tried to escape marriage to a heretic by going into a convent, and ultimately the negotiations broke down. When Buckingham, who had already been created Duke in expectation of a successful outcome to the mission, returned to England in October 1623, he and the unwanted suitor were furious against Spain. Thenceforward the King and Parliament were in perfect agreement in their attitude to Spain and Roman Catholicism. Indeed, so unnerved was the King by the failure of the proposed Spanish match, that he condescended to ask the counsel of parliament in foreign affairs, although when they had offered advice before he had regarded it as an affront to his prerogative. He now laboured to build up a coalition to restore his son-in-law. In June 1624 an offensive treaty was signed with the Dutch, a marriage was sought for Charles with a French princess, now that France was effectively ruled by Cardinal Richelieu whose policy was to oppose the Habsburg

Emperor; and a force was gathered under Count Mansfield, a soldier of fortune, to fight on the Continent. As payment for parliamentary support, the King agreed to an important act against monopolies, one of the major parliamentary grievances of the reign.

Actually the King's new foreign policy fell between two stools. He might have concentrated on an alliance with France against Spain or he might have inspired a Protestant military alliance dedicated to recovering the Palatinate. Instead he took on more than he could finish. Mansfield's hastily raised and poorly equipped army was unwelcome to both the French and the Dutch and soon was broken by starvation and disease. On the other hand, so far as domestic policy during the reign is concerned it was not such a failure from the point of view of the monarchy as has sometimes been supposed. Broadly, King James had maintained the rights of the executive against the encroachments of an independent-minded House of Commons which had still to make good its claim to freedom of speech. By various financial ingenuities and by sticking until near the end to a peaceable policy he had prevented the Crown from depending unduly on parliamentary grants. Thus the Commons had not been able to better materially their constitutional position and in their aggressive Protestantism and little-Englandism had shown themselves to be a source of much foolishness. But the King saw the danger signals ahead and warned his heir that he would have his 'belly-full' of parliaments and impeachments.

If it lay in shadow as compared with the wonderful age of Elizabeth I, his was by no means an inglorious reign, which passed, on the whole, in peace and prosperity, though we should remember it chiefly as the epoch of Shakespeare and Bacon at the fullness of their powers – and of the good ship, *Mayflower*, which sailed with its load of Puritan emigrants to America in 1620. King James I died in March 1625, and King Charles I and the ineffable Duke of Buckingham entered upon their dubious heritage.

CHAPTER V

King Charles I and the 'Eleven Years' Tyranny'
1625–40

KING JAMES I, it has been said, had 'a genius for getting into difficulties', but was 'not without a certain shrewdness in stopping just short of catastrophe. If he steered the ship straight for the rocks, he left his son to wreck it'. (Gwatkin). Probably this interpretation of the reigns of the first two Stuart Kings attunes rather too easily with the old-fashioned notion that the Great Civil War in the mid seventeenth century was entirely the fault of absolute monarchs who had made bloated claims of power against an ill-used nation; but it is certainly true that even if he grew lazy in his last years and was ludicrously complacent towards his favourites, King James had been a statesman, while his son was no statesman and was handicapped from the beginning by serious weaknesses of character. Not that he was without virtue; he was 'sober, grave and sweet' and was handsome and dignified, though flattered before posterity by the portraits of Van Dyck. He was a patron of the arts, induced both Van Dyck and Rubens to come to England and accept knighthoods, built up a noble collection of paintings that were later sold to pay Roundhead debts, and delighted to show foreign visitors the masterpieces for which his agents had scoured Europe. A good father and a faithful husband, he might, save for that unsullied respectability, have made an excellent Italian Duke. But his lack of insight and humour, his customary curtness and his intellectual shortcomings were poor protection against the coming storms. He was guided by sentiment and prejudices, he was shifty and unstable; and he usually surrendered himself to advisers of second-rate capacity. Moreover in confronting the political problems of his reign, he had two special disadvantages.

In the first place, he was even more friendly than his father to Roman Catholics, and even more strongly opposed to the Puritanism which now pervaded the House of Commons. Two months after his accession, he had married a fifteen-year-old French wife, Henrietta Maria, the sister of King Louis XIII, and had secretly promised to relieve the English Roman Catholics of their disabilities. The bishops who took his fancy were High Churchmen. King James had at least appointed the Puritan, Abbot, as Archbishop of Canterbury, whose career was clouded after he killed a keeper when aiming at a deer. But when Abbot died in 1633 King Charles selected in his place William Laud, the Bishop of London, an avowed opponent of the Puritans. Laud had been a pupil of Bishop Lancelot Andrewes and together with Richard Neile, the Bishop of Winchester, later Archbishop of York, whose chaplain he had been, he had sustained the new movement in the Church which laid stress upon the beauty of holiness and questioned the doctrine of predestination. In the Netherlands a theologian named Arminius had also attacked predestination in the early seventeenth century; consequently Laud and his friends were nicknamed 'Arminians' and because they refused to deny that Roman Catholics were true Christians they were also rudely dubbed 'spawn of the Papists'. The King favoured Laud's point of view and in due course was to use him as his chief adviser. But at the outset of the reign he had not even a man as able as Laud for a Minister. The disgraced Bacon was dead; John Williams, a supple bishop who had succeeded him as Lord Keeper, was removed from his office and told to go to his see of Lincoln and stay there; and Buckingham, who 'lay the first night of the reign in the King's bedchamber', remained to mismanage the war.

This war with Spain was King Charles's second disadvantage. He could scarcely be said to have inherited this from his father since he and Buckingham had themselves promoted it eagerly after they had been humiliated in Madrid. They were now launched on an ocean of costly enterprises. By the treaty with the Dutch they had promised to supply them with 6,000 English soldiers and the useless army of Mansfield was still on their hands. Finally, they were expected to attack Spain from the sea, while the Dutch harassed the Spanish Netherlands (modern Belgium). Consequently King Charles was compelled at once to summon parliament and to ask the Commons for money. He erred, however, in failing to explain to them in detail why he wanted it, so that they only voted a subsidy of £140,000, less than a quarter of what was needed for the war, and turned smartly to matters of religion. They clamoured for the enforcement of the laws against Roman Catholics (which the King had secretly promised to cancel), the introduction of measures to promote Puritanism, and violently criticized the writings of an 'Arminian' rector named Richard Montagu, who was wittier and sharper than Laud, and had the bad taste to deny that the Pope was Anti-Christ, a widely-held view among Puritans. The King immediately disclosed his views by appointing Montagu his personal chaplain and ordering the Commons to stop their attacks; later he made Montagu Bishop of Chichester.

Owing to the plague, which had returned to London in its full horror, as during the first year of King James I's reign, Parliament after an adjournment met again that August in Oxford. It did so in a bad humour. In July when many members of the Commons had already scattered owing to the plague they had been begged for large grants of money. But they distrusted both the wisdom and competence of the Duke of Buckingham, now the leading Minister. On 8 August, taking the bull by the horns, the Duke of Buckingham himself addressed both Houses in the hall of Christ Church College, assuring them that he was 'a faithful, true-hearted Englishman', that he never took action without the advice of the Privy Council or Council of War, and that the King would certainly execute the existing laws against the Roman Catholics. He then required that the navy should be made ready for an assault on Spain. His audience was unimpressed by such speciousness and before the Commons even fulfilled its promise to grant 'tonnage and poundage' (that is, customs duties) to the King for one year – instead of, as normally, for his lifetime – Parliament was dissolved.

The King and Buckingham now hoped that their actions would speak louder than words. By cashing Henrietta Maria's large marriage portion and, if necessary, by selling the crown jewels, they planned to supply the needs of the navy; and the navy, in its turn, they reckoned might, by acquiring booty on an Elizabethan scale, supply their needs. But that autumn an expedition to Cadiz under command of an admiral who had never before put to sea, failed. True, a land force marched towards the port, but the ill-equipped and undisciplined troops got drunk on Spanish wine and after re-embarkation the whole expeditionary force ran short of supplies and was afflicted by sickness. Afterwards the fleet was dispersed by storms and limped back to Plymouth with many men half-dead.

While this fiasco occurred and Buckingham, though Lord High Admiral, was busy in an ambassadorial capacity at The Hague negotiating fresh treaties with the Dutch and the Danes, King Charles was quarrelling with his wife and the country from which she came. The young French princess had pictured herself as carrying a torch of freedom to her Roman Catholic co-religionists. Since it was a Protestant ceremony and she had refused to take part in the coronation service the King had been compelled to appear by himself clad in white as being married not to his wife but to his people. Subsequently he had demanded that her French attendants should be removed and it was not until after a series of scenes slightly reminiscent of *The Taming of the Shrew*, during which Henrietta Maria learned that her best chance of getting what she wanted was to appear to be submissive, that a way of living together was found between the royal husband and wife. Meanwhile the treatment of his sister annoyed the French King as did also the refusal of a number of English ships hired by him to act against his rebellious Protestant subjects, the Huguenots.

As King Charles I was thus raising enemies abroad, his

financial troubles, after the collapse of the Cadiz expedition, remained unsolved. In February 1626 he called a new parliament, first taking care to appoint leading opposition members in the previous parliament, such as Sir Edward Coke and Sir Thomas Wentworth, as sheriffs so as to disqualify them from election. The new House of Commons, however, found a passionate champion in Sir John Eliot, a Cornishman, who at one time had been the friend of Buckingham. Eliot demanded an inquiry into the Cadiz disaster, asked about the causes of the misunderstanding with France, and sought to impeach Buckingham.

At this time the King also succeeded in annoying the House of Lords by his unwise treatment of the Earl of Bristol who had formerly been the English ambassador at Madrid and whom the King blamed personally for the failure of his mission in his father's reign to marry the Infanta. Having previously asserted that the Earl was innocent of any crime, the King now charged him with treason, but Bristol defended himself to good purpose and helped to magnify the unpopularity of Buckingham. In May Eliot carried his case against Buckingham up to the House of Lords. He made a speech comparing Buckingham to Sejanus, the wicked adviser of the tyrannous Roman Emperor Tiberius. The King sent Eliot and Dudley Digges, his chief supporter in the impeachment proceedings, to the Tower and ordered that the case against Buckingham should be heard in the prerogative court, the Star Chamber, where he was acquitted. The Commons refused to be frightened, denied the Crown a fresh supply of money, and was dissolved. The King then levied 'tonnage and poundage' without parliamentary sanction and tried to raise a 'forced loan' or capital levy. The Lord Chief Justice who questioned the lawfulness of the forced loan was dismissed and those who would not pay it were imprisoned on the King's order. Five of the Knights so imprisoned applied in 1627 for a writ of *habeas corpus* on the ground that they had not been charged with any specific offence. The judges remanded the Knights, but the constitutional question whether the King could or could not

imprison his subjects without showing cause was left un-
determined.

In that same year the country drifted into war with
France as well as with Spain. The reasons for the breach
with France were numerous and complicated. Cardinal
Richelieu had desired an English alliance. But the encouragement given by England to the Huguenot rebels, quarrels
over trade and shipping, and the annoyance of the French
King with King Charles for his behaviour towards Henrietta
Maria and with the Duke of Buckingham because of a
foolish if unsuccessful attempt to make love to the French
Queen all contributed to frustrate Richelieu's policy. In
1626 a treaty was concluded between France and Spain
and just before Christmas Admiral Pennington, the English
naval commander in the Downs, was ordered to attack and
sink French ships lying at anchor in Le Havre. King
Charles relied upon the overwhelming English supremacy
at sea and the support of the Huguenots to bring the war to
a speedy and profitable end. In June the Duke of Buckingham taking up in earnest one of his protean parts, that of
Lord High Admiral, sailed with ninety ships and some
10,000 men to relieve the besieged Huguenot town of La
Rochelle on the west coast of France by capturing the Isle
of Rhé, separated by a strait two miles wide from the mainland. The investment of St Martin, the chief town on the
island, which was defended by only a small French force,
was prolonged and ignominiously unsuccessful, and in the
late autumn the Duke led his dispirited expedition back
home.

For a third time the King was driven to summon parliament. Various novel methods of raising money had been
examined by his advisers and then abandoned as unwork-
able. In the elections to the new House of Commons it was
inevitable that the men who had resisted payment of the
recent forced loan, such as the Five Knights, should be
chosen, and that Buckingham's failure at the Island of Rhé
should find them eager to condemn and protest. Bishop
Laud, who preached the sermon when Parliament met in

March 1628, took as his text 'Endeavour to keep the unity of the Spirit in the bond of peace', which was more optimistic than appropriate. The King instructed the two Houses to provide means for meeting 'the common danger'. As the nation was now committed to a hazardous war with both France and Spain, his attitude was comprehensible. But the Commons insisted on voicing their grievances before voting supplies. They decided to draw up a protest against imprisonments without cause shown, against forced loans, martial law, and the compulsory billeting of soldiers. This was like drafting a report on civil defence while the bombs were still falling. But though the King found such behaviour amazing, the M.P.s thought it both necessary and agreeable. The only debate – and it was a long one – among themselves was how they should proceed. Sir Thomas Wentworth favoured enacting legislation, while others wanted to confer with the Upper House and pronounce joint resolutions. But the Lords would not accept the Commons' drafts about arbitrary imprisonment and when Coke headed a committee to draw up a Bill, Wentworth thought his phraseology was too outspoken to exact assent from the King. In the end after much argument a clever idea of Coke's was adopted: it was decided to frame a 'Petition of Right' which adapted to public use a private procedure, inviting the King to waive his prerogatives in favour of the normal course of law. The Petition was also put through the usual legislative stages, being read three times in each House. It asked the King for 'recognition of a claim that every subject of the Crown had been wronged in certain specific matters, and that, in future, the law should be observed'. (E. R. Adair.) On 7 June the King finally gave his assent to the Petition of Right in a form acceptable to the Commons, but whether that form really gave it the force of law has been disputed. The Commons now moved on to censure such divines as had unduly exalted the King's prerogative (for example, Dr Sibthorpe, who had ventured the opinion that the King himself possessed legislative powers), to threaten Buckingham, and to remonstrate over impositions. This session was notable for a vain attempt by Wentworth to purge the evils from Buckingham's administration without reducing the real strength of the King and his government. On 26 June, to save Buckingham from impeachment, the King prorogued Parliament.

Buckingham had escaped the vengeance of a parliament thirsting for his blood only to die at the hands of an assassin. Political agitation had spread throughout the country. 'Who rules the kingdom?' asked a satire nailed to a post in the City of London. 'The King. Who rules the King? The Duke. Who rules the Duke? The Devil. Let the Duke look to it.' A naval lieutenant named John Felton with genuine or imaginary grievances of his own, was also persuaded by the agitation and with a tenpenny dagger killed the Duke when he was in Portsmouth preparing another expedition for the relief of La Rochelle. The Earl of Lindsey took command of the fleet that had been making ready, but it was unable to break past the moles that the French besiegers of La Rochelle had pushed out from the harbour and on 18 October the Huguenot stronghold surrendered to Richelieu and the war between England and France was practically at an end.

In spite of the death of Buckingham Parliament met again in January 1629, still in an angry mood. During the recess many merchants who had refused to pay taxes which the Commons regarded as illegal had either been arrested or had their goods seized. One of these merchants, John Rolle, whose property was confiscated was a member of parliament. Moreover 'the Commons noticed that the Petition of Right had been printed and circulated with the King's first unmeaning answer affixed; one of those petty acts of dishonesty by which Charles convinced the world that he could never be held to a promise.' (F. C. Montague.)

The Commons plunged forthwith into the alluring topic of the Church. The King had published a declaration enjoining peace and unity and leaving it to Convocation to settle ecclesiastical disputes. But Sir John Eliot averred that so long as the High Church bishops held sway such a declaration was only calculated to bring in 'popery and Arminianism' and poison the pure waters of the Calvinist faith. The Commons, therefore, ignoring such mundane matters as finance and war, settled down with ardour to sort out problems of theological interpretation and announced that they would not allow the religion of England to be changed, that is from the sense in which they preferred it should exist. Francis Rouse moved that 'first it may be considered what new paintings are laid on the old face of the whore of Babylon to make her more lovely and draw more suitors'. Oliver Cromwell, the new member of parliament for Huntingdon, whose fiery countenance and plain clothes attracted some attention, accused Bishop Neile of preaching 'flat popery'. The King ordered a short adjournment and when the Commons reassembled on 2 March the Speaker declared that the King required a further adjournment, but this was resisted on all sides. Two strong young members, one of whom was Denzil Holles, thrust the Speaker back into his seat and held him down. 'God's wounds!' cried Holles, 'you shall sit till we please to rise.' Never before had the King's right to adjourn parliament whenever he wished been called in question. The Speaker was then required to put three resolutions to the House which Eliot had prepared, but he refused, and Eliot threw a piece of paper containing his resolutions into the fire. The King then sent the Serjeant-at-Arms to seize the mace, the symbol of the House's authority, and he was followed by the Usher of the Black Rod with a royal message commanding obedience. Holles recollected the purport of Eliot's resolutions and himself put them to the House. They ran: (1) Whosoever brought in innovations of religion or favoured Popery and Arminianism should be considered capital enemies to the kingdom. (2) Whosoever should advise the taking and levying of tonnage and poundage without parliamentary consent should likewise be considered capital enemies. (3) Any merchant who paid tonnage and poundage thus levied should be deemed a traitor to the liberties of England. The resolutions were carried by acclamation and the House then voted its own adjournment. Parliament was not to meet again for eleven years.

We may pause at this point to weigh the significance of English political history in the first thirty years of the seventeenth century. We have seen how from the time King James I took the road from Edinburgh to London the House of Commons had pressed its novel claim to take the leading part in the State. The House of Lords had occupied that position in the fifteenth century when it had contained the richest landowners in the kingdom and had even used the Commons as a mouthpiece of its desires. In the sixteenth century the Commons became, in Professor Bindoff's view, 'the Tudors' chosen instrument for translating the national will into legislation of unprecedented importance, volume, and complexity'. The rise or enlargement of the gentry in the later half of the sixteenth century and the early half of the seventeenth century had fortified the Commons who grew conscious of their strength and wealth. 'We could buy the Upper House (His Majesty only excepted) thrice over,' boasted a member of the Commons in 1628. Greedy for wider political powers, they wrested from the King's counsellors the initiative in legislation, they demanded complete 'freedom of speech' (which both King James I and King Charles I would not recognize), and they asserted their right to dictate to the King on religion and foreign policy, subjects which Queen Elizabeth had held to be peculiarly her own affairs. They put forward all these demands not in the name of a brave, new world, but as their lawful rights, broad-based on precedent. The Petition of Right was the logical outcome of this conservative approach: 'it enacted nothing new. It merely set out the law in the sense in which the [parliamentary] opposition understood it'. (Holdsworth.) But though the Calvinist squires and lawyers who filled the Commons in the reigns of King James I and King Charles I might honestly have believed that all they were seeking to do was to preserve the pristine purity of the English Church and State, both their ultimate aims and their immediate programme were in fact revolutionary. The parliamentary leaders, Pym, Eliot, Rouse, and the rest, forged the Commons into a revolutionary tool with which to transform the constitution as it was handed down by the Tudors. Their hands may have been the hands of Essau, but the voice was the voice of Jacob.

After he had dissolved Parliament in 1629 King Charles I published a reasoned defence of his conduct and promised to uphold the true religion as established in the Church of England 'without admitting or conniving at any backsliding either to Popery or schism', and also, to maintain contrast, he ordered the arrest of nine members of parliament including Eliot for seditious words and violence to the Speaker. In the end all the prisoners, though condemned by the Court of King's Bench, were released, some even without making any act of submission, but no such mercy was displayed towards Eliot. It is clear that the King blamed Eliot for Buckingham's death. In close confinement the strength of this sincere and uncompromising idealist waned. In October 1632 he applied for leave of absence from the Tower to recover his broken health, but this was refused. By the end of the next month he was dead. And by Eliot's friends his untimely fate was laid at the door of the King.

It has been said that for the next eleven years the King was his own Prime Minister. This is one of those simple generalizations which scarcely survive serious scrutiny. For Prime Ministers hardly existed before the eighteenth century and Kings had always been the makers of policy. It is true, however, that the King possessed no outstanding minister on whom he could rely. His Lord Treasurer, Lord Portland, was a well-intending nobody. Sir Thomas Wentworth who, anxious to promote efficient government, had offered his services to the Crown after the death of Buckingham, though generous with advice, was rarely in London. Only William Laud, who became Archbishop of Canterbury in August 1633, was constantly in Whitehall, but he was absorbed in reforming the Church on his own pattern.

In foreign affairs the policy of the King ought to have been to preserve peace if only because in the absence of parliament he did not have the means to wage war. In fact he still struggled to win back the Palatinate for his sister's husband and to assert British sea power. But he kept on feebly changing his plans: at one time he tried to make an arrangement with Spain, at another with the United Netherlands, to gain his objective in Germany; yet he had little to offer and less to hope for. It is true that, when peace was reached with Spain in November 1636, the Spaniards secretly promised help to recover the Palatinate, but the promise was not worth the paper it was written on, even though the price King Charles was prepared to pay was war on the Dutch to divide up the independent Netherlands that Queen Elizabeth had helped to set up. Nothing came of all this, although later the King gave indirect assistance to Spain by ordering the Royal Navy to enforce dominion over the Narrow Seas and convoy Spanish merchant vessels across them. Actually the King's best chance of doing good in Germany was to ally himself with the King of Sweden, the great Gustavus Adolphus, who had in September 1631 at Breitenfeld inflicted a crushing defeat on the Imperial armies. Gustavus Adolphus asked for the aid of the English fleet in safeguarding his communications with his homeland base while he fought in Germany and for an English-paid contingent to serve in his army. King Charles rejected the advice of the majority of his Privy Council which was in favour of accepting these terms. In the summers of 1635, 1636, and 1637 English fleets sailed into the North Sea partly to frighten Dutch fishermen, partly with the more worthy aim of ensuring that the Belgian coast should not pass into the hands of the rising French or Dutch States. The policy of keeping Belgium out of the hands of a strong continental power was of course consistent with the historical aims of England throughout modern times, but the main result of showing the flag was to worsen relations with our former allies, the Dutch, who were now becoming our chief commercial and colonial rivals.

To pay for these fleets as well as to meet the ordinary expenses of government without parliamentary aid the King employed a number of financial devices unpalatable to the wealthy classes. His principal source of revenue was customs duties; after the conclusion of peace with France and Spain there was a marked trade revival and the yield from these duties increased. In his defence published after the dissolution of parliament he had justified his taking 'tonnage and poundage' by precedents dating back to Edward IV in addition to levying impositions and although protests continued, on the whole, merchants pocketed their scruples, ignored the previous warnings of the Commons, and paid up. Freeholders owning land worth £40 a year or more were fined for not taking knighthoods; the royal forests were enlarged; grants made by the Crown of Scottish lands were resumed; the royal jewels were pawned; and monopolies were sold to companies or corporations (instead of to individuals, as this had been forbidden by the Act of 1624). Finally ship money, a direct tax assessed on real property, was revived and levied to pay for the fleet. In October 1634 a first ship money writ was issued to the citizens of London, to which nobody objected except the victims, but when in August 1635 ship money was extended to the entire kingdom there were loud protests on high-principled grounds. But in all his expedients the King strove to keep within the letter of the law. On the question of ship money he had first consulted the judges, after having taken the precaution of replacing the Lord Chief Justice by a more complacent nominee. None the less in 1637 John Hampden, a Buckinghamshire squire, contested the exaction as a point of principle in the Court of Exchequer. In deciding the case in the King's favour the judges were by no means unanimous, although only two out of twelve found in principle for Hampden. But the reasons given by some of the judges for their verdict in favour of the Crown caused perturbation, for it appeared as if no man were left with anything that he might call his own since the prerogatives of the King were inflated beyond all expectation or limit. The amounts collected for ship money (and the actual collection had unavoidably to be assigned to the classes that were least inclined to pay it) fell away steadily after the Hampden case.

The broad social and economic policy pursued during the 'Eleven Years' Tyranny' was largely influenced by the need for money and it would be ridiculous to deny that this was the uppermost consideration in the minds of the King's Ministers. Yet to begin with at least a beneficent social policy was aimed at. Attempts were made at administrative reform. Some concern was shown for the unemployed, for orphans and debtors. During the period of unparliamentary rule it was exceptional to find places where a poor rate was not levied while special efforts were made to find or create work for the unemployed. Writing in 1900 a historian of the early English poor law claimed that 'from 1631 to 1640 we had more poor relief in England than before or since'. Wentworth who took up his post as President of the Council of the North at the end of 1628, after he had been created a baron, though his methods were drastic and despotic, conferred on that unruly region much peace and prosperity. Unfortunately when he left the North to become Lord Deputy in Ireland in 1633 he still retained his presidency and his good work was to some extent undone. The Court of Star Chamber burst into vigorous action against enclosers of arable land who were held responsible for a rise in the price of corn and were heavily fined, and it became almost a popular institution. 'Last year's famine', Bishop Laud instructed an Essex farmer in 1631, 'was made by man and not by God, solicited by the hard-heartedness of men.' Apart from these efforts in the social field, Wentworth autocratically put down abuses in Ireland and the King's ships suppressed piracy off both the Irish and English coasts. Some naval historians maintain that the modern British navy dates from King Charles I's reign and that if it had been better employed it might have outdone the triumphs of Drake and Blake. Finally this was a brilliant decade in seventeenth-century English art.

Probably the mass of the people were quite satisfied with the interval of autocracy. There is no evidence that any widespread anxiety existed for the recall of parliament. The cause of its meeting again in 1640 was not social or constitutional discontents but more trouble over religion. With the promotion of Laud to the Primacy, the control of the Church passed to the High Church group who were unquestionably a minority. Laud was an honest idealist. Son of a Reading clothier – of 'mean extraction', as his enemies called it – he had forced his way upwards as much by ability as through luck. Conscientious and hard-working, he suffered from a lack of tact and humour; he had few friends, but then how many really successful men ever have intimate friends? As soon as he reached Canterbury he and his former patron, Archbishop Neile of York, set about imposing uniformity and purging their sees of Puritan manifestations in a thorough manner. Thoroughness was in fact Laud's watch-word, as it was Wentworth's; far from their thoughts were the notions of back-pedalling and procrastination dear to the other royal advisers such as Portland. Archiepiscopal visitations took place everywhere to ensure that the altar stood at the eastern end of the churches, that paid lecturers should not invade the parishes to preach puritanism, that the services set out in the Common Prayer Book were used, and that extreme sabbatarianism was stamped upon. Puritan pamphleteers like William Prynne who proved that all plays were mortal sin, Henry Burton, and Dr John Bastwick, and a bright Bible-fed London apprentice named John Lilburne who distributed their wares were savagely punished by the Star Chamber. Archbishop Laud spread his wings throughout Whitehall. A Privy Councillor, an active figure in the Star Chamber, head of the Commission for the Plantations (or Colonies), and a leading adviser to the King on foreign affairs, he found with regret that he did not have sufficient time left also to attend to the Treasury, and after Portland's death obtained the appointment of his own nominee, William Juxon, Bishop of London, to look after the national finances in the spare time from his ecclesiastical duties. Since several of the King's Ministers lived or died Roman Catholics and High Church bishops stalked the capital engrossing important secular offices, it was scarcely surprising that the Puritan leaders were able to proclaim that Popery was again rampant at Court. The King's more tender behaviour to his Roman Catholic Queen and the admission into England of a Papal Agent gave substance to this accusation.

The King's zest for uniformity in the Church was now injected with fateful consequences into Scotland. Edward Hyde, who was later to be the chief Minister of King Charles II, wrote in his autobiography how in 1639 'England enjoyed the greatest measure of felicity it had ever known', lapped in peace and plenty, with strong fleets commanding the seas and the trade of the whole world entering her ports:

In this blessed conjuncture ... a small, scarce discernible cloud arose in the North, which was shortly after attended with such a storm, that even rooted up the greatest and tallest cedars of the three nations; blasted all its beauty and fruitfulness; brought its strength to decay, and its glory to reproach ...

At the beginning of his reign by an act of revocation annulling grants of property made for more than eighty years King Charles turned against him the Scottish nobility who had been his father's supporters in his contest with the Calvinistic hierarchy. King James I indeed managed to introduce episcopacy of a sort into Scotland, though the Scottish bishops exercised little power. The Presbyterians' hold on Scotland provoked the reforming passion of Laud and his master and in 1637 they attempted to thrust a new prayer book, modelled on the English Book of Common Prayer, on the tough and convinced Scottish Calvinists. In July 1637 the reading of the new liturgy in St Giles' Cathedral in Edinburgh was drowned by outcries of protest and a woman threw a stool at the Bishop which nearly hit the Dean. Riots radiated from the Scottish capital throughout the land, and in February 1638 King Charles was informed that if he wished to insist on the use of the new prayer book he would need an army of forty thousand men. The Scottish

Protestants subscribed to a National Covenant binding them to reject all religious alterations not approved by a free assembly of the Kirk. In spite of elaborate negotiations by the Duke of Hamilton, a personal friend of the King, the Scottish Covenanters were adamant and they raised a force under an experienced general, Alexander Leslie, a flaming sword to defend their drab but beloved faith. King Charles I accepted the challenge and scraped together an army, half the size needed, but it recoiled before what was virtually a nation at arms, where even the women took up pistols or worked on the frontier fortifications. A truce was patched up at Berwick in June 1639 but the King would not countenance the Covenanters' demand that their General Assembly should be recognized as supreme over the bishops. 'No bishop, no king', muttered the ghost of his father. He ordered the Scottish Parliament to be prorogued and to assist him in renewing the war summoned his ablest servant, Wentworth, from Ireland. Wentworth's advice was uncompromising – and was backed by Laud. To pay for another 'Bishops' War' against the unconquerable Scots he must call a parliament in England. In that unexpected way the 'Eleven Years' Tyranny' came to an end.

CHAPTER VI

The Great Civil War

1640–49

HAVING advised King Charles I to call a parliament in England to rescue him from his difficulties, the Earl of Strafford hastened back to Ireland, though he was smitten with gout, in order to engineer a good example there. On 16 March 1640 the Irish Parliament did as it was instructed and voted a sum of £180,000 to the King. Later a Convocation of Clergy, which, to the embarrassment of loyal bishops with seats in the House of Lords, was sitting at the same time as the new Parliament, was to offer £120,000. Even these sums, though no trifles by seventeenth-century standards, were not enough for the King's urgent wants. He felt obliged to ask the Commons for £840,000 so that he might have at least a million as a war chest to sustain the fight against the Scots. The new House of Commons, which met on 13 April, refused to provide so large an amount until their grievances had received attention.

Strafford, a stranger to the capital, had miscalculated – though not unnaturally. He had imagined that a patriotic parliament, alive to the fact that the Scots were the traditional enemies of the English people and that their land might always afford a base to continental foes, would succour the Crown in its hour of danger. Yet the men who gathered at Westminster felt no such impulse and were conscious of many a justifiable complaint to air after the 'Eleven Years' Tyranny'. Moreover they had a polished leader. Inevitably after so long an interval the majority of the House of Commons were men who had never sat there before. But John Pym, with his peaked beard and studious manner, was an old hand. He was not far off sixty and had delivered his maiden speech some twenty years before. After the Lord Keeper, Finch, had pleaded for aid against the Scots, Pym departed from precedent and spoke for two hours. He was a moderate man, a man of the middle. So far as the records show, he had paid his 'ship money' and contributed to the 'forced loan' without protest. But the House of Commons was his forum and with all the art that comes from experience he put the case against the Crown, detailing their dissatisfaction in Church and State and persuading his fellow members that they must not vote the King any supplies before they had proposed remedies and obtained redress. Strafford, who had returned to London, found an answer. He counselled King Charles to appeal in person to the House of Lords, which, after a speech from the sovereign, voted that supply ought to precede grievances. That was bound to provoke the Lower House whose right alone it was to vote taxes. Sir Henry Vane, an enigmatic figure who had succeeded the eighty-year-old Sir John Coke as Secretary of State, now went to the Commons on 4 May and offered to yield over ship money if the King were given the supplies he wanted. The Commons were divided over the suggested bargain and seemed prepared at any rate to offer some sort of grant in return for the abandonment of ship money. Speaking for his master, Vane spurned compromise: it was all or nothing. Furthermore the Commons showed themselves anxious to insist on peace with the Scots. The following morning the King summoned a Privy Council. As it was timed for six a.m., both Strafford and his friend, Archbishop Laud, were understandably late. By the time they arrived the King and the majority of his counsellors had agreed that it was hopeless to expect any help from Parliament. And against the instincts of Strafford, the decision was taken to dissolve the two Houses less than three weeks after they had met. The 'Short Parliament' broke up in anger.

Meanwhile the Scottish war had to be carried on. Desperate means were proposed to raise money. The City of London was required to make a loan; Strafford, who was rabid for drastic measures and effective action, suggested that the King should hang some of the aldermen to stimulate contributions from the others. However the City Government as such refused a loan, nor did any foreign nations or the Papacy give a lift to the King in his distress. Though every possible method was examined, from impounding Spanish bullion in the Tower to debasing the coinage, the King could obtain little help. Moreover his commander-in-chief fell sick and Strafford, who had been appointed his deputy, was also in bad health and had to be carried north in a litter. 'Pity me,' he wrote to a friend, 'for never came any man to so lost a business.' The Scots crossed the border and met little resistance. After a whiff of cannon fire at Newburn on the Tyne the royal army – such as it was – fled and the King was compelled to invite a council of peers to negotiate with the Scots, who occupied Newcastle on 29 August. In October the King's commissioners met the Scots at Ripon and quailed before their demands. They were obliged to leave the Scots in control of the counties of Durham and Northumberland and to undertake to pay their army until another English parliament met. With the Scottish army occupying the North of England, King Charles I had no alternative but to throw himself on the mercy of elected representatives. But he was unable to fashion a friendly instrument of his desires. Indeed there are indications that Pym and his friends successfully planned to strengthen their following in the new House. The electors were reluctant to choose courtiers and the wealthiest part of the country declared against the King. The bulk of the 'Short Parliament' which had resentfully dispersed in the spring, was chosen again and on 3 November the 'Long Parliament', one of the most famous in English history, met in a black mood, determined not on reform but on revolution.

Pym, in spite of all his undoubted moderation, had proclaimed in his two-hour speech in the Short Parliament that 'a parliament is that to the Commonwealth, which the soul is to the body. . . . It behoved us therefore to keep the faculty of that soul from distemper.' Since to the Puritan the soul was supreme in the body, this was clearly to intimate that parliament ought to be supreme in the state. Now at the opening of the Long Parliament Pym announced that the King's Ministers, headed by Strafford, had broken the 'fundamental laws' and must be punished. But what were those 'fundamental laws'? They were an idealized conception of a customary law tested and approved by time. But they were as much a figment of the imagination as the 'state of nature' that the political philosophers invented to justify their ideal forms of government. What Pym was preaching under the guise of conservative reform was the subversion of the constitution.

Strafford, who was a brave man, came unhesitatingly to the capital to face his accusers. 'I am tomorrow to London,' he told a friend, 'with more danger beset, I believe, than ever man went out of Yorkshire.' He was not without hopes that by bringing counter-accusations against Pym and his friends he might preserve the existing system of monarchy. If he could not do that, then perhaps the sacrifice of his own life would provide a foundation on which a new partnership between the King and Parliament might be built. But the Commons were disinclined to harmony. Strafford was charged on the evidence of Sir Henry Vane's notes, filched from his desk by his son, of planning to bring over an Irish army to subject England to the King's will. There was no corroboration of this charge from the other Privy Councillors. Strafford defended himself in the House of Lords with immense skill against all his prosecutors. In the end the Commons were driven to condemning the Earl not by a judicial process but by legislation – by a bill of attainder. But would the King give his assent to this death warrant for his servant? 'Upon the word of a king,' King Charles I wrote to Strafford two days before the Bill was passed, 'you shall not suffer in life, honour, or fortune.' Nevertheless Strafford offered himself to his master as a sacrifice. The King was under revolutionary pressure. With the Scottish army still encamped in the North and a mob shouting for blood in Whitehall, he feared for both his family and his throne. On 10 May 1641 he was persuaded to yield to those threats. On the same day he signed a bill whereby the Parliament could not be dissolved without its own consent.

So on 12 May Strafford died for his king. The Commons were pitiless towards the man whom they regarded as the 'arch apostate' and they had no compunction in applying to him the same ruthlessness he had used upon others. Archbishop Laud had also been arrested and sent to the Tower of London and was likewise to be put to death in 1645, at the age of seventy-three, by act of attainder. Strafford had asked to see Laud before he went to the scaffold in order to obtain the old man's blessing. He was informed that this would require parliamentary sanction; and he proudly refused to ask for it. But as he was led to his execution he saw the Archbishop at the window of his cell. Laud raised his hands in blessing and then fainted away. King Charles's other Ministers were also executed or fled abroad. The King was now powerless – he gained nothing whatever by his weak surrender of his Ministers. 'Reformation goes on . . . as hot as a toast,' rejoiced a member of parliament. Throughout a long summer session the Commons enacted every measure they wanted. A 'triennial act' had already been passed laying it down that a parliament must automatically be called once every three years; nearly all the prerogative courts, such as the Star Chamber, were abolished; all taxes levied without parliamentary consent were declared illegal; a Scottish treaty was signed on the Covenanters' own terms. As soon as the armies were disbanded in August, the King left England for Scotland in the delusive hope of raising a Royalist party there. But, as usual, he had miscalculated: it was in England and not in Scotland that a party was beginning to form to defend Church and King.

When Parliament met again in the autumn of 1641 a rebellion had broken out in Ireland, the direct consequence of the lifting of Strafford's firm hand. The native Irish rose in Ulster and soon the rebellion spread throughout the land and brought with it so many cruelties as to earn for it among the English Puritans the name of the 'great massacre'. The Commons dared not place under the royal command an army to suppress the rebellion, for might not the distrusted and humiliated King use it against themselves – just as

Strafford had prepared, so they thought, to employ the Irish army against them? Hence since action was essential, the royal prerogatives must be further reduced. Pym resolved that the army to fight the Irish must be managed by officers and ministers approved by parliament. At the same time the majority of the House of Commons expressed itself in favour of abolishing the English bishoprics altogether. In the previous session a bill to this effect had received a second reading. Oliver Cromwell, now a prominent member in the Lower House, urged that the Book of Common Prayer should be done away with, that the investiture of new bishops should be prevented, and a number of bishops who had been impeached by the Commons should be prohibited from voting in the House of Lords on the future of their offices. Early in November the Commons drew up a Grand Remonstrance to the King in which they set out all that had gone amiss since his accession, a statement of the reforms that parliament had achieved, and a list of the things which in their view still remained to be done. At the same time they petitioned the King to deprive the bishops of their votes in Parliament. The Grand Remonstrance had been approved by a significantly small majority, 159 votes to 148. Moderate men, like Lord Falkland, Edward Hyde, and Edmund Waller, had been convinced that reform had gone far enough and was turning into revolution. Thus the King, who came back to London after the failure of his mission in Scotland, became aware that there were still 'champions of the prerogative' to be found. He therefore returned a non-committal answer to the Grand Remonstrance and issued a proclamation upholding the Church of England. He further offended the Commons by ordering that the guard they had placed round the House to protect them should be withdrawn.

The wildest rumours now swept the Westminster air, many blowing across the Irish sea. The House of Lords resisted the Commons' proposals to take complete control of the army away from the King and to abolish the bishops altogether. The Commons, supported by the City of London mob, on the other hand, believed that the 'papists' were rising in England as well as in Ireland to destroy the Protestant religion. Men marched the streets of the capital crying out: 'No popery! No bishops! No popish lords!' The Commons impeached thirteen bishops and prepared to impeach the Queen – or so the King believed. That was too much for him. The King thought that he also would impeach. He determined to charge five members of the Commons, including Pym, with attempting 'to subvert the fundamental laws, with inviting the Scots to invade the kingdom of England, and with raising tumults in order to compel parliament to join them in their treacherous designs'. This action was not only unconstitutional and unconvincing, but, what was worse, ineffective. When the King entered the chapel of St Stephen's, where the Commons sat, he discovered that 'the birds were flown'. Nor would the City of London disgorge the missing members. Although for a moment King Charles, ever vacillating, staggered before the stubborn temper of his capital, civil war was now certain. Early in 1642 he left London for Kent to see off the Queen to the Continent where she was going to seek allies or obtain munitions. In March he went to York, whither he ordered the Lord Keeper to remove the courts of justice. Parliament meanwhile voted that the kingdom should be put in a state of defence and named new lords lieutenant in the counties. In June the two Houses dispatched to the King in York their proposals for a settlement. In the 'Nineteen Propositions' they set out a new English constitution under which parliament would become the supreme power in the land: no Privy Councillors or Ministers of State or even guardians of the royal children were to be appointed except with parliament's approval; judges were to hold office during good behaviour; the army was in effect to be put under parliamentary control; parliament was to determine the future of the Church. The 'Nineteen Propositions' were an ultimatum by men who were ready for war. Immediately after they had been rejected by the King the two Houses appointed a Committee of Safety, enlisted a force of 10,000 men for active service under the command of the Earl of

Essex, and declared that the King was the aggressor. On 22 August with his sons and his nephews and such followers as he could muster, Charles I repaired to Nottingham and the civil war started.

What were the causes of the Great Civil War? Oliver Cromwell once said that he had not been convinced at the outset that the causes were religious, but he had come to that conclusion in the end. Superficially religious differences lay at the bottom of everything. Had King Charles I and Archbishop Laud not tried to impose a prayer book and strengthen the episcopacy in Scotland, the Long Parliament need not have been called when it was; and if the Scottish Covenanters, thus provoked, had not invaded England successfully, Pym and his friends would never have been able to strike down Strafford and fasten their will on the King. Had it not been for the ill-treatment of the native Catholics in Ireland, dating from the time of Queen Elizabeth or earlier, the screw might not have been turned on the royal prerogatives to such a point that King Charles was presented with the alternatives of attacking the Commons in the citadel of their privileges or forfeiting his throne as he had inherited it. Finally, if Laud had not pushed through a policy of ritualistic reform in the Church of England which had offended the dearest feelings of all who were touched by the Puritan creeds, Parliament would not have found a body of supporters in the country ready to follow their leadership against a ruler to whom all the glorious traditions of the English monarchy still clung. Yet when all that is said, it still has to be recognized that it was a real shifting of economic power within the community that made the civil war possible. It is significant that Cromwell himself did not at first consider that religion lay at the root of the Civil War. He was right: for it was not the case. Well before Queen Elizabeth died the rise of a vociferous new gentry and the demands uttered in the Commons, which they had reinforced, to express opinions on matters that had never before been their concern showed that the monarchy of the Tudors had ceased to offer an acceptable method of government.

As early as 1615 Sir Walter Ralegh had argued that the centre of social gravity had moved and that political power was moving with it. It has even been contended that the position of the gentry before the civil wars had been improved at the expense of the aristocracy which underwent a 'crisis' and that this can be demonstrated statistically, but the argument has been questioned. What is clear is that the Crown was relatively poorer than it had been say a hundred years earlier and consequently weaker. Therefore the Stuart monarchy and its methods of raising revenue were open to attack by well-to-do critics. Outside Parliament the political nation was open to conviction about the need for change. A war of propaganda preceded the civil war. To give one instance: John Hutchinson, a Nottinghamshire gentleman, who had sought office in the Star Chamber and had hitherto played small part in public affairs 'about the time when the Irish massacre was acted' (according to his wife), 'finding humours beginning to be very stirring, applied himself to understand the things then in dispute, and read all the public papers that came forth between the King and Parliament, besides many other private treatises, both concerning the present and foregoing times'. Thus he became convinced of the justice of the parliament's cause. In the early volumes of Clarendon's *History of the Rebellion* we can observe on the other side the importance which the King and Royalists attached to setting out their case on paper. But it was of course only the upper and middle classes who were sufficiently literate to master this propaganda. Politically it was a one-class society. The mass of the people, the men on the verge of the subsistence level or below it, the people who had been relatively well looked after during the 'Eleven Years' Tyranny', were scarcely involved. At the time of the battle of Marston Moor a patrol found a farm labourer on the field of battle and told him to clear out as King and Parliament were at war. 'Whaat!' he explained, 'has them two fallen out then?'

But within the governing classes the divisions of loyalty when the crux came were pronounced if often fortuitous. Up to the time of the Grand Remonstrance the bulk of the

members of the House of Commons, including such later stal-
wart royalists as Edward Hyde, were critical of the King's
policies. Afterwards, as a recent examination of the membership of the Long Parliament has disclosed, the House was
fairly evenly divided but not along any obvious social or economic lines. Lawyers, country gentlemen, and university
graduates were to be found on both sides in almost equal pro-
portions. Among the merchants there was a number of
royalists, while among the King's servants there were future
parliamentarians. Yet it is perhaps unwise to draw any general conclusions from the membership of the Commons, for it
may not have been a microcosm of the nation. Nevertheless
one can point to several county families, for example the
Cromwells and Montagues in East Anglia whose different
branches ranged themselves on opposite sides in the civil wars.
Some broad generalizations, however, appear to hold good.
A constitutional revolution in the City of London prevented
the King from obtaining the help from the City authorities
which previous experiences had led him to expect; and
Charles I found many of his adherents in the less commercial-
ized and industrialized parts of the country. Most of the
bigger towns, particularly the weaving districts and ports,
supported Parliament. Whether, as some historians have argued, the Puritan majority in the House of Commons was
able to claim that it was the 'soul' of the kingdom and the
arbiter on its 'fundamental laws' because it was conscious of
possessing greater economic power and therefore having a
right to a larger share in the government or whether – as
others suggest – it made the claim because it contained a radical element jealous of the Court has been disputed. Men are
sometimes moved by principles, whatever class or party they
belong to. But unquestionably the comparative poverty of the
monarchy contrasted sharply with the growing wealth of
many of the King's subjects who could fairly be called middle
class (John Pym and John Hampden were good examples)
and this surely was an important factor in the political
exuberance of the Commons which led to the civil war.

Though the resources on which the parliamentary forces

could draw at the outset of the civil war were considerable, the King's side had some advantages and the two parties were not badly matched. For in the spring of 1642 neither side possessed an army. If the only competent militia, that of the City of London, was at the disposal of Parliament, the King was able to form a useful cavalry from the outdoor staffs of the nobility and gentry. And the cavalry was the decisive weapon in seventeenth-century warfare, the shock troops who invariably decided the battle. Both sides contained experienced officers who had fought on the continental mainland, but no outstanding generals: Essex was competent but pessimistic; Prince Rupert, the King's nephew, was a daring cavalry leader but with limited experience of command. The navy, so carefully nurtured by the King and fed with ship money, promptly went over to the parliamentary side which controlled most of its bases and was able to draw on such customs duties as could be levied at the ports.

The war got slowly under way. Since the Parliamentarians controlled most of the east and south-east, while the Royalists dominated Wales and the west, the fighting in its early stages was concentrated chiefly on the north and midlands. The King marched from Nottingham into Wales recruiting, while the Earl of Essex moved from Northampton towards Worcester. The first important battle of the war was fought between the forces of Essex and Rupert at Edgehill in Warwickshire; neither force gained a notable advantage and both suffered big losses, but afterwards Essex withdrew on London and the Royalists occupied Oxford which remained their capital for the rest of the war. In the late autumn the Cavaliers advanced on London and Prince Rupert stormed Brentford which was only lightly held. This was a crucial phase. The frightened Londoners rushed out to reinforce the Earl of Essex's army at Turnham Green and the Royalists recoiled to take up their winter quarters in the Oxford area.

In the following year, not being able to grasp the easy victory which they at first expected, the Parliamentarians opened negotiations with the King but on such hard terms that they courted refusal. Now a longish struggle seemed in prospect. The fortunes of war swung at first one way and then the other. The Royalists had victories in Cornwall and Gloucestershire while Essex occupied Reading and Sir Thomas Fairfax, known to history as 'Black Tom', took Wakefield in Yorkshire for the Parliament. But by the end of the campaigning season of 1643 the King could claim to control about three-quarters of the country and stern efforts had to be exerted by the Committee of Safety to improve the Roundhead position. They imposed two new taxes – assessments (a land tax) and excise – to raise money, and they entered upon a treaty with the Scots. Just before the death of their leader, John Pym, at the end of 1643 Parliament signed a Solemn League and Covenant with the Scots and early in 1644 a Committee of Both Kingdoms was set up to direct the war. The intervention of the Scots was in the long run decisive. The King was forced on to the defensive, while no fewer than five armies took the field on behalf of Parliament. In the late spring King Charles I ordered Prince Rupert to leave a successful campaign he was waging in Lancashire to advance to the relief of York which was being besieged by three of the opposing armies. On 2 July at Marston Moor Rupert made ready to attack a force greatly superior to his in numbers but was beaten largely by the brilliance of Oliver Cromwell's 'Ironside' cavalry from the eastern counties and the Scots under David Leslie. Later in that month York surrendered to Parliament. But the Royalist cause was not yet lost. Another Cavalier victory was recorded in Cornwall and the Marquis of Montrose raised a force of Scottish Royalists and began winning a series of remarkable victories in Scotland.

Some of the Parliamentary commanders were reluctant to pursue to its destined end the campaign against the royal armies in England. The Earl of Manchester, for example, who commanded one of the parliamentary armies, argued that after Marston Moor the King would be compelled to bow to terms. Cromwell, however, who was Manchester's lieutenant-general, believed that once the decision had been submitted to the test of battle, there must be no hanging back until victory had been won. Cromwell publicly accused his superior officer of incompetence (an accusation only permissible among amateur soldiers) and a fierce quarrel between the two Houses followed, each House backing its own man. Finally a compromise was suggested. All members of Parliament who held commissions were invited to lay them down so that the army could be put under the command of simple soldiers. It was ultimately agreed to form a 'New Model Army' based on the remnants of previous armies and place it under the command of General Fairfax. In April a Self-Denying Ordinance was passed and Essex and Manchester reluctantly gave up their commissions. When Cromwell, who had been sent with his regiment to join Sir William Waller in the west of England returned to London as if to surrender his command too, he was at once ordered to march towards Oxford to prevent the forces of the King and Prince Rupert from joining. A blockade of Oxford opened in May, and early in June Cromwell became lieutenant-general under Fairfax after a special petition to Parliament from the Council of War. On 14 June the two armies of Fairfax and the King met in the greatest battle of the first civil war at Naseby in Northamptonshire. Once again the King's men were outnumbered and conquered mainly by the torrential charges of Cromwell's cavalry. On 11 September Prince Rupert surrendered Bristol, the one big port held by the Royalists, and the next day Montrose was at last defeated at Philiphaugh. In the following year Lord Hopton, perhaps the ablest of Cavalier commanders, yielded to Fairfax in Cornwall and on 24 June 1646 Oxford capitulated by royal order after King Charles I had fled to seek refuge with the Scots at Newark. The Scots however were little pleased with his arrival. When he rejected the hard conditions they tried to exact, they came to terms with the English Parliament. In return for £400,000 they agreed to withdraw from England and to hand over His Majesty to the English Commissioners. The King's only hope now was that the victors would fall out among themselves. And this soon happened.

The New Model Army, which in alliance with the Scots had been victorious in the first civil war, had been formed to a large extent out of troops raised by Cromwell in a group of eastern counties, known as the Eastern Association. Many of these men, though staunch Puritans, were of a different persuasion from the Scottish Presbyterians. They were in fact Independents (forerunners of the modern Congregationalists) who held that each individual congregation should be responsible to God alone, and they did not admit the right of any general assembly to establish a uniform discipline throughout the realm. The eastern counties had been the centre of the early Independent movement. When in July 1643 Parliament had appointed an ecclesiastical commission to frame the future religious organization of the country Cromwell and others had come forward to press for an effective Independent representation. But because they required military aid from the Scots both Houses of Parliament had subscribed to the Solemn League and Covenant and promised to bring the Churches of England and Scotland to the nearest possible religious uniformity. The only concession allowed to the Independent point of view was that existing congregations should not be touched. Cromwell himself, who was known as 'the Great Independent', had never been convinced that the employment of the Scottish Covenanter Army was necessary to win the civil war and after the war had been won he continued to urge religious toleration on Parliament, notably in a letter he wrote to the Speaker after the battle of Naseby: 'He that ventures his life for the liberty of his country,' he said, 'I wish he trust God for the liberty of his conscience, and you for the liberty he fights for.' This sentence was omitted when his dispatch was printed.

Thus between the New Model Army, filled with sectarians, and the predominantly Presbyterian House of Commons (from which of course the Royalists had withdrawn) a gulf was fixed. And to religious differences were added financial squabbles when Parliament decided to reduce the size of the army and compound for arrears of soldiers' pay at the end of the first civil war. Early in 1647 Parliament voted to reduce the garrison in England and to keep no officer except Fairfax with any rank above that of colonel. This was a direct insult to Cromwell. Moreover the army that had now to be sent to serve in Ireland was put under the command of two Presbyterians. Discontent broke out in the New Model Army when a deputation from the House of Commons arrived in Saffron Walden in Essex to invite volunteers for Ireland. The officers protested at the new arrangements and the soldiers resolved to follow their example and to petition Parliament for redress. Eight cavalry regiments appointed 'Agitators' or agents to represent their point of view. Cromwell, who had resumed his place as a member of parliament, went down with other officers to Saffron Walden to investigate the reasons for the discontent and managed to patch up a temporary agreement for which he received the thanks of the House. But after a new financial arrangement had been completed, religious complications followed. The King, now a prisoner of Parliament, had at length offered to accept the establishment of Presbyterianism as the national religion for a period of three years. (This was in answer to a list of proposals, originally known as the 'Propositions of Newcastle'.) The Presbyterian leaders in Parliament, though not displeased, were well aware that the army would resist the scheme and therefore reopened negotiations with the Scots to protect them against their own army. At the same time the Commons delayed the fulfilment of the terms agreed for the disbandment of the New Model. Waves of anger lapped the army and the 'Agitators' actively conspired against disbandment and set up printing presses to publish statements of the soldiers' case. One regiment broke into open mutiny, which was quelled with difficulty. Before the middle of 1647 the Parliament and the Army were at daggers drawn.

Under these circumstances King Charles I, now in custody at Holmby in Northamptonshire, was a third party rejoicing. But the Army thought they would lay hold of his person as a point in the debate and a cavalry contingent under the radical Cornet Joyce went to Holmby and removed the King to Newmarket. He accompanied Joyce not unwillingly for he saw that events were moving in his favour. Indeed the Army now declared that the Commons ought to be 'purged' and should fix a date for their own dissolution. Henry Ireton, Cromwell's son-in-law, drew up a novel scheme of government known as the 'Heads of the Proposals' which was informally submitted to the King as an alternative to Parliament's 'Propositions of Newcastle'. This scheme, while it made the King's power subservient to that of Parliament, also lessened the power of Parliament by making it more amenable to the control of the constituencies and by establishing 'liberty of conscience' as an unalterable right. The 'Heads of the Proposals' embodied the wishes of the army gentry, of men of property like Cromwell and Ireton; but the 'Agitators' put forward in October a far more revolutionary plan known as the 'Agreement of the People' which provided for manhood suffrage, new parliaments every other year, and a redistribution of the constituencies and made no mention whatever of the King or the House of Lords. While the King was trifling with the army leaders, he entered into more serious negotiations with commissioners from Scotland who promised him that if he would agree to their religious terms they would restore him to his throne; they also urged him to make his escape. In November 1647 King Charles I escaped from the Army's custody and fled to the Isle of Wight where he thought he had a friend in the Governor, Colonel Hammond. He was made an honourable prisoner in Carisbrooke Castle. While he was there he signed an 'engagement' with Scottish commissioners on the terms that they proposed. Earlier in the year the English Army had marched on London, compelled leaders of the peace party to run away and vainly tried to come to terms with Parliament and the King. Thus England was reduced to a state of chaos and a second civil war began.

Though this political confusion, a growing public discontent with the Long Parliament, and the King's secret alliance with the Scots might have seemed to provide reasonable grounds for Royalist hopes of revenge, in fact the war soon went against them. Risings on the King's behalf in Wales and in Kent and Essex were ill coordinated and the Scottish Engagers did not invade England until July. The New Model Army was still intact and Cromwell, at last convinced that no arrangement could be reached with the King – a point on which he had changed his mind throughout 1647 – rose to his greatest heights as a general. After suppressing the revolt in Wales, he rode north to meet the Scots and their Royalist allies. In the battle-and-rout of Preston he obtained a conclusive victory, while Essex was regained by General Fairfax. As the second civil war was in progress, the leaders of the peace party in parliament continued placidly to negotiate with the King in the Isle of Wight. But the Army had now had enough, and Ireton drew up a 'remonstrance' demanding justice upon the King and the establishment of a republic. Cromwell, who in 1647 had still been anxious to preserve the monarchy in some form, now thought it unwise to deal any more with King Charles I, who was 'the capital author of all our woes'. In December 1648 Colonel Thomas Pride, a former drayman, acting on behalf of the Council of the Army, again 'purged' Parliament leaving only a militant 'Rump' at Westminster. The Rump decided to set up a High Court of Justice to try the King for innumerable and hitherto unheard-of crimes. The Act was carried by a mere 26 votes to 20 in the depleted House of Commons and the Lords were not consulted. Many of the 135 Commissioners named in the Act refused to serve. But Cromwell, now convinced that King Charles I was a Man of Blood, brushed aside all resistance. 'We will cut off the King's head with the crown on it,' he is said to have told his fellow commissioners.

When the trial opened in Westminster Hall on 20 January 1649, King Charles refused to plead as he would not recognize the jurisdiction of the Court or indeed of any court. 'The King', he exclaimed, 'cannot be tried by any superior jurisdiction on earth. But it is not my cause alone, it is the freedom and liberty of the people of England.' On 27 January he was sentenced to die, though many of the commissioners refused to sign the death warrant. It was mainly by Cromwell's personal efforts that a plausible number of signatures was collected. Lord Fairfax would not approve the death sentence and his wife screamed from the public gallery during the trial: 'Oliver Cromwell is a traitor!' On Tuesday, 30 January, with the winter sun gleaming on him, King Charles I stepped out through a middle window of the Whitehall Banqueting Hall on to the scaffold and after he had handed his solitary jewel, the George and Garter, to Bishop Juxon he laid his head on the low block. At four minutes past two the blow was struck. The citizens of London who watched the event were silent.

CHAPTER VII

Oliver Cromwell and the Interregnum
1649–60

FOR eleven years, from 1629 to 1640, England had been governed without a parliament; now for another eleven years, from 1649 to 1660, it was to be governed without a monarchy. Soon after the execution of King Charles I the monarchy and the House of Lords were abolished and England was named 'a Commonwealth or Free State'. A Council of State, composed of forty-one members who had to be elected every year, was appointed to carry out executive and administrative duties, working by means of a number of committees. Law-making remained with the Rump Parliament, that had been so often 'purged' on the pretext of impurities that only some ninety members now remained. Thus the new government was that of a select few or oligarchy and no clever phrasing could make it appear otherwise.

On the new Great Seal these words were inscribed: 'In the first year of freedom by God's blessing restored.' But the new republic, born, as it were, by mistake – for the English republicans were a small minority lifted into influence by the obstinacy of the dead King – was coldly received by the outside world. No thrill of hope such as later greeted the French Revolution was felt at its birth. Whatever constitutional forms might be invented, the realities of power rested with the great men of the Army (known as 'the Grandees') and a group of their civilian friends. In the rank-and-file of the victorious Roundhead forces discontent soon showed itself. The soldiers looked for inspiration to John Lilburne, nicknamed 'Freeborn John', the same man who as an apprentice in the reign of the late King had been whipped and pilloried for distributing tracts against the bishops. In his career were many strange changes – he had become a colonel, a financial speculator, and a soap manufacturer. But he was always aggressive and noisy and a leader and a hero. Not long after the King's execution of which, though a radical republican, he had by instinct disapproved, he published a pamphlet bearing the title *England's New Chains*. Parliament was begged not to abdicate in favour of an arbitrarily chosen Council of State and Cromwell was held up for special abuse. Lilburne was then arrested and committed to the Tower. Cromwell said in the Council of State, thumping the table, 'you have no other way to deal with these men but to break them or they will break you.' Cromwell and his son-in-law, Ireton, were perturbed at the threat of anarchy implicit in social and constitutional reforms advocated by Lilburne and his followers, who were known as Levellers. They reckoned that if a constitution based on manhood suffrage and a freely and annually elected parliament were established then the poor would govern the rich and the institution of private property be destroyed. Point was given to their outlook when a small group of men who called themselves 'True Levellers' suddenly emerged in Surrey as the first preaching and practising communists in English history. They took hold of a small plot of public land and began to dig and plant it with the intention of sharing its fruits in common. It was not long before their ardent hopes were dashed by wealthy neighbours who pulled down their houses and trampled on their corn. But their innocent and indeed touching experiment was declared proof of the anarchy of all 'Levelling'.

About the same time the discontent aroused in the army by the new government culminated in a number of mutinies. A Leveller named Trooper William Thompson raised the standard of revolt in Banbury, and Cromwell and Fairfax had to ride through the night to round up Thompson and his comrades at Burford in Oxfordshire. After the mutiny had been broken, Cromwell prepared to go to Ireland at the head of an army organized to meet the Royalist-Catholic

combination which was in full cry there. For the new republic had to contend with enemies in Ireland and Scotland as
well as at home and in continental Europe. Though auto-
cratic Spain was the first to show friendliness to the new republic, many foreigners were shocked at the execution of the
King. Prince Rupert, who was as dashing on sea as on land,
collected a fleet of Royalist privateers and was to find hospitality in Portugal. France, the United Netherlands, and Russia were at first well disposed to the cause of royalism, while
in Scotland the Covenanters were aghast at the treatment
meted out to their Presbyterian brethren by the Independents of the English army and inclined to come to terms
with the exiled King Charles II if he would but swear to
advance their religion. Charles II, a lively lad of nineteen with several love affairs already to his credit, preferred to wait and see the outcome of events in Ireland
before selling himself to the changeable dignitaries of the
Kirk.

The Marquis of Ormonde, working on behalf of the King
in Ireland, had managed to build a coalition out of mixed
and even hostile elements. Not only the Anglo-Irish Royalists but native Irish and even some of the Scots in Ulster
had rallied beneath his flag. For a moment it seemed as
though they would both be able to dislodge the slight Parlia-
mentarian hold on Ireland and send over an expedition to
Wales as well. However the oddly compounded alliance
soon broke asunder. Colonel George Monk, one of the parliamentary commanders in Ireland, concluded a secret
neutrality treaty with the leader of the Ulster Irish, while
another such commander, Colonel Michael Jones, repulsed
Ormonde with heavy losses from Dublin. Thus when in
August 1649 Cromwell landed in Ireland with his well-
equipped veteran army he was able to concentrate rapidly
in Dublin and thence move swiftly north or south with his
forces supported from the sea against the Irish Royalists.
On 3 September he began the siege of Drogheda in Lein-
ster, a seaport into which many of the finest troops in the
Irish coalition had been thrown. When his summons was

disregarded, he ordered an assault and refused any mercy, so that almost the entire garrison was put to the sword. According to the laws of war, Cromwell was permitted to order the slaughter of the besieged for forcing him to storm a position incapable of defence. But he felt obliged to justify his action to the English Parliament on two grounds: first that 'this was a righteous judgement of God upon these barbarous wretches who have imbrued their hands in so much innocent blood' (that is, the massacres of 1641) and, secondly, that 'it would prevent the effusion of blood for the future.' The first line of defence may appear nauseating to our supposedly more humane generation, though the second line of defence was precisely that put forward as the case for dropping atomic bombs on the Japanese in 1945. After this, Cromwell turned south to besiege Wexford where the massacre of Drogheda was repeated. From Wexford Cromwell marched farther into Munster where two towns were abandoned by their garrisons and where the Governor of Ross wisely surrendered after a breach had been made in the walls. By now winter was also advancing and the English soldiers were hit by disease and by scarcity of supplies. Before the next campaigning season had fully developed Cromwell was called home to meet another royalist menace from Scotland. But the Ulster army was routed in June 1650 and afterwards Ormonde resigned his command. The war continued until 1652 and harsh methods were employed against the Irish who adopted characteristic guerilla tactics. Thus Cromwell's name came to be associated in Irish minds with starvation as well as slaughter and no later concessions made by English governments in the way of free trade or representation at Westminster could ever wipe his awful curse from the memories of Irishmen. To the Puritans the Irish who fought against their armies in the years 1649–52 were the same as the men who had carried out the 'great massacre' of 1641, while the desire of the Roman Catholics to attend Mass did not come within their definition of 'liberty of conscience'. So there was no let-up on either side. Nothing could smooth away, hide, or bury the bitterness of those years which has helped to shape Irish history ever since.

King Charles II had waited in Jersey for tidings that would justify his going to Ireland in person. But as the bad news of Cromwell's victories flowed in, he was compelled to reopen discussions with the Scottish Covenanters. After the execution of his father, he had been proclaimed King of Scotland but on humiliating terms. The Covenanters wanted a minister-ridden monarchy that would fasten their religion throughout the British Isles. King Charles clung to hopes of succour from abroad, success in Ireland, or even help from the gallant Montrose. But Montrose was hanged on an Edinburgh gallows in the spring of 1650 and the young King was driven back on his last resource. On 23 June 1650 he swore to the Covenant, abandoning the cause for which his father had died and bartering religious bondage against his chance of regaining the English throne with Scottish arms. The Rump Parliament had long been aware of the danger to the new Commonwealth from Scotland and Cromwell had been recalled from service in Ireland because General Fairfax could no longer be trusted; 'Black Tom' had refused to swear allegiance to the republic or make any gesture that might express his approval of the killing of the late King. Moreover he was opposed to conducting an offensive war against the Scots when (like the rest) he had signed an agreement as binding as the Solemn League and Covenant. Cromwell, after he had arrived in England in June, exerted every effort to induce the commander-in-chief to change his mind. But Fairfax decided at the early age of thirty-eight to renounce what was in fact the most influential post in all the land. His former second-in-command, who was now over fifty, therefore succeeded him and marched north in the company of General John Lambert as his chief of staff. The crowds cheered as the Roundhead veterans rode towards the border. But Cromwell observed to Lambert: 'Do not trust to that, for these very persons would shout as much if you and I were going to be hanged.' Cromwell's troops were much inferior in number to those of the Scots, under the command of the experienced David Leslie. Leslie took up an excellent position covering Edinburgh. King Charles II came up to inspire his followers, but was told to go away, and the war was run for him by a committee in which Presbyterian ministers predominated. At the end of August Cromwell was obliged to withdraw from the area north of Edinburgh to Dunbar by the sea on the road to England. At the battle of Dunbar on 3 September 1650 Leslie was outmanoeuvred and beaten and Cromwell then laid siege to Edinburgh itself. The Scottish leaders retired to Stirling and King Charles II was crowned a covenanted King at Scone. When the next campaigning season opened, Cromwell was taken ill and stalemate developed. Eventually he advanced and occupied Perth and the Scottish army fell into a trap set by him and crossed the border into England. The Scots moved down through Lancashire, losing rather than gathering men as they went. Cromwell followed them and caught them at Worcester, again on 3 September, in 1651, and there they were surrounded and overwhelmed. The invading forces were almost annihilated. King Charles II managed, after many adventures, to escape abroad, and the victorious English General was invited to return to London and honour Parliament with his advice.

Cromwell had now become the leading figure in the land. A small country gentleman by origin, descendant of the younger branch of a family that derived its fortunes from the dissolution of the monasteries in the time of King Henry VIII, he had been converted to puritanism at about the age of thirty. Though he became a member of parliament when he was under thirty and had been active in local affairs, it was not until he was over forty that he had turned energetically to politics and discovered his genius as a soldier. We really know very little of his early life, of the compulsions which made him, although an ardent predestinarian, into a believer in that 'liberty of conscience' for which he had pleaded in his Naseby dispatch. Conservative by temperament – save in that one respect – he possessed a powerful personality and an infinite capacity for seeing things through once he had settled on his course. In many ways, like most statesmen, he was an opportunist, but when he took his chances he described them as having been 'dispensations' by God from on high. Soon after the battle of Worcester he became impatient with the Rump Parliament and eager for constitutional reform and a competent executive. In November Parliament had agreed only to dissolve after another three years: to Cromwell and his friends that seemed to be a very long time. Though the third civil war, if we may call it that, had ended with the battle of Worcester, the capitulation of Limerick in Ireland on 27 October 1651, and the defeat of Prince Rupert's fleet by Blake, a constitutional settlement awaited peace abroad, for in the early summer of 1652 war had broken out between the new English Republic and the United Netherlands.

The Dutch had at first reacted violently against the execution of King Charles I, but later a feeling had shown itself on both sides that the two sister republics should be allies and not enemies. An English mission was sent to The Hague early in 1651 to conclude a treaty with the Dutch States-General, but difficulties arose over political as well as commercial questions, and in October of that year the English Parliament passed a Navigation Act which forbade the importation of goods into England from Europe except in ships owned by Englishmen or in ships belonging to the exporting country, and also laid it down that goods from outside Europe might not be carried except in British or colonial ships. This Act was aimed against the Dutch who had a large carrying trade though their trade with England had been falling. It is doubtful if the Act played much part in the war that followed. This was mainly a maritime and commercial war and arose almost spontaneously out of the bickering between naval seamen and merchantmen on both sides. Many Englishmen had never forgotten the way in which the Dutch had in 1623 tortured and put to death a number of English traders at Amboyna in the Banda Islands, and the English East India Company was one of the most

persistent advocates of a war of revenge. During the naval
war between the two nations English warships built by King
Charles I had an opportunity of blooding themselves and
under the command of Robert Blake, a sturdy republican
admiral, they inflicted big losses on the Dutch and crippled
their world-wide commerce. Cromwell told the Dutch commissioners who came to seek peace: 'You have appealed to
the judgement of Heaven. The Lord has declared against
you.' The Dutch Calvinists did not quite see it in that way,
and Cromwell himself and a number of his friends were
averse from pressing too hard a war against a sister Protestant state, as it savoured to them of murder in the family.
But the English naval successes impressed the rest of Europe
and enabled negotiations for treaties of alliance with various
other governments to be opened.

Meanwhile the Anglo-Dutch war had interrupted political developments in England. Schemes for the reform of the
law – and in particular of the Chancery law – on which the
army leaders had set their hearts, hung fire; the Roundhead
army, now deprived of occupation, broke up and spilled its
contents into the labour market, causing much unemployment; while the soldiers who remained under arms clamoured for the settlement of their arrears. The dissatisfaction
of the army with the small and unrepresentative Rump
Parliament was voiced by its leaders, notably by Major-
General Thomas Harrison, a religious fanatic, and by
Major-General John Lambert, who had hoped to succeed
Henry Ireton as Lord Deputy of Ireland on the latter's death
in 1651 and had been disappointed. Both these men urged
Cromwell to get rid of Parliament, which had long promised
to dissolve itself, but whereas Harrison wanted the country
to be ruled by a group of saintly men who should stay at the
helm until Christ came in person to rule His people, Lambert sought a reformed parliament on the lines of the 'Heads
of the Proposals'. 'I am pushed on by two parties', Cromwell said, 'to do that, the consideration of the issue whereof
makes my hair stand on end.' For some months he acted as a
mediator between the army and parliament and also played

with the idea of restoring some form of monarchy, perhaps with the youngest son of King Charles I as a figurehead.

Throughout the early months of 1653 Cromwell hesitated as to his right course, even as he had hesitated throughout 1647 on whether he should finally break with King Charles I. He exerted his influence to moderate 'the preaching people' who were 'violent against this Parliament' and urged the officers to make no move until peace had been concluded with the Dutch. Nevertheless he was said to have been offended because his opinions about peace with the Dutch had not been accepted by Parliament, and in April he was concerned in a scene in the Commons when his demand for a new assembly was countered with the reply that there was 'no more fitting moment to change the Lord General'. On 19 April 1653, at a large meeting held in Cromwell's lodgings between members of parliament and army officers, the commander-in-chief proposed that Parliament should for the time being devolve its trust upon 'men well-affected to religion and the interest of the nation'. But the parliamentarians wanted to pass a Bill for successive or continuous parliaments to take effect from the following November. The meeting broke up without any agreement being reached. Next day Cromwell was informed that in defiance of the Army the Rump was pushing through the Bill. Learning of this, he went down to the House and after a brief speech in which he charged the members with self-interest and injustices, he ordered his soldiers to expel the Rump, and later also dissolved the Council of State. Thus the Long Parliament which had first raised the sword against the King perished by the sword, and for five-and-a-half exciting years Oliver Cromwell became the chief figure in the English Commonwealth.

The tragedy of Oliver Cromwell was that he was never able to find a constitutional basis for his government. A patriotic Englishman, he regarded his fellow countrymen as a Chosen People who were the apple of God's eye, and he was anxious to do right, to preserve order, and to promote Christian well-being. But how could a soldier, raised to prominence by revolution after a series of civil wars and kept in power by his army, become a constitutional ruler? Yet the history of these five-and-a-half years is the story of how a military ruler sought respectability. As it has well been said, he could not get on with parliaments and he could not get on without them. In the first instance he took the advice of Harrison and invited a select number of proved Puritans to form an Assembly of Saints, 'the well affected men' to whom he had urged the Rumpers to hand over their powers. The members 'looked for the long-expected birth of freedom and happiness'. But, alas, they thrust on with their reforms too eagerly and unthinkingly. For example, they abolished the Court of Chancery in a day before they had invented a substitute for it. They condemned the payment of clergy by tithe, but found no other means of paying them instead. In general, in trying to replace the Common Law by the Law of Moses they made the mistake of attacking property, while many of them were tactless enough to prefer listening to the advice of City preachers to that of the general who had created them. 'I am more troubled now', General Cromwell observed, 'with the fool than with the knave.' So he turned from Harrison to Lambert and under the spur of Lambert the Assembly of Saints (also known to history as Barebone's Parliament, after the name of one of its members) committed suicide in a placid if undignified way. On 12 December 1653 the moderates gave back their authority to the leader from whom it had come, on the ground that their opponents were out to destroy the law, the clergy, and private property. Lambert was ready with a new and better constitution. Under his guidance the Council of the Army produced an 'Instrument of Government' which made Oliver Cromwell 'Lord Protector' of the Commonwealth of England, Scotland, and Ireland and conferred executive powers on a Council of State containing both civilian and military members headed by Lambert. This Council was intended to act as a check upon the Protector: he could not make war or peace or approve ordinances without its advice. A parliament including representatives of Scotland and Ireland as well as of England was to be elected on a revised franchise and with new constituencies and was to be responsible for law-making and taxation. But when parliament was not sitting the Lord Protector and the Council of State could do much as they liked. Finally embodied in this, the first written constitution in our history, were clauses guaranteeing liberty of Christian worship 'provided that this liberty be not extended to Popery and Prelacy, nor to such as, under the profession of Christ, hold forth and practise blasphemy and licentiousness'.

The new Lord Protector started by trying to establish peace everywhere. On 5 April 1654 a treaty was concluded with the Dutch on very favourable terms. At home he tried to pacify both the republicans who disliked the Instrument of Government as smelling of monarchy and the royalists who wanted no king but a Stuart. On 14 April Cromwell moved with his family into Whitehall Palace and in May was lucky to escape assassination in the City. In August a feeble royalist invasion of Scotland was suppressed, so that by Sunday, 3 September, the anniversary of the victories of Dunbar and Worcester – and of the massacre at Drogheda – Cromwell was able to meet his first Protectorate Parliament and to unroll before it an impressive list of his doings. 'According to the opinion of all the world', wrote an impartial observer, 'the Crown is only wanting to this government to establish and confirm the authority upon the head of the Lord Protector.'

To be eligible as electors under the Protectorate county voters had to possess real or personal property valued at £200 instead of, as previously, a freehold of forty shillings. Thus the men who came to the new House were far from having democratic sympathies, and Cromwell's opening speech, in which he justified his rule as defending the 'good interest' and the 'natural magistracy' of the nation against the Levellers and extreme sectarians, might have seemed well calculated to appeal to them all. But however conservative in their personal interests, the House contained several republicans and a large number of Presbyterians who had their own good reasons for criticizing the 'Instrument of

Government'. Cromwell was compelled to tell the recalcitrants that they must not interfere with the 'fundamentals' of the Protectoral government. All but thirty members then signed a pledge to accept these 'fundamentals', but the remainder soon fell with a good will to tearing the rest of the constitution to pieces. To ensure their own independence (as they had been warned by the fate of their predecessors) they were zealous to wrest control of the army from Cromwell and, if they could not do that, to restrict its size and reduce its pay. Impatient with the failure of parliament to abandon constitutional criticism and tampering with the army in favour of immediate problems of government, the Protector dissolved the assembly at the earliest possible opportunity in January 1655.

During the twenty-one months that followed this dissolution, control of foreign and domestic policy was entirely in the hands of Cromwell and his Council of State and military rule was established. Plots against the regime were organized by both royalists and Levellers and a dangerous rising in the Salisbury area was used as an excuse for the administration of England and Wales by eleven Major-Generals who divided the country among them. Juries were hand-picked; newspapers were suppressed; additional taxation was imposed; and municipal corporations were 'purged'. But Cromwell discovered, just as King Charles I had done, that it was impossible to raise sufficient money to govern without the aid of parliament. Thus in July 1656 writs for the second Protectorate Parliament were issued. Although the Major-Generals had made a gallant effort to secure the return of members favourable to the Government, many known enemies of the Protector were elected. England was now again at war with Spain, Cromwell having sent an expedition in the winter of 1654 to attack the Spanish West Indies in the name of Protestantism and in the interests of piracy. But his commanders only succeeded in taking the then undeveloped island of Jamaica and failed to intercept a Spanish treasure fleet. Now therefore Cromwell had to appeal to the new Parliament to contribute to the cost of the war – again as had the Stuart Kings – and the majority were convinced that they were also expected to set the stamp of their approval on the rule of the unpopular Major-Generals. By a perversion of a clause in the Instrument of Government which permitted the Council to determine whether persons elected were of 'known integrity, fearing God and of good conversation', about a hundred members opposed to the executive were excluded from the House and a number of others voluntarily withdrew. In the hope of putting the Government on a legitimate basis a proposal was put forward to make Cromwell king. Among the middle-class representatives, particularly the lawyers, the feeling was that a monarch was more clearly subject to law than a Protector and that in return for this 'feather in his cap' Cromwell might drop his Major-Generals. Oliver Cromwell was certainly not 'wedded' or 'glued' to forms of government, as he himself admitted, and he was sorely tempted by the offer of a crown, though certainly not for reasons of personal ambition, for he honestly thought it might aid stability. Early in 1657 he did in fact suddenly throw over his Major-Generals, but the leaders of the army (among whom of course were these very Major-Generals) and many of the rank-and-file would not allow him to become King. After interminable discussions between the members of the parliament who promoted the project and the Protector, the offer of the throne was at last refused in May 1657; instead a new written constitution known as the 'Humble Petition and Advice' which enlarged the powers of parliament and reduced those of the Council of State replaced the Instrument of Government. Under this new constitution the Protector received the right to nominate his own successor, was given the title of 'His Highness', and was asked to choose members of a second chamber instead of the old House of Lords: it was indeed a monarchy without a monarch.

Cromwell was now growing prematurely old under the strain of political affairs. He devoted much of his time to organizing a war against Spain in Europe with France as his ally and in forwarding various schemes, of which little came, for a European Protestant alliance. His last Parliament met, according to the terms of the 'Humble Petition and Advice' on 20 January 1658. But Cromwell's ablest supporters had now been wafted into the new Second Chamber and members of the republican opposition, who had been allowed to resume their seats, returned with undimmed enthusiasm to constitutional debates, attacking the 'Other House' with vigour. Cromwell was afraid that the republican chiefs would ally themselves with discontented soldiers and to prevent this went down to Westminster in a hackney cab and rebuked the two Houses for their failure to keep faith with him while an enemy was ready to invade the country. 'I do dissolve this Parliament', wound up the Lord Protector, 'and let God judge between you and me.' 'Amen', answered the unrepentant republicans. Once more Cromwell was forced to fall back from the assistance of parliament on to the support of the army. Though it was said that the leaders of the army had sworn to live and die with the Lord Protector, it was not long before rumours arose that a new parliament would have to be called, so desperately was the Government in debt. But somehow his Government carried on through the summer of 1658 and in the early autumn, at the age of fifty-nine, the Lord Protector expired.

Oliver Cromwell died hated by all save a few intimate friends and admirers, such as his competent little Secretary of State, John Thurloe, and it is only in the last hundred years that he has been given the honour due to him in English history. What were his achievements? In the first place, he raised English prestige abroad from the depths to which it had dropped in the reigns of the first two Stuart Kings. Though his foreign policy may have been wrongly conceived and inconsistent – his alliance with France against Spain, for example, upset rather than set right the balance of power on the continental mainland – the English redcoats distinguished themselves on fields of battle which have since become, unhappily, all too familiar to the British army, and captured the port of Dunkirk of later fame. The Government of the Lord Protector was treated by the French monarchy and indeed by all the European rulers as an equal, and thus England, with her fine navy, her flourishing commerce and her intrepid soldiers, became, for good or ill, a Great Power. When in the reign of King Charles II the nation sank to being not the equal but the paid satellite of France, even faithful royalists, like Samuel Pepys, were heard to sigh for the famous days of Oliver.

In the second place, in all his political compromises and even during the period of Puritan military government which he imposed, Oliver Cromwell never departed from the principle that he held dear, that of 'liberty of conscience'. This principle was ingrained within him. Soon after the battle of Dunbar, arguing with those who said that if you gave people liberty freely to preach the Gospel of Jesus Christ error might step in, Cromwell answered: 'Your pretended fear lest error might step in is like the man who would keep all wine out of the country lest men should be drunk.' And in a speech to Parliament in 1654, he said: 'Notions will hurt none but them that have them.' In those two sentences is the essence of the modern ideas of toleration; can we think of any other ruler of his time who would have talked to parliament or to his people in that sort of way? Indeed whatever concessions he may have made to dictatorial methods in a nation split asunder by civil wars, Cromwell in his heart believed in what most people mean by freedom, the freedom of the mind, the freedom of the spirit. He maintained that it was 'an unjust and unwise jealousy to deprive a man of his natural liberty upon a supposition that he may abuse it: when he doth abuse it', he added, then 'judge'. Cromwell believed that the mind was the man. He thought they all have a right within limits to seek truth in their own fashion. He said in an immortal phrase: 'To be a Seeker is to be of the best sect after a Finder, and such a one shall every faithful humble Seeker be in the end.' It is true that Cromwell's idea of 'liberty of conscience' was narrow by modern standards. It did not, for instance, apply to Roman Catholics or even to the Anglicans. But it embraced both the Quakers and the Jews so long as they did not defy civil authority. Those political and economic freedoms which came down to us with the spirit of nonconformity we owe in no small measure to the precepts of Oliver Cromwell.

Finally, Cromwell sought to give the English people both peace and order. Though he has been called a tyrant, in fact his aim was to avoid 'arbitrary' government. In this he was not very successful. Passions were too fierce for politicians to settle down under any revolutionary rule (though no doubt many were indifferent). Thus the constitutional experiments he tried to operate failed, and when he himself died, there was no one capable of carrying them on.

General John Lambert thought, and many of the Ironside Army thought with him, that he ought to have been Oliver's political heir: and in Cromwell's own lifetime men were heard to argue whether the throne would descend to 'John' or to 'Richard', Cromwell's elder son. Cromwell, like so many great men, wanted to be a dynast and named Richard as his successor, but the new Lord Protector, though not devoid of astuteness, was a mild and lazy country gentleman quite unprepared to ride in the whirlwind or direct the storm. Oliver's other son, Henry, though no Puritan, was the real heir to his genius, but was left to govern Ireland and write letters home. Richard Cromwell's Parliament was opposed to military rule, but within eight months the military chiefs, headed by Fleetwood, Richard Cromwell's own brother-in-law, overthrew the Cromwellian Protectorate with some assistance from the irreconcilable republicans inside and outside Parliament. These conspirators decided, for want of any better solution, to recall the Rump Parliament which Oliver Cromwell had dissolved in 1653, and so in May 1659 forty-two members of that ancient assembly found themselves at Westminster no doubt rubbing their eyes to discover themselves again after so many weary months the rulers of the fair land of England. They did not moderate their pretensions and were far from ready to accept the advice of Lambert or any other grandee. So in October Lambert retorted upon them, like his late master, by marching his troops to the House of Commons and dissolving it.

This state of confusion or anarchy made inevitable the restoration of King Charles II who had long been awaiting his opportunity across the Channel. But the instrument of his restoration was a Cromwellian officer, who had moved from being a colonel in Ireland to being a general in Scotland: George Monk had been unflinchingly loyal to Oliver Cromwell and would have prevented the fall of his son if Richard had displayed the slightest wish to save himself. 'Richard Cromwell forsook himself,' said Monk, 'else I had never failed my promise to his father or my regard to his memory.' Monk had no ambitions for himself, though his loyal army would have done as he ordered; but he would not have Lambert as his leader; he told 'Lambert in so many words that what he was prepared to tolerate in Oliver Cromwell he could not stomach in a lesser man'. So early in 1660, having had (as he said) 'a call from God and His people', and defying Fleetwood and Lambert, he marched from Coldstream on the Scottish border to London, gathering adherents and opinions as he came. He sought political stability at any price and was opposed to military rule. At length he decided in favour of calling a 'free parliament', which meant, as he knew, the restoration of the King. For the Presbyterians, like Lord Fairfax, who were now allowed to resume their old seats in both Houses of Parliament, had never been republicans and had always wanted a monarchy on terms. King Charles II met their wishes half-way by announcing in his Declaration of Breda (4 April 1660) that he would grant 'liberty to tender consciences' and leave to Parliament the punishment of such as should be excepted from a general pardon as well as the settlement of property problems arising out of the political upheaval. In May a mission from the new royalist parliament went to Holland to invite King Charles II to return home. On 29 May 1660, after years of poverty and adventure, he entered his capital to claim his inheritance.

CHAPTER VIII

A Ferment of Ideas
1640–60

FOR twenty years, from 1640 to 1660, religious enthusiasm and political idealism so swept English thought that by comparison for the following twenty years they seemed almost to disappear, overshadowed by wit, cynicism, and science. But already in the whole of the first half of the century which, as a recent writer has said, was 'perhaps the most profoundly and thoughtfully religious in English experience since the Middle Ages', religion and politics had been the topics dearest to prose writers and gradually submerged pure literature. The mid century was an earnest epoch, neither polite nor humanist; we have already remarked how John Donne had abandoned his love poetry rather shamefacedly in favour of religious conceits and how, though scientific notions had begun to stir doubts in the minds of the more intelligent, the Bible remained, from Bacon to Locke, the unchallenged fount of truth.

It had been primarily the Court that had given encouragement to the wonderful group of dramatists headed by Shakespeare and Ben Jonson in the early part of the century and had patronized the Metaphysical Poets such as John Donne and George Herbert (just as it was the Court that had inspired a period of brilliant artistic achievement in the decade 1630–40 when Van Dyck was flourishing). Moreover under Archbishop Laud the leaders of the Church of England had approved, within limits, of drama, poetry, and sport. Donne and Herbert were beneficed clergy of the Church. When the Court and Church were overthrown, plays and poetry went down with them. The Puritans had long boycotted drama as immoral; the works of only one or two poets, such as Spenser, were allowed into pious households; and, as for the Court, it was dubbed by Mrs Hutchinson, who spoke for her party, 'a nursery of lust and intemperance'.

Even before the Long Parliament met in 1640, plays and poems were, as Sir Herbert Grierson has written, merely 'a sparkling side-stream' beside the huge river of religious treatises, volumes of sermons, and political and sectarian tracts that poured from the presses. Afterwards the river became a torrent, so that every faith and creed had its pen-men, and booksellers were stocked with expositions and refutations of every conceivable variety of the Christian doctrine. Much of this literature was for the day and no more. But in some cases, as in Milton's *Areopagitica*, it touched the heights; in others, as in the writings of George Fox, the founder of the Society of Friends, and of Richard Baxter, a moderate Calvinist, it was highly serviceable; in other cases still, such as in the pamphlets of Lilburne, Prynne, and Winstanley, the prose was lively and inexhaustible, if nothing more, though their biographers sometime stake bigger claims. Apart from Milton (and later Bunyan), Fox's *Journal*, and Baxter's autobiography, the most consistently fine writing of a religious character came not from the Puritans but from a number of liberal-minded theologians at the two universities.

The first patron of these 'rational' theologians was Lucius Cary, Lord Falkland. Though he himself was something of an orator, a poet, and a soldier, he was above all one of those personable young men who (like the celebrated Edwardian hostesses) have a natural gift for attracting brilliant company. At first the poets of Ben Jonson's circle clustered round him, but after his father's death, his home of Great Tew near Oxford became the meeting place of a notable theological group: Falkland's house, wrote Clarendon, 'within ten or twelve miles of the university looked like the university itself by the company that was always found there'. Among this company were to be found future bishops of King Charles II's reign, some who were to be hot against the nonconformists, others of a more obliging temper. But the two most distinguished members of these gatherings never reached bishoprics: they were William Chillingworth of Oxford, Falkland's 'most intimate and beloved favourite', and the 'ever memorable' John Hales of Eton College. Falkland himself had had a Calvinist upbringing and when he first entered the House of Commons had been critical of the King's policies, but he became a moderate Anglican and loyal Cavalier and after being appointed Secretary of State was killed at the age of thirty-three fighting for the King. His spirit of moderation was reflected in the writings of Chillingworth and Hales. These theologians argued that there were only a limited number of fundamental beliefs required of Christians, and other doctrines need not be fastened tightly on them on account of authority or tradition. They held to the middle road. In common with Archbishop Laud they rejected the doctrine of predestination; but in common with the Puritan sectarians they abided by the Bible, as interpreted by 'right reason' (that is, their own). In his book, *The Religion of Protestants* (1637), Chillingworth urged the principle of religious 'latitude' or of agreeing to differ over many points of religious theory so long as men believed in Christ. He himself objected to the Athanasian Creed and refused to admit on his deathbed to the anxious Puritan who tended him that a Turk or a Papist might not be saved. Chillingworth reached these broad views partly in reaction against the teaching at a Jesuit seminary which he had attended as a young man; Hales came to much the same conclusions after listening to the theological controversies at the Synod of Dort in Holland. Hales argued that dogmatic differences were not religious differences: he pleaded for 'liberty of judging'; he rejected the High Anglican point of view in regard to the power of bishops and the meaning of the Communion; and he maintained that it is 'the unity of the Spirit in the bond of peace and not identity of conceit which the Holy Ghost required at the hands of Christians'. Chillingworth died in 1644 and Hales in 1658. Both were royalist in their political sympathies and owed as much to the friendship of Laud as of Falkland. Their teachings were better suited to the Church of England, as conceived by Queen Elizabeth and by Hooker, than to any other imaginable Church. Although Laud had required outward uniformity, he had allowed scope for variety of belief, whereas the Calvinists were rigorous in their requirements in dogmas, morals, and discipline. The rational theology of Falkland, Chillingworth, and Hales would have opened the door to all Christians. Nor did they stand alone: Jeremy Taylor in his *Liberty of Prophesying* (1647) also argued in majestic prose that religious differences of opinion were inevitable, but that the reason for disunion was not variety of opinion, but lack of charity. Let Christians adhere to the Apostles' Creed and they might leave the interpretation of Scripture to their reason guided by divine revelation. Edward Stillingfleet, who, like Taylor, was to survive the Interregnum and become a bishop, in his *Irenicum* (1659) likewise quotes with approval from the Epistle to the Philippians: 'Let your moderation be known before all men.' Finally, the group of theologians who flourished at Emmanuel College, Cambridge, mostly in the reign of King Charles II (although one of their number, John Smith, died in 1652), and were influenced by the Neoplatonic philosopher, Plotinus, and also to some extent by Descartes, carried the latitudinarian doctrines, but on a slightly higher plane, forward into the Restoration world.

The 'liberty of conscience' which the Oxford 'rational theologians' and the Cambridge 'Platonists' preached was, as we have observed, a belief shared by Cromwell. Indeed one can trace a close connexion between him and the protagonists of these ideas. One of the members of the Cambridge group, John Worthington, was made Vice-Chancellor of the University by the Lord Protector; another, Ralph Cudworth, was frequently consulted by him; and a third, John Wilkins, married his sister, Robina, in 1656. During the Interregnum the Cambridge thinkers were content to concentrate on purely theoretical teaching, but they also sought toleration. Several passages in Cromwell's speeches, where he pressed the doctrine of 'liberty in non-essentials', show how closely he agreed with them.

The 'Cambridge Platonists' were mostly brought up in a Puritan environment. But those among the Puritans themselves who favoured 'liberty of conscience' were a minority. The right wing of the English Puritans, the Presbyterians, though they might not believe in a Church-ruled State to the same extent as their Scottish brethren, were neither tolerationists nor democrats nor even republicans. What they wanted was their strict system of Church organization buttressed by a limited monarchy. In his *Sovereign Power of Parliaments* (1643) William Prynne declared that Parliament was above the King and could depose him if he broke faith, but he defended kingship, while every Calvinist writer from Calvin onwards condemned popular government. It was only among the Independents and left-wing Puritans that religious ideas led towards liberal political thought. Because they wanted liberty for Christians, they came to believe in wide liberty of thought; because they held that all Christian believers were equal in the sight of the Lord, they came to advocate political equality. And finally because they admitted the right of each Christian to value the word of God by the light of his own reason, they came to be individualists: a true church, according to John Milton, might consist of a single member.

The doctrines of religious liberty, political equality, and individual freedom were first put forward altogether by John Lilburne and the Levellers and embodied in the paper constitutions which they discussed with members of the Council of the Army in 1647 and 1648. John Wildman, Lilburne's first lieutenant, asserted that 'every person in England hath as clear a right to elect his representatives as the greatest person in England'. Thus the 'Agreement of the People', which was drawn up by Wildman, would have guaranteed manhood suffrage, frequent parliaments, and freedom of conscience for all. But the Independent Grandees or 'middle party' among the Puritans were doubtful about the wisdom of manhood suffrage: they wanted parliamentary supremacy, but not a democratic republic. For they feared if such a democracy were established, the poor would rule it and it might happen that 'the majority may by law, not in a confusion, destroy property . . . there may be a law enacted that there shall be an equality of goods and estates'. Hence what these middle-class Independents wanted was a franchise based on property and a government composed of an aristocracy of chosen Christians. In the writings of men as different as Henry Vane the younger, John Milton, and Algernon Sidney and in the speeches of Cromwell, Ireton, and Haselrig the case was put not for a democratic government founded on popular consent, but for the rule of the virtuous, selected by men of standing. On the other hand, neither Lilburne nor Wildman asked for anything other than a more representative form of government with certain rights or 'fundamentals' guaranteed, as in the United States constitution of today, by a written instrument. Lilburne was above everything else an individualist and the accusations made against him by contemporaries that he wanted economic communism do not bear examination.

A few seventeenth-century pamphleteers did however take up a more radical position than that of Lilburne, while being numbered among his friends and supporters. Modern historians have tried hard to prove that in William Walwyn, Richard Overton, and Gerrard Winstanley are to be found ancestors of our modern Communists. Walwyn certainly exercised considerable influence on Leveller thinking. He was of the opinion that in an ideal community all private property should be abolished. He reached this conclusion from his study of primitive Christianity, but he did not believe it to be practical politics in the seventeenth century. We know little about the political thought of Overton. His main claim to be associated with modern Communists rests on an anonymous pamphlet supposed to have been written by him in which, like Milton, he taught that the body and soul were inseparable and remained dead until the Day of Judgement. Winstanley was a more complex character and we know rather more about him than about Overton. He was the leader of the 'True Levellers' or 'Diggers' who tried to put communism into practice on a patch of land at Cobham in Surrey. After this experiment he wrote in a pamphlet called *The Law of Freedom* (1651) that man first fell from his innocence when he began to buy and sell; he therefore urged that the land should be set free to oppressed commoners and a 'common stock' be created to pay for all. The appearance of Winstanley and his Diggers at Cobham and his outspoken agrarian communism made him a ten-days' wonder, but afterwards he disappears from history.

In our own lifetime historians of many nationalities from Americans to Russians have seized upon these obscure pamphleteers and bloated them into veritable Platos, Rousseaus, and Marxes. But a sense of proportion may be used. What these men had in common was not a premature bent for Marxist ideology, but a touching faith in the value of Christian revelation to inspired individuals, in the virtues of Primitive Christianity, and in the immediacy of the Second Coming of Christ. Lilburne, who defended private property and distrusted the all-powerful State, ended his adventurous career not as a fighting democrat but as a peaceable Quaker. Walwyn, who derived his belief in communism from the Christian doctrine of loving one's neighbour, hoped not for a proletarian revolution but for conditions of apostolic simplicity when the Millennium came round the corner. Winstanley, like Lilburne and Walwyn, furnished the matter in his tracts out of 'openings from God' and thought that the old world was vanishing under the fierce glare of inspired reason. But his 'reason' was not that of nineteenth-century agnostics, any more than Overton's 'materialism' was that of twentieth-century Leninists: his light of reason was 'the candle of the Lord' as understood by the Cambridge Platonists and the Quaker followers of George Fox.

A Puritan sect which achieved a notoriety out of proportion to its numerical strength in the middle of the seventeenth century was that of the Fifth Monarchy Men who exerted influence on Cromwell in 1653 and caused anxiety to the Restoration Government in 1661. Members of this sect sincerely believed that the Second Coming was due at any moment and that until that event occurred they were the men entitled to rule the country. Thus they preached in an exaggerated if nebulous form the republican doctrines shared by all the Puritan Millenarians. They were indeed the veritable revolutionaries, fearless soldiers of Christ ready to trample down man-made laws and set up a fanatical government, if only they were allowed to do so. How important were the Levellers and other radicals? What the Levellers stood for was the sovereignty of the people (except for servants and beggars), religious toleration, equality before the law and economic freedom. The Levellers were a minority and the extreme radicals who wanted 'the world turned upside down' were inspired eccentrics. Their doctrines still seem fantastic today. But they were the true revolutionaries of their time who would have destroyed Anti-Christ, prepared for the Second Coming and established a brave new world. They wanted the rule of the Godly, as Cromwell did, but the difficulty was to define it. And their aim to overthrow established society merely strengthened existing governments both during the Interregnum and after.

The political writings of these Levellers and sectarians are really of most interest because they disclose the complaints of the common people – for instance, against tithes and the delays of the law – and because of the way their authors groped after a better life in a Golden Age. But they had little practical significance at the time and no serious effect on the later history of political philosophy. Two political philosophers whose principal works were published during the Interregnum did however profoundly influence contemporary and subsequent political thought: they were Thomas Hobbes, the Sage of Malmesbury, and James Harrington, erstwhile friend of King Charles I. Though Hobbes and Harrington did not agree with each other, both contributed strands to that Marxian faith which now sways so much of the modern world, Hobbes by his materialist outlook on life and society, Harrington by his economic interpretation of history. Hobbes was an out-and-out materialist. 'The universe is material,' he wrote, 'all that is real is material and what is not material is not real.' He did not, like his notable contemporary, Descartes, believe in the duality of body and mind: to him the body was all and 'conceptions' were caused by the impression of external objects on the organs of the body; conceptions in turn caused appetite and fear, 'which are the first unperceived beginnings of actions'. Men are therefore guided, he thought, by a lust for power or by a fear of the consequences of the struggle for power. Because they are afraid of each other and so as to prevent self-destruction in a war of all against all, they are compelled to agree together to confer all their power and strength upon one man or one assembly of men who can reduce all their wills to one. This sovereign, whom they create voluntarily without imposing any conditions upon him, is the Great Leviathan or Mortal God. What he orders is the law; what he decides is justice. For the subject to rebel against the sovereign is useless, because if he does so, he simply destroys the State and lets social life revert into war and anarchy. It is possible to argue against the material bases of Hobbes's thought, but once they are granted his conclusions inexorably follow. Moreover they were superficially well suited to the age in which he lived. The world into which this rather timid man but daring philosopher was born seemed plunged into a perpetual anarchy. Only some sort of strong-arm politics directed by an indivisible and unchangeable sovereign of untrammelled powers and genuine strength of will could, it seemed to him, restore peace and prosperity. Thus Hobbes's theories lead to the all-powerful, all-embracing State such as existed before the war in National-Socialist Germany and now exists behind the Iron Curtain: and Hobbes himself did not care in his lifetime whether the sovereign was a Cromwell, a republican Council of State, or a Charles II.

Harrington's *The Commonwealth of Oceana* (1656) was dedicated to Cromwell and opens with an attack on Hobbes: he asks what is the good of an all-powerful sovereign unless he has an army on which he can rely. But 'an army is a beast that has a great belly and must be fed: wherefore this will come to what pastures you have, and what pastures you have will come to the balance of property, without which the public sword is but a name or mere spitfrog'. The notion of a 'balance of property' was central to Harrington's teaching. He believed that a stable society depended on a direct relationship between the distribution of property and political power. The basis of his State therefore was to be an 'agrarian law' providing that no one should possess land above the value of £2,000 in England or £300 in Scotland. No one owning property worth £2,000 should be allowed to buy more; marriage portions should be restricted and property divided equally among children. Harrington believed that by thus restricting and dividing property he was 'cutting with the grain' because property in his time had already become more widely diffused. Kings and peers had lost their power because they had been obliged to sell large parcels of property. In his opinion the alienation of estates by the English kings had imperilled the absolutism of the crown and the civil wars had been caused by a conflict between the old and the new landed classes. Now, however, he wanted to establish an aristocratic republic securely based on a socialistic division of property. By keeping power in the hands of the steadier section of the community, which engaged in agriculture, he hoped to avoid an extreme form of democracy. A Senate of mature property-owners was to make and debate laws, while an assembly, elected by universal suffrage, was to be allowed to vote on them, for 'a popular assembly without a senate cannot be wise and a senate without a popular assembly will not be honest'. Harrington advocated the use of the ballot in general elections and in parliamentary voting. He wanted the Senate (much as in the United States today) to be a permanent institution from which one-third of the members had to withdraw from office every year. By combining in one constitutional system the agrarian law, two Chambers with different duties, universal suffrage, indirect election, and the ballot, Harrington intended to accept the principles of democracy while losing none of the advantages of aristocratic government. Harrington's *Oceana* was so superior to any other detailed constitutional scheme put forward during the Interregnum that it immediately influenced nearly all other political theorists of that age, royalist and republican alike. The remnants of the Leveller Party that had virtually disappeared after the death of Lilburne as a convinced Quaker swallowed Harrington's ideas whole, and even John Milton in a book published in 1660 adopted the principle of rotation of offices for that grand aristocratic council which was to him the perfect form of government.

Milton, the 'mighty organ voice of England', was the third outstanding author of the Interregnum, with Hobbes and Harrington. All three of them survived into the reign of King Charles II. Hobbes died in 1679 in his ninety-first year, luckily for him in his bed. Harrington, after being wrongfully imprisoned for alleged plotting against the new Government, went insane and died in 1677. Milton, the youngest of the three, long blind, was struck down by gout in 1674. He was indeed unique even in that age of remarkable thinkers. Known to history as the one great Puritan poet, he might, had he died before the civil wars, have been hard to distinguish from the group of Cavalier poets of King Charles I's reign; though he was at one time a Presbyterian apologist, he broke away in all essential doctrines from that party after it had become dominant in the land; a 'regicide' who enthusiastically approved of the execution of the Martyred King, he survived to publish his best works in the reign of the Martyr's son; an epic poet who wrote of the battle between God and Satan, his work, as modern critics have shown, is yet personal and even heretical to a high degree.

Milton was born in 1608 and dedicated by his parents (as were Ruskin and John Stuart Mill) to a life of culture and scholarship, although, as was natural then, his ultimate destination was expected to be the Church. He managed, however, perhaps by his excessive intellectualism, to make himself unpopular at Cambridge and never obtained a fellowship, and he declined to enter the Church. He started his career as a poet by writing lyrics in the manner of Spenser, but after a short visit to Italy determined to devote himself to a heroic poem in English with an elevated moral purpose. The meeting of the Long Parliament and the events that followed diverted him for the time being from his path. Instead he concocted a number of pamphlets of varying quality in which he assaulted the bishops and defended the Presbyterian faith. But thenceforward he moved away from rigid Puritan orthodoxy. His marriage to a girl of half his age, who left him a month afterwards for her mother, persuaded him to write pamphlets urging divorce for incompatibility: the banning of these divorce pamphlets by the Presbyterian authorities induced him to write his *Areopagitica* in favour of the liberty of the press; and his *Tractate of Education* was also 'a song of hope' written for those revolutionary times. In August 1645 Milton's first wife returned from her mother and bore him a number of children and he relapsed into a private and quiet life from which he emerged just before the execution of King Charles I to publish *The Tenure of Kings and Magistrates* so as to convert to republicanism the Presbyterians who had objected to killing the King as not being 'the act of their party'. Milton maintained that the people may 'as often as they shall judge it for the best either choose him or reject him or depose him, though no tyrant, merely by the liberty and right of freeborn men to be governed as seems to the best'. The self-appointed apologist of the Independent cause was rewarded with the office of Latin Secretary to the Council of State and set to work on propaganda in defence of the new republic – that council of the elect which he so much admired. But by 1655 he had lost his sight and had more or less been pensioned off. Probably his blindness and the efforts of some influential friends enabled him to escape severe punishment at the Restoration: he suffered only a short period of imprisonment, though early in 1660 he had published his *Ready and Easy Way to Establish a Free Commonwealth*, an optimistic essay written in a pessimistic tone. For these were, he thought, 'the last words of expiring liberty' and were greeted with a storm of abuse.

In comparative poverty and fortunate obscurity Milton lived on with his third wife (his first died in 1652, his second in childbirth) to complete his greatest work, *Paradise Lost*, in 1665 and have it published in return for £5 in 1667. This magnificent Christian epic of the expulsion of Adam from the Garden of Eden written to 'justify the ways of God to men' has caused paradoxical comment down to our own day. Dryden considered that Milton had in fact made the Devil his hero instead of Adam; Blake said Milton was 'of the Devil's party without knowing it'; and one modern critic has claimed that 'his genius was inverted, so that what objectively appears evil in the demonic verse of *Paradise Lost* is subjectively good'. It is difficult to accept all this. We prefer the interpretation that in *Paradise Lost* Milton himself contended with Satan, while in *Paradise Regained* (1671) Christ was the victor 'not only over Satan but over Milton himself' (J. H. Hanford). But perhaps the noblest expression of Milton's inner struggles was *Samson Agonistes*, completed not long before Milton died, in which occur the lines:

> Now blind, disheartened, shamed, dishonoured, quelled,
> To what can I be useful, wherein serve
> My nation and the work from Heaven imposed?

The poetry of Milton, that eccentric Puritan, (as that of John Donne, the witty servant of the Anglican Church) took a very modest place in the reign of King Charles II, with its emphasis on science and comedy, a Broad Church and a resurgent Roman Catholicism. Yet we can see now that the Interregnum was by no means an intellectual backwater: the ferment of ideas that then arose was finally absorbed into English history.

CHAPTER IX

King Charles II and the Wars against the Dutch

1660–74

WHAT did the Restoration of King Charles II in 1660 in fact restore? First of all of course it restored the monarchy. But it was not the Elizabethan monarchy. All the acts of parliament to which King Charles I gave his assent before he left his capital (except that excluding the bishops from the House of Lords) retained their full validity. Consequently many of the devices which until that time had been perfectly legally used by the King to uphold his prerogative and to enable him to govern and raise money without parliament's aid were abolished for all time. The prerogative courts were not reconstituted. Unparliamentary taxation, such as ship money and forced loans, stood condemned. The criminal jurisdiction of the Privy Council had vanished. The King could no longer order the arrest of members of Parliament without showing cause. In fact, the monarchy had almost become 'constitutional'. Secondly, Parliament was restored, but on the old basis. Cromwell had tried all sorts of experiments with his parliaments: among other things the constituencies had been altered, the franchise had been changed, and members had been summoned to it from Scotland and Ireland. Although some of the new King's advisers recognized the strength of the case for reforming the franchise, nothing was done about it in the seventeenth century. Union with Scotland waited until 1707, with Ireland until 1801. When in 1677 King Charles II tried to create a new parliamentary borough (as previous monarchs had done so often) a storm of protest arose from the Commons and the 'prerogative was never again exercised' (G. N. Clark). Thirdly, the Church of England was restored with its full panoply of bishops and deans, but it was no more a comprehensive church, for many of the Puritans were to be driven from it. On the other hand, the Church, like the country, never entirely lost its puritan undertone. Thus in spite of the Restoration being, in theory at least, 'unconditional' neither King nor Parliament nor Church was left unscathed by the fire of revolution. And both the monarch and his ministers were aware that they dared not take the road back to the old Tudor methods of government. Their policies were always tempered by the knowledge that behind them lay the precedent of a civil war and an anointed monarch's execution; while King Charles II was determined not to go on his 'travels' again.

The new King was a man of charm, wit, intelligence, and accessibility. Years of exile and adventure had taught him that virtue lay in compromise and dissimulation and little was to be gained from strict adherence to principles. Though capable of application, he was congenitally lazy and self-indulgent. He had a sense of occasion and of humour and, unlike his father and his brother, he knew when to yield. 'To the patriotism, moral courage, and self-sacrifice which have been eulogized by his more recent biographers he made no claim' (Ogg). His chief minister was Edward Hyde, Earl of Clarendon, an honest and austere man, 'in his nature inclined to pride and passion', who would have been more at home in the respectable court of King Charles I than in the immoral Whitehall of his son. Clarendon's daughter was married to the King's brother, James, and at the outset of the reign he seemed firmly stationed on the steps of the throne. The King governed through a large Privy Council over which he himself usually presided, but after a while all matters were first referred to committees of the Council: one of these committees, that for foreign affairs, is sometimes held by historians to be the direct ancestor of the modern Cabinet, though no Prime Minister in the modern sense existed. But the machinery of government was, on the face of it, still that of the Tudors. Yet James Harrington had rightly seen that new wine could not be poured into old bottles; for he had averred that however royalist a parliament might meet, in seven years it would turn republican again. And so it proved.

Clarendon's triumph had been to procure the Restoration without the assistance of foreign arms. The price he had to pay was to persuade the King to promise in his Declaration of Breda to leave to parliament the settlement of all the knotty points arising out of the recent upheaval. The first of these was the question of an act of pardon and indemnity. The Convention Parliament which had recalled the King (and continued to sit until December 1660) eventually exempted under thirty persons from the general pardon and of these only thirteen were executed. This merciful conduct (which was approved and in fact supported by the King and Clarendon) was wise, for it enabled the army, a possible source of unrest, to be disbanded without serious danger, although a small rising in 1661 was made the excuse for retaining in service General Monk's regiment which was to be known to later generations as the Coldstream Guards. The land settlement was a very much trickier problem. Property belonging to the Crown and to the Church which had been confiscated by the Commonwealth was restored by statute, and royalists whose lands had been confiscated outright were entitled to try to get them back again by special petition or by ordinary process of law, if they could. But royalists who had been compelled to sell their land because of the crippling fines imposed by the Interregnum governments or for other reasons received no compensation. Although such researches as have hitherto been undertaken by historians appear to suggest that there was little change in the distribution of land among the great propertied families as a direct result of the civil wars, it is certain that a number of the smaller royalists did not get back all their lands, while some of the purchasers among the Cromwellian officers and puritan merchants managed to cling on to property that they had bought for a song in the revolutionary heyday. The tendency during the second half of the seventeenth century among men with land was for the rich to grow richer and the poor to grow poorer. Many big landowners, such as the Earl of Bedford, were able to increase the size of their holdings by buying from small needy squires; the enclosure of open fields advanced without interruption, as it had done ever since the days of the 'Eleven Years' Tyranny', while in an age of rising rents the small yeomen and leaseholders had a struggle to make both ends meet. In the end the Crown, which was compelled to sell most of its remaining land and yield up profitable feudal rights, had to come to terms with a group of very wealthy men – and, when civil war again threatened, the families who had fought for King Charles I turned against his son, James. But Charles II did not allow events to go so far, though by the land settlement of the Restoration, in which he had to acquiesce, he committed his first great act of ingratitude against men who had served him faithfully in his exile. Out of the complicated property pattern of the Restoration emerged the Whig magnates and disgruntled Tory squires – new and effective actors on the stage of English history.

Besides dealing with the question of landed property rights after the civil wars the Convention had to provide the King with money. The King's debts amassed in exile and the State's debts amounted to about £3,000,000 or the equivalent of nearly three years' ordinary revenue. Recognizing the urgency of disbanding the army the Convention voted taxes to meet the soldiers' arrears of pay, but they did not provide enough to do much else. Afterwards the Commons voted customs and excise on ale and beer (and on the new-fangled drinks, tea and coffee) to the King, indirect taxes which together with certain other traditional sources of revenue were reckoned to yield £1,200,000 a year. In 1662 an unpopular hearth tax was added. Apart from the fact that the King's expenses were larger than this vote, the amount actually raised usually fell short of the sum promised by Parliament, often by as much as one-third. King Charles II therefore was constantly in debt and this indebtedness finally helped him into the arms of the King of France who offered him subsidies for collaborating in his foreign policy. Half the excise was voted to King Charles for life and the other half to the Crown in perpetuity. That was considered to be a fair return for the abolition of the Court of Wards, the means by which King Henry VIII had kept hold of certain feudal dues belonging to the Crown and exacted by it from the tenants-in-chief since early times. By surrendering these dues King Charles II bade farewell to feudalism and entered upon a more modern world – but not Mr Gladstone's world in which budgets were usually balanced. While the King thus resigned his position as the biggest territorial landlord, he also had let go of a means of levying taxes on other wealthy landowners. So changes in methods of public finance, as well as changes in the ownership of landed property, strengthened the power of the wealthy English magnates at the expense of the Crown and ushered in a new era in history.

One other big question remained to be settled in 1660, namely the future of the Church. The Convention contained a large number of Presbyterians who had helped to restore the King and were yet hopeful that in any religious settlement concessions would be made to their point of view. On 25 October the King published a declaration in which he conferred temporary freedom on all practising Christians and on 5 April 1661 a conference of Anglican and Presbyterian leaders gathered at Savoy Palace to work out an agreement about worship and belief. But before the conference ended the first parliament of the new reign, known to history as the Cavalier or Pensionary Parliament, had been elected and summoned. The number of Presbyterians in the House of Commons was seen to have shrunk and the majority of the Cavalier M.P.s were devoted to the Church as well as to the King and distrusted political compromises. The idea of 'comprehension' which had been favoured by the more moderate Presbyterian ministers such as Richard Baxter (who was actually offered a bishopric) and by the latitudinarian theologians within the Anglican fold was pushed aside. A series of acts of parliament, usually known together as the Clarendon Code, imposed grave disabilities on the dissenters. The Corporation Act of December 1661, for example, excluded from municipal bodies all who refused to renounce the Covenant, to take the sacrament according to the rites of the Church of England, or to swear not to resist the King. In April 1662 a revised Book of Common Prayer was promulgated and in May an Act of Uniformity insisted that clergy who did not assent to the new liturgy must give up their livings. On 24 August 1662 a large number of dissenting clergy, variously estimated at between one and two thousand, were driven from their parishes. At the same time a licensing act gave large powers over the press and printing into the hands of the Archbishop of Canterbury and the Bishop of London. When the King attempted to soften the severity of all these new laws by publishing in December 1662 his first Declaration of Indulgence the Commons were furious and nothing came of it. On the contrary: a bill allowing the King to 'dispense with' the Act of Uniformity was dropped; a Conventicle Act provided for penalties against people who attended services not conducted according to the rubric of the Common Prayer Book; and in 1665 the Five Mile Act banned nonconformist preachers from living in or even visiting any place where they had formerly officiated.

The Clarendon Code created English Nonconformity, but not, as has sometimes been said, dissent, for that, as we have seen, dates from at least the beginning of the century. How far the Code was enforced is not clear. For its enforcement depended, as did so much of the national administration in the seventeenth century, upon the inclinations of the Justices of the Peace, and in some parts of the country they were sympathetic to the Nonconformists, just as in Lancashire they had been sympathetic to Roman Catholics. On the other hand, the civil disabilities suffered by the Nonconformists – such as their exclusion from the universities – were to become permanent for many years. And one reason for the extraordinary success of the Nonconformists, notably of the Quakers, in business enterprise was that they were thus diverted from the ordinary duties and pleasures of citizenship.

Clarendon won unenviable notoriety for the introduction of this penal legislation against the former Puritans. In fact he was not an enthusiastic supporter of it, although he neither resisted it nor reduced its severity. It represented in the first place the wishes of the Anglican majority in the House of Commons who had good reason for feeling bitter against the dissenters; but it was also promoted by the King's Privy Council because it was thought that dissenters' meeting places were possible and indeed likely centres for plotting against the restored King. In actual fact – except for the Fifth Monarchy Men who staged a wild and hopeless rising in the City of London in 1661 – the Nonconformist sects were singularly peaceable. If there was any serious plotting to revivify the republican cause in the early years of the reign, it took place among the disbanded soldiery and the employees of the Post Office (or General Letter Office) where John Wildman, the former Leveller, exerted influence. The ordinary chapel-goer might well have been provoked by the Clarendon Code, but reform and not revolution was his aim.

Although Sir Henry Bennet (later Lord Arlington), who carried a sign of his loyalty in a scar on a once wounded nose and succeeded an older royalist as Secretary of State in October 1661 was an ambitious rival to Clarendon and agreed with the King's desire for toleration, it was foreign policy and not religion that brought about the downfall of the Lord Chancellor. As with the so-called Clarendon Code, the Earl was blamed for policies for which a case could be made and for which he was by no means solely responsible. For example, the marriage of the King at Portsmouth in May 1662 to a Portuguese Princess with a face of limited aesthetic value had seemed at first sight a good piece of business, as she had brought a handsome dowry including Bombay and Tangier, but her childlessness offset her dowry. Again, the sale of Dunkirk to France in October of that same year did not seem unwise, since its upkeep was expensive and it would have been impossible to defend this bridgehead on to the Continent from an attack on the land side; but Dunkirk had been the trophy of Cromwell's redcoats and its loss was regarded as an affront to national pride. Finally, the war against the Dutch which broke out in 1665 might have been more popular if it had not dragged on so long. This second Anglo-Dutch war, like the first of 1652-4, was brought about by trade and maritime rivalries and old disputes over colonies outside Europe: it was 'the clearest case in history of a purely commercial war'. (G. N. Clark.) Although the English navy under the command of James, Duke of York, won one or two victories over the Dutch, its enemies had an inconvenient way of recovering from disasters. Moreover they had allies, though somewhat reluctant ones, in the French, and were able in 1665 and 1666 to take advantage of the confusion caused in English administrative circles by the Great Plague and the Great Fire of London. The Plague, of which 68,000 persons died in London alone, was of the usual bubonic type, brought in by black rats and carried round by their fleas. The Fire, unlike the Plague, was not an unmixed evil. It started in Pudding Lane, extended very rapidly owing to an adverse wind, and destroyed nearly the whole of the City proper. Many old lath-and-plaster houses were burned down and rebuilt in brick and thus a condition which had contributed to the spread of plague was eliminated. In any case, whatever the reason, the Great Plague was the last of its kind. The Great Fire also afforded an opportunity to Sir Christopher Wren to rebuild London and particularly its churches on nobler lines.

By the winter of 1666, when the Thames was filled with ice, the Commons had become tired of the Dutch war and perturbed about its cost, and peace negotiations were opened. King Charles II had prematurely ordered the bigger ships of the navy to be laid up. The Dutch, on their side, though more or less deserted by their French allies, determined on a daring operation. Not only did their vessels sail up the Firth of Forth in the spring of 1667, but in June the great Admiral de Ruyter successfully carried out a carefully prepared plan, bombarded Sheerness, attacked Chatham, sending fireships into the dock, and sailed away suffering little loss, taking in tow the *Royal Charles*, the flagship of the English fleet. In July an inconclusive peace was signed at Breda.

The country had been deeply humiliated and sought a scapegoat. It had not far to look. After the disaster at Chatham crowds had assembled outside Clarendon's house in Piccadilly, broken the windows, and pulled up the trees. He had been criticized for the severities of the legislation against the Nonconformists and for the sale of Dunkirk to France; now he was accused of mismanaging the Dutch war, of which he had disapproved, and for the financial scandals arising out of it, for which he was not responsible. He had many enemies. As early as July 1663 an attempt had been made to impeach him. He was hated by 'the buffoons and ladies of pleasure' that consorted with the King. He had always distrusted the House of Commons, seeing in it the successors to the hot-blooded republicans of the Long Parliament, and its members retorted their wrath upon him. The Cavaliers thought they had been insufficiently considered by him, the Roman Catholics and Puritans that he had considered them too much. The King, egged on from below stairs, had tired of a domineering old man and abandoned him to the malice of his enemies, as his father had abandoned Strafford. Clarendon was dismissed, impeached, and banished, and retired abroad to complete his distinguished *History of the Rebellion*. The Commons, which had already instituted the principle, in voting money for the recent campaigns, of appropriating supply to that purpose alone – thereby creating a constitutional precedent – now appointed a Committee of Accounts to see how the money had been spent. This Committee exposed various scandals. Thus by 1667 the loyal Commons had awoken from its dream of Restoration bliss into a day of political realities.

Clarendon had no immediate successor as first Minister. The King took upon himself the direction of foreign policy, using as his instruments such advisers as he thought suitable. The principal Secretary of State, Lord Arlington, and Sir William Coventry, who as Treasury Commissioner had advised the laying up of the fleet in 1667, only just managed to escape impeachment with Clarendon for the inglorious results of the Dutch war. Coventry lost his office two years later, but Arlington, though frightened, survived. It was at first thought that George Villiers, second Duke of Buckingham, now the King's Master of Horse, might step into Clarendon's place. Buckingham, son of Charles I's favourite, a wit and a sceptic, made himself personally agreeable to the King, but lacked application and set more store by popularity than anything else. Bishop Burnet said of him that 'he had no principles either of religion, virtue or friendship'. Principle was not a notable characteristic of Restoration statesmen and Burnet was more to the point when he added that 'he was true to nothing; for he was not true to himself'. When Buckingham was commissioned to bring over one of the King's mistresses from France, he forgot all about her and left her stranded at Dieppe; it was left to Arlington to dispatch the requisite yacht. Thus Arlington was the more serious character of the two. An industrious worker, a proven royalist, an experienced diplomatist, he had a Dutch wife (descendant on the wrong side of the blanket of the royal House of Orange), but though distrustful of France he had no consistent policy; he died a Roman Catholic. Another of the King's leading Ministers at this time, whom he made Lord Chancellor in 1672, was Lord Ashley, later Earl of Shaftesbury, friend of the philosopher John Locke who acted as his physician, and a man as famous for the smallness of his body as for his indomitable courage: he even defended Clarendon. Other Ministers were the Earl of Lauderdale, the King's adviser on Scottish affairs, a former Presbyterian, and Sir Thomas Clifford, a *protégé* of Arlington, who, like his patron, died a Roman Catholic. The initials of these five men, Clifford, Arlington, Buckingham, Ashley, and Lauderdale, spelt 'Cabal' and therefore the period that followed Clarendon's dismissal is sometimes spoken of as that of rule by the Cabal, but this group was in no sense exclusive or in any way whatever analogous to the modern Cabinet.

In the years 1668 to 1670 King Charles II wavered between two foreign policies, but his ultimate aim was to obtain good terms of alliance from the French King whom he admired and envied. In 1667 the French had gone to war with Spain, claiming the Spanish Netherlands after the death of King Philip IV, a Habsburg, as the rightful inheritance of his daughter, the French Queen. King Charles II then decided to conclude an offensive and defensive alliance with the United Netherlands so as to prevent the whole of the Belgian coastline from falling into French hands and to make King Louis XIV more amenable to compromise. A treaty was therefore made with the Dutch in January 1668 and welded into a Triple Alliance with Sweden in April. But meanwhile the French King had arranged a secret treaty with the Emperor, head of the Habsburg family, whereby his gains in Belgium were defined and the partition between them of the whole Spanish Empire, which included large parts of Italy as well as Belgium and much of the New World, was projected when the Spanish Habsburg line ended, as it was expected to do at any moment. Thus Louis XIV had good reason for being willing to make peace with Spain in the spring of 1668 (for why bother over a small part of the Spanish Empire if the bulk of it might be coming his way?) – and the Triple Alliance contributed little to his decision, but left him angry with the Dutch on whom he was provoked to take his revenge.

During 1669 Louis XIV concentrated all the efforts of his superb diplomatic machine on isolating the Dutch. For he believed it necessary to suppress or neutralize the upstart republican merchants of that country in order to seize vast territories when the feeble Spanish King, Charles the Sufferer, who had succeeded in 1667, should die. Meanwhile King Charles II continued to flirt with Holland and Spain, but all his inclinations lay towards alliance with France. By the beginning of 1670 after secret negotiations, partly initiated through a private correspondence with his beloved sister, Minette, who was married to the brother of Louis XIV, a road to agreement with France had been opened. A Roman Catholic breeze blowing through the English Court may or may not have stimulated this change of policy.

By that time King Charles II's brother, James, Duke of York, had become a convert to the Roman Catholic Church and, according to his account, King Charles II had announced in that same year his intention of joining the Church and of carrying his subjects into it along with him. Be that as it may, in May 1670 King Charles II concluded a secret treaty with France known as the Treaty of Dover, because it had been signed there when his sister, Minette, came over to pay him a friendly visit before returning to France to die. By the terms of this treaty King Charles undertook publicly to declare his adhesion to the Roman Catholic religion as soon as convenient and Louis XIV promised to aid his ally with money and soldiers to enforce the reconversion of England to the faith. The two Kings furthermore agreed to attack Holland, their former ally, and in return England was to receive the island of Walcheren if the war were won. The treaty was signed by four Ministers, Arundel, Bellasys, Arlington, and Clifford, of whom the first two were Roman Catholics in life and the other two at death. From his other Ministers the King carefully concealed the Treaty. But all his Ministers were willing and in fact eager to revenge themselves on the Dutch. Consequently both Ashley and Buckingham commended the desirability of the proposed war of aggression and in December Buckingham was sent over to Paris to conclude another treaty with the French King, assenting to the attack on Holland. This 'simulated treaty' of December 1670, as it is called, was as effective for its immediate purpose as the 'secret treaty' of June; and whether the King seriously intended to carry out his promise of forcibly converting England to Roman Catholicism is still disputed. It has been plausibly suggested that both King Charles and Arlington were too experienced statesmen to imagine that such a task would be easy and only committed themselves, in guarded phrases, to the project to improve the conditions which they obtained from France. Whichever way one looks at it, the Treaty of Dover was one of the most discreditable instruments in the history of English diplomacy;

and it did not achieve the objects at which it was aimed.

The third Anglo-Dutch war opened in March 1672. It was preceded by a Declaration of Indulgence issued by King Charles II in which he suspended all the penal laws both against the nonconformists and the Roman Catholics – a sop to Cerberus – thus in his own way fulfilling the promises of the Treaty of Dover while softening the blow to Protestants by ensuring wider liberty to nonconformists. Two months earlier the Government had temporarily suspended payment of interest on money borrowed from London bankers, causing bankruptcies in the City. The King raised further funds by selling off his capital. But in spite of such financial expedients, the new war was no more of a success than the previous one against the United Netherlands. The Dutchmen under the command of William of Orange prepared to defend themselves against the unprovoked aggression of the French and English by manning their river barrier running southward from the Zuider Zee, while on 7 June De Ruyter fought an important battle against the English and French fleets at Southwold Bay which postponed the danger of an amphibious operation against their exposed flank. Nevertheless it was touch-and-go for them. King Louis XIV failed to be bold when boldness might have paid and the Dutch had time to pierce the walls of their dykes and flood strategic watercourses. William was elected to the highest position in the country, that of Stadtholder, and John de Witt, who almost up to the time of the assault had pinned his hopes to the good faith of the French, was murdered.

When the English Parliament met early in 1673 after an interval of three years it was in no amiable frame of mind. True, foreign policy was the King's affair and the Dutch were the traditional enemies and trade rivals of England. But the war had started suddenly while Parliament was not sitting and the House of Commons, though royalist still, was fiercely anti-Catholic. It objected strongly to the second Declaration of Indulgence and in return for granting a sum of money – £1,200,000 spread over eighteen months – obliged the King to abandon his Declaration and demanded the enactment of a bill whereby every holder of office, military or civil, should be compelled to take the sacrament according to the rites of the Church of England. The King yielded and gave his assent to this Test Act; the Duke of York, who had been Lord High Admiral, felt obliged to resign, and so did Clifford, now Lord Treasurer. The war went badly for the English. After the drawn battle of the Texel in August, the blockade of the Dutch ports had to be lifted and the possibility of an invasion of Holland from the sea was finally ended. Although the French King tried to bribe members of parliament and the King met the wishes of the Commons by enforcing the penal laws against Roman Catholics both Houses of Parliament urged the need for peace. King Charles II told King Louis XIV that he was acting under compulsion and in February of the following year he withdrew from the war and accepted modest peace terms in the Treaty of Westminster. 'England was virtually content with a return to the position existing before the war. That was all Charles II had gained by a gamble, by his war expenditure of six millions, and by the sacrifice of thousands of lives.' (G. N. Clark.) By a secret article of the Treaty of Westminster King Charles II agreed not to aid the enemies of the Dutch, but he left a number of English troops in French service under the command of his natural son, the Duke of Monmouth. This was typical of the tortuous diplomacy that characterized the King's foreign policy in those years.

Just as the English failure in the first Dutch war of the reign had caused the overthrow of Clarendon, so the second Dutch war ended with the break-up of the Cabal. Clifford was succeeded as Lord Treasurer by Sir Thomas Osborne, an anti-French and robust Yorkshireman, and Shaftesbury lost his office as Lord Chancellor in November 1673 because of his unconcealed disagreement with the domestic and foreign policies of the King. Shaftesbury told the emissary who came to collect his seals of office that he was laying down his gown and girding on his sword. The remaining members of the Cabal did not stay much longer at their posts. Buckingham and Arlington attacked each other and the House of Commons attacked both. At the request of the Commons the King dismissed Buckingham who drifted into opposition and Arlington resigned his Secretaryship and soon afterwards was made Lord Chamberlain. But the Commons did not stop there. Bills were read or passed to determine how members of parliament should be elected, to extend the remedy of *habeas corpus*, and to ensure that the Duke of York's children should be brought up as Protestants. Before the latter could be passed, the King prorogued Parliament in February 1674.

The year 1674 therefore is a dividing line in the history of the reign of King Charles II. The exultantly royalist House of Commons of 1661, consisting of a mixture of greybeards and youngsters warmly welcomed to their places by the King, had been transformed, partly by numerous by-elections, but even more by the impact of events into a disillusioned gathering about to enter on 'a middle age of republican pugnacity'. (Ogg.) To the minds of some of the King's advisers it was indeed almost indistinguishable from the Long Parliament of terrible memories and it seemed as though the forecasts of Harrington and the forebodings of Clarendon had been fully realized. Between the Roman Catholic atmosphere of the Court and the anti-papal fury of Parliament lay a deep gulf. At the same time the period of personal rule by the King ended in utter failure. It is true that a few gains by way of naval prestige and colonies had been exacted from the Dutch, but on the whole the two Dutch wars and the pro-French policy of the King had yielded little advantage. Even the secret subsidies which the King was paid, amounting to perhaps £740,000 over six years, had been negligible compared with the heavy costs of the war. The Dutch were alienated without the French being gratified; Parliament had been angered and frightened without Roman Catholics or Nonconformists being relieved of their disabilities; the most powerful politicians with experience of affairs had been driven out into the ranks of the opposition. Now King Charles II, like Cromwell and the earlier Stuart monarchs, was forced back on to the assistance of Parliament. Osborne, who was created Earl of Danby in 1674, set about restoring the position of the monarchy by proclaiming a doctrine of 'Church and King' like 'a Clarendon in a minor key' (Feiling), and courting the majority in the House of Commons. He hoped by weaning the King from his Catholicizing tendencies and bringing his foreign policy more into line with public opinion to stave off discontent, put the national finances in order, and sustain a clear and patriotic programme. His hopes, as we shall see, were vain. For the executive was now distrusted by its own supporters. So deep was the confusion, so wild the passions of the time that only by an ace was civil war to be averted in the last years of the reign and the King allowed to die in Whitehall instead of once more in exile.

CHAPTER X

The Beginnings of Political Parties
1674–85

IN the second half of the reign of King Charles II the English political world was peopled by the Court party, loyal, if sometimes exasperated, supporters of Church and King, and those who opposed the Government, boldly calling themselves the Country party. The leader of the Court party, Lord Danby, the new Lord Treasurer, aimed at promoting the Protestant interest at home and abroad, at keeping on friendly terms with the Dutch and breaking with France, and at suffering 'no diminution nor embezzlement of the revenue either in England or Ireland'. Finance was his speciality. He had made his mark as the sole Treasurer of the Navy after its accounts had got into a shocking muddle at the end of the Dutch wars and he hoped by putting the national finances on a sound footing to maintain the independence of the Crown without being beholden to an inquisitive parliament. He regarded the House of Commons as a body to be corrupted or tricked and was the first English statesman to use bribery in an organized way to ensure the functioning of government, thus fathering a tradition that was to be followed in the eighteenth century by Sir Robert Walpole and the Duke of Newcastle. Danby was as respectable in his private affairs as he was unscrupulous in his public life. And even there he was not without principles. He had a mind and a policy of his own. But he no more enjoyed the confidence and loyalty of his master than Clarendon or Arlington had done. Behind the scenes the King's brother, the Duke of York, the King's French mistress, now the Duchess of Portsmouth, and even the disgraced Arlington and Buckingham all exercised varying degrees of influence. The complicated pattern of politics in the years after the fall of the Cabal is largely explained by their uneasy partner-ship.

When Parliament met in April 1675 Danby hoped in return for repressive measures against both Roman Catholics and Nonconformists to the benefit of the Church of England and the promise of prosperity nursed by peace to obtain a grant of money for the upkeep of the navy and exact a 'non-resistance' oath from all members of parliament and office holders by which they would swear not to try to alter the government in church or state as by law established. But Parliament was not compliant. Some members even at-tempted on somewhat vague grounds to impeach Danby himself, and a motion demanding the recall of all English troops serving abroad was defeated by only one vote. Just as it appeared as if the 'non-resistance' test might be agreed to by both Houses, a violent quarrel developed between them and the session came to a sudden close.

During the recess foreign affairs began to exert a baneful influence on domestic policy. King Louis XIV had been forced on to the defensive in his war against the Dutch who had found allies in Spain and the Empire – indeed almost the whole of Germany had now turned against him. Al-though he had consented, with such grace as he knew how to muster, to England's withdrawal from his side as an ally in 1674, he was anxious to keep King Charles II available as a mediator of peace, at heart attached to his interests. To suit this purpose the English Parliament with its anti-French majority had to be rendered powerless. On 27 August 1675 a secret agreement was signed between the two Kings in which Charles II promised that if Parliament were to make a vote of money to him conditional upon a war against France, he would dissolve it and receive a subsidy of £100,000 a year from Louis XIV.

The two Houses when they met again in October showed themselves to be about evenly divided between the Court party, manipulated by Danby, and the Country party, led by the former members of the Cabal, Buckingham and Shaftesbury. To put an end to the influence of Danby,

Buckingham and Shaftesbury moved in the House of Lords that the existing Parliament which had sat for nearly fifteen years should be dissolved. In this they were rather oddly joined by the Duke of York who hoped that his fellow religionists, the Roman Catholics, would thus be saved from persecution. But the King preferred not to dissolve parliament as he feared worse things rather than better from his point of view; instead he prorogued it for fifteen months. Thus the successes of Danby's Administration in 1675 had been of a negative character. The opposition had not been able to bring him down; on the other hand, it had voted the King no money.

While Danby fought this drawn battle at home, he suffered a further rebuff in his foreign policy from the King. In February 1676 Charles II signed a second agreement with France in which the two monarchs promised to give no aid to each other's enemies nor to make treaties without each other's consent. Danby refused to countersign this treaty which was copied out by King Charles in his own handwriting and then sealed by him. Having thus covered their rear, the French began an offensive in Spanish Flanders, defeated the Dutch at sea, and repulsed William of Orange before Maastricht. So when the English Parliament met again in February 1677 the 'overweening power' of France had again become a reality, and later Danby told the King that 'when men's fears are grown both so general and so great as now they are by the successes of France, neither his Majesty nor any of his Ministers shall have any longer credit if acts do not speedily appear some way or other to their satisfaction'. The majority in the Commons, who had begun the session by voting the King a large sum to build ships for the navy, soon demanded that he should ally himself with the Dutch and join the coalition against France. Up to that point things had gone well for the King, for the opposition leaders in the Lords had overreached themselves by questioning the legality of the Parliament and had been sent to the Tower of London for their pains and Danby had pacified the Commons with new measures against the

Roman Catholics. But King Charles II, like his father and grandfather before him, refused to have his foreign policy dictated to him by the Commons and after uttering a stern rebuke adjourned Parliament in May. In August he completed a third secret agreement with King Louis XIV promising not to recall Parliament for a further year in return for yet another subsidy. He was now in desperate need of money; his debts amounted to over two million pounds and even Danby was agreeable to getting something out of the French, though he would have liked more.

But seldom in English history was the foreign policy of the executive so much at variance with the wishes of parliament. The feeling in the country against France became too strong even for the King. After concluding no fewer than three secret compacts with the French King, Charles II suddenly tacked by agreeing to the marriage of William of Orange, the indomitable foe of France, with his fourteen-year-old niece, Mary, daughter of the Duke of York. It was an astonishing turnabout hard to gloss over. For this marriage was popularly and rightly recognized to be a blow against France – though King Charles II offered an involved and unconvincing explanation to the French ambassador – and meant his compelling his brother, now an avowed Roman Catholic, to agree to his daughter marrying the most popular Protestant hero in Europe. In defence of his foreign policy during these years it has been said that King Charles wanted money and peace (as most of us do). It has been urged that Louis XIV really received little in return for his subsidies, which in any case were small in relation to King Charles's debts, and that England became an arbiter in Europe. But modern historians who have studied these complicated manoeuvres most closely are not of the opinion that any such consistent policy or triumphant achievement can be assigned to King Charles II. Rather they are inclined to the view that he lived from hand to mouth, hoped for the best, tried not to provoke parliament too much, and would always have preferred to range himself behind the admired 'Sun King', if his subjects would but have let him. That this in fact was the case is shown by what happened next. In December 1677 a formal treaty was concluded between England and Holland, following the marriage of William and Mary which had taken place in November, whereby the two countries agreed to enforce terms of peace on France and Spain. Thirty English men-of-war were equipped for action, English troops in French pay were recalled, and an expeditionary force was prepared. The English Parliament was summoned to meet in January 1678, even though King Charles II had promised the French King not to call it until May. But the French King struck back by alienating the Dutch republicans from William of Orange and by bribing English members of parliament to oppose their own King. Moreover in March King Charles II ordered Danby to write to Ralph Montagu, the English ambassador in Paris, telling him to offer English assistance in securing French peace terms in return for a three-year subsidy. In May the French accepted a secret arrangement along these lines, though no English Minister dared put his signature to the treaty.

When the Parliament that had been adjourned met again on 23 May, the King told it that peace was imminent and that the English forces were to be disbanded. However there was a further delay and English reinforcements were actually sent to Flanders. But now at last in August 1678 the peace of Nijmegen was signed between the French and the Dutch without English influence counting for anything much in the pacification. By this treaty Louis XIV reached the height of his success in Europe. On the other side, the constant changes in King Charles's foreign policy, his humiliating blackmail of the French Court, his ignoring of his Ministers' advice, and his flouting of Parliament reduced the prestige of his country to its lowest point. And many Englishmen were becoming convinced that a secret conspiracy had been engineered to establish a Roman Catholic despotism in the kingdom with the aid of French arms. This view was set out by the poet, Andrew Marvell, in his *Account of the Growth of Popery and Arbitrary Government in England* which was published anonymously in 1677. Though, as we have seen, King Charles II had not really purposed quite such an extreme policy as that, yet he had drawn very near to it in signing the Secret Treaty of Dover in 1670, and if the one-time 'Cavalier' Parliament had come to fear arbitrary rule, suspect a 'popish plot', and distrust the monarch and his brother, then the King had only himself to blame for it. Danby's policy of rallying the country behind the old royalist battle cry of Church and King lay in ruins and the curious and melodramatic train of events that filled the remainder of the reign followed logically from all that had gone before.

Advantage was now taken of the fear of Roman Catholic resurgence and arbitrary government on the French model which had transformed the character of the political world by two extraordinary university doctors, Titus Oates and Israel Tonge, who came forward to reveal a gigantic plot (which they themselves had invented) against the King and his subjects. Oates was an Anglican clergyman who had been thrown out of a naval chaplaincy for immorality. But a long and impressive chin, a real familiarity with the teachings of the Spanish Jesuits, an imaginary doctorate in the University of Salamanca, and an infinite capacity for bold lying combined to make him a plausible discloser of popish conspiracies. Dr Tonge, for his part, boasted a real degree at Oxford and a genuine rectory in London and was a botanical scholar of note; but he also had an anti-Catholic mania congenial to the temper of his times and possibly believed in the tissue of lies unfolded to him by his younger friend, Oates. After some preliminary skirmishings Tonge obtained an interview with the King who passed him on to Danby. Tonge described to Danby an elaborate Jesuit plot to murder the King by either shooting, stabbing, or poisoning as appeared most convenient. The assassination, he said, was to be followed by a massacre of Protestants and then James, Duke of York, was to be put on the throne with a Jesuit Junta. At first all this was not taken too seriously. But the charges were also laid before a London magistrate, named Sir Edmund Berry Godfrey. About a month after Oates and Tonge had made their depositions before him, Godfrey was found dead on Primrose Hill with a sword sticking through his back. It was at once proclaimed that Godfrey had been murdered to close his mouth and three innocent men, alleged to have been commissioned as assassins by an Irish priest, were put to death for the crime. That explanation of Godfrey's death does not stand up to investigation. A duplicate copy of Oates's accusations was already before the Privy Council and the sword was in fact thrust through Godfrey's body after death. Probably Godfrey either committed suicide or was murdered by a personal enemy. He had warned Edward Coleman, the Queen's Roman Catholic secretary, with whom he was friendly, about Oates's charges, which had mentioned him by name, and Coleman who had engaged in some indiscreet but not necessarily treasonable correspondence with foreign Jesuits had in consequence partly destroyed it. Possibly therefore Godfrey, who was a melancholy and conscientious man, came to believe that he had committed a dereliction of duty.

In any case it was symptomatic of the temper of the times that even before Godfrey's alleged murder a full meeting of the Privy Council, presided over by the King, had thought fit to examine the matter. A special meeting of the Council had been called on a Sunday (a fortnight before Godfrey's death) and though the King had caught out Oates in a couple of lies, the confidence of the Councillors in Oates's information was not shaken, and both Coleman and Sir George Wakeman, the Queen's doctor (another Roman Catholic), were put in prison and other arrests were to follow. The Oates–Tonge dossier had been lent a little weight by the circumstantial evidence unearthed, such as the remains of the Coleman correspondence: and because of this it resulted in the judicial murders of Jesuits and Catholics, forced the Duke of York into exile, destroyed the Cavalier Parliament, raised the Earl of Shaftesbury, as opposition leader, to the pinnacle of power, created the party system and imperilled the throne itself. But if the rubbish purveyed by a perjured informer had such extraordinary consequences, the King himself was responsible. The truth was stranger than fiction. For a plot had actually existed, signed and sealed not by the Pope but by the King's Ministers; it dated not from 1678 but from 1670. The policy of the Secret Treaty of Dover by which the King had agreed to accept French money to support him if he declared himself a Roman Catholic was a far more sensational plot than either the fantasies of the shifty Oates or the lucubrations of the bemused Dr Tonge.

Such was the atmosphere of fear charged with passion in which Parliament met again in October 1678. Five Catholic peers were committed to the Tower and impeached; a bill was introduced and passed excluding Roman Catholics from both Houses; and Shaftesbury proposed that the King should be asked to dismiss the Duke of York from his Council. On 28 November Oates appeared before the bar of the House of Commons and brazenly accused the Queen of treason. Finally, Ralph Montagu, formerly the English ambassador in Paris, produced in the House the letter which Danby had written on his master's orders, seeking French money in return for English help in foreign policy. The Commons demanded the removal of the Queen from Whitehall Palace and proposed to impeach the Lord Treasurer. However, the King won a temporary respite by first proroguing and then dissolving Parliament. Thereby he saved his Queen, his brother, his Ministers and the powers of the throne. But how different was the outlook from what it had been eighteen years before when the long parliament of his reign first met. Then it had appeared as if the conciliatory policy followed by Clarendon at the Restoration would establish internal peace for years and that the Roundheads would be crushed for ever. Nor was it the persecution of the nonconformists which had caused the rise of an opposition to the Court. For the penalties against them had been materially relaxed after the fall of Clarendon. It was not so much the dissenters, but the old secular republican group, the ex-soldiers and their like, who now grouped themselves round Shaftesbury and Buckingham and took advantage of the distrust created by the Francophil and Catholicizing policy favoured by the King to insist on paring the powers of monarchy as Pym and Eliot, long since dead, had been wont to do.

The general election of February 1679 was a panic election fought for the first time largely on party lines and resulted in a defeat for the Court. The King was obliged to bow before the facts. He supinely acquiesced in the judicial murders, he sent his brother into exile abroad, he disbanded much of his army, he dismissed the unfortunate Danby (who was not really the villain of the piece), and he appointed an entirely new Privy Council which included not only his less offensive Ministers but also the opposition leaders headed by Shaftesbury himself. The new Council has sometimes been hailed as an interesting constitutional experiment. But as it consisted of fifteen officials and fifteen members of the opposition it was both unwieldy and impotent and its intention was, to borrow a phrase from later history, mainly 'to dish the Whigs'. The King privately observed: 'God's fish, they have put a set of men about me, but they shall know nothing.' Moreover Shaftesbury and his friends were by no means satisfied. In May they introduced a bill to exclude the Duke of York from the throne, laying it down that if the King were to die without issue he was to be succeeded by the next Protestant heir. The Bill passed its second reading in the Commons by a majority of 79 votes. The King would not stand for that. Six days later he prorogued and afterwards dissolved his second parliament.

The first Exclusionist Parliament, as it was to be known, did one useful piece of business. On the day that it was prorogued the King gave his assent to a Habeas Corpus Amendment Act. The writ of *habeas corpus* whereby a prisoner could demand that he should be brought before the courts and have his case examined was a well established right of Englishmen, but a number of ways had been found of evading its use in the case of political prisoners. The philosopher,

James Harrington, for example, had been removed from the Tower of London when his sisters applied for *habeas corpus* and sent out to a rocky island where the writ did not run. The new act put an end to such anomalies and deprived the executive of powers that might have been employed in support of arbitrary government.

The King had survived the first thunderclaps of the rising storm. Parliament had voted him money, the Exclusion Bill had not been passed, and Danby, though languishing in the Tower, had not been impeached. Two sections of the opposition had begun quarrelling with each other, for not all were in favour of 'exclusion'; some, such as George Savile, Marquess of Halifax, an able and philosophical statesman known to history as 'the Great Trimmer', were willing to let the Duke of York come to the throne provided that his powers were limited by statute: for example, that he was deprived of all ecclesiastical patronage. The King's chief advisers were now Halifax, Sunderland, an ambitious politician *par excellence*, and Arthur Capel, Earl of Essex, who did not remain long in office. When the King took the decision to dissolve parliament in July his Council was split asunder, though Shaftesbury was not dismissed until October. The opposition now found a Protestant hero and a rival to the Duke of York in the King's illegitimate son, James Scott, Duke of Monmouth. Monmouth was a handsome and romantic soldier who had fought much in France and had that very June put down a rising of Scottish Covenanters at the battle of Bothwell Bridge. Some of his supporters claimed that he was not even illegitimate, that proofs of his father's marriage to his mother were to be found in a black box. A descendant of his has published a book powerfully arguing in this sense. But the one person who seems to have had no doubts whatever about his being a bastard was his father, who was in a position to know. For though King Charles II loved Monmouth, he was inflexibly determined that his brother should succeed to his throne, and that if possible the Stuart monarchy should carry on unimpaired after his death. The legitimate succession was a principle to which King Charles adhered until the end. For a moment that summer it seemed indeed as if his time had come. He was taken seriously ill: the Duke of York returned post haste from his exile in Brussels. It proved a false alarm, but so imminent were the dangers of a disputed succession that the King was persuaded to deprive Monmouth of his post of commander-in-chief and to order him to leave the country, which he did, though he returned against orders before the year was out. James, on the other hand, was allowed to come back from Brussels and take up residence in Edinburgh as the King's Commissioner.

Though the King had thus been loyal to his beliefs after his fashion and practically abandoned the policy of concession to the opposition which he had adopted after the madness of the Popish plot, the year 1680 was still critical for the royal cause and reminded contemporaries who had lived long enough of the rumblings of 1640. Passions were stirred by a new imaginary disclosure of Roman Catholic conspiracy, but this proved to be but a poor relation of the Popish Plot. When Monmouth returned to London he was greeted with bonfires and the ringing of bells and the King was compelled to relieve him of his remaining offices and to declare publicly that he was not the lawful heir.

When the third parliament of the reign at last met in October, the King appealed to it for money and arms, since Tangier, an expensive jewel in the Queen's dowry (it was voluntarily and unwisely abandoned later), was now under attack by the Moors. Before that the King had resumed his old policy of trying to extract promises of help from France. The French King was now engaged by dubious legalistic means, backed by a strong army, in extending the territory on his frontiers at the expense of his weaker neighbours and consequently was glad of such friends as he could buy. But King Charles II had not at first been able to conjure any money out of him and instead had concluded a treaty with Spain as an earnest of his good intentions and had also promised to do anything that was wanted to protect the Church of England. The Commons were not to be cajoled.

They proceeded to pass a new and more stringent Exclusion Bill which was rejected in the House of Lords largely because of the advocacy of Halifax, who had left and was now about to rejoin the King's Government. Shaftesbury, bold as ever, tried to indict the Duke of York as a 'popish recusant' and the King's mistress, the Duchess of Portsmouth, as a common nuisance. Shaftesbury now had a well-organized following both in London and the country. In the City flourished a political club called the Green Ribbon, while gatherings in Fleet Street inns saw the old republicans creeping out of the shadows. This was the time when the names 'Whig' and 'Tory' came into common use – Whig (meaning a Scottish outlaw) for the exclusionists and supporters of Shaftesbury, Tory (meaning an Irish robber) for the anti-exclusionists, the men who were faithful to the established Church and the hereditary monarchy. If Shaftesbury, with his club headquarters, was the founder of the Whig party, the imprisoned Danby, who had built up the royalist caucus in the Commons, was the father of the Tories. But lines of demarcation between the two parties were not sharply defined: some politicians would only stomach the succession of a Roman Catholic monarch with limited rights, some wanted Monmouth as their king, some favoured the Duke of York's Protestant daughters, a few hoped for a republic. Even the King's own Ministers had no clear and agreed policy, while the leaders of the opposition were frequently at loggerheads among themselves. Nevertheless out of the turmoil of those times the party system emerged and survived. The general elections had been fought out by parties centrally directed. The differences between Whigs and Tories were understandable and their leaders were known. For good or ill it was a main contribution of the reign to constitutional history.

Having been thwarted of the Exclusion Bill, the Commons at the end of 1680 impeached Lord Stafford, an aged Roman Catholic nobleman, for his alleged part in the Popish Plot. With his execution in December one of the most disgraceful episodes in the story of the House of Commons and the English Bench was finished. On 10 January 1681, when the Commons were happily absorbed in passing a resolution that the Fire of London fifteen years earlier had been the work of the 'papists', Black Rod knocked at the door, and the second Exclusionist Parliament was dissolved.

The King now shook himself free from his normal lethargy and with the help of Lawrence Hyde, the second son of the great Clarendon, took a course that attuned with all his natural instincts. He opened negotiations, soon to be successful, for another secret agreement with the French monarchy, in which he promised to abandon his treaty with Spain, signed only a year before, in return for the assurance of the French King's friendship and of his moral and material backing if Charles was threatened with civil war. At the same time he summoned a new parliament to meet in Oxford hoping that there, freed from the menace of Shaftesbury's London mob, he might obtain cooperation in return for some last moment compromise on the succession question. He even negotiated with Shaftesbury, but the Earl had now committed himself to the succession of the King's eldest illegitimate son, the Duke of Monmouth, in place of the Duke of York. The Whigs flocked to the university city in armed bands, so fearful were they of the loyal regiments. The London members stuck the motto 'No Popery! No Slavery!' in their caps and were defiant to the end. The third Exclusionist Parliament and the fourth of the reign was soon dissolved. It was the last parliament to meet in the reign of King Charles II.

To the 'Whig frenzy' succeeded the 'Royalist reaction'. 'From the end of the Oxford Parliament the Cavalier spirit rose from its dust again.' (Feiling.) By the violence of their behaviour after the disclosure of the alleged Popish Plot, the Whigs had overreached themselves. The humiliated King had invoked the sympathy of his subjects and the Crown regained much of its popularity. Even the Duke of York shared in this revived loyalty. And the resurgent royalist rank-and-file, embittered children of the Cavaliers, determined that concerted parliamentary opposition to the King, hitherto unknown in English history save as a prelude to revolt or revolution, should be destroyed. The Court party prepared to make the law courts the instrument of its revenge. Chief Justice Scroggs, who had presided over the Popish Plot trials, was dismissed and replaced by a more agreeable dignitary, while other judges were dismissed and replaced. But one obstacle remained to be overcome, the independent London juries. The judges no longer possessed the power to intimidate juries and when an attempt was made to punish for treason an obscure Protestant joiner named Stephen College, who was charged with uttering seditious words, the Middlesex Grand Jury threw out the bill. But the trial was then removed to Oxford where College was found guilty and perished as the first Whig martyr. Flushed by this triumph, in July the King's advisers had Shaftesbury arrested for treason. But the Whig chief was acquitted in spite of the biased summing-up of the new Lord Chief Justice. Yet that victory for the opposition was largely offset when the Poet Laureate, John Dryden, published that November his wonderful satire, *Absalom and Achitophel*, in which Monmouth, the Whig candidate for the succession, and Shaftesbury, his sponsor, were held up to ridicule. The Tories recovered their nerve. The doctrine of the inviolability of hereditary monarchy had many rigid defenders who even argued that to depose or exclude a ruler for his religion was a 'Popish' and not a 'Protestant' doctrine. The King 'whom God in wrath' might give us 'is not in our power to change', explained the high-principled Leoline Jenkins.

In this reluctantly loyal atmosphere the Duke of York was allowed to return from exile in May 1682. The moderation of Halifax the Trimmer was neutralized by the return to the Privy Council in July of the unprincipled Earl of Sunderland, who was soon restored to his post of Secretary of State of which he had been relieved at the time of the second Exclusionist Parliament. It was decided to carry the City of London over to the King's side by hook or by crook. The surrender of the City Charter as well as the charters of other towns was demanded. Since the Crown had originally granted these charters, some technical excuse could always be found for requiring their recall – indeed Cromwell's Government had done this too. Once the municipalities had been remodelled in the Tory interests, suitable juries could be appointed and other benefits flow in. But this was a slow process. So far as London was concerned a quicker method was found. In 1682 owing to the splitting of the Whig votes the Lord Mayor of London was a Tory. He was prevailed upon to revive an ancient custom whereby he was entitled to nominate one of the City sheriffs merely by drinking to him at the annual feast. He raised his glass to a Tory freeman. Aghast at such daring tactics the Whigs were thrown into confusion and after four months two Tory sheriffs were installed in office. The fate of the Whiggish juries was settled and the Whig leaders in fright for their lives turned from open opposition to conspiracy. Monmouth, who had at the prompting of Shaftesbury undertaken 'progresses' or half-royal tours in the north of England that autumn and won an enthusiastic welcome, was arrested at Stafford as a disturber of the peace. And Shaftesbury himself, who had gone into hiding after his discharge from prison, fled to Holland, where he died suddenly in the house of an Amsterdam merchant, disappointed but smiling.

While Shaftesbury was in hiding in London, he and other Whig leaders, among whom were William, Lord Russell, the Earl of Essex, and Algernon Sidney, an aristocrat republican, had discussed the prospects of revolution and a messenger had been sent to Scotland to examine whether an alliance might be arranged between the English Whigs and the Scottish Covenanters, whose leader, the ninth Earl of Argyll, had been condemned to death for treason, but had escaped abroad. These talks did not reach a very advanced state, partly because the conspirators themselves were divided over their objectives, some wishing to put Monmouth on the throne, others aiming at forcing the King to consent to the exclusion of the Duke of York, and a third party wanted to restore the Cromwellian republic. But in an age when 'informing' was a recognized, if not highly paid, profession it was inevitable that these conspiratorial conversations should be disclosed to the authorities. The informers of course embroidered on the truth. In June 1683 Josiah Keeling, a bankrupt oilman, and Robert West, a seedy barrister – opposite numbers of Oates and Tonge – came forward to tell their story of an imaginary plot to assassinate the King near Rye House in Hertfordshire when he was on his way to or from the Newmarket races. The plot was as much a fabrication as Oates's Popish Plot had been, but it served its purpose. The Whig leaders and a number of old soldiers were arrested; a search was made for arms and a couple of rusty cannon were discovered in a London cellar. One of the arrested Whigs, Lord Howard of Escrick, turned King's evidence and the Earl of Essex committed suicide in prison. The manuscript of a theoretical republican treatise was found at the home of Algernon Sidney. On such circumstantial evidence Russell and Sidney and a number of smaller fry were found guilty and executed. Sidney 'died stoutly and like a true republican.' The Plot enabled the Tories to complete their revenge and their political opponents were thrown out of all their offices whether in the municipalities, in the militia, or on the magistrates' bench. The University of Oxford declared itself in favour of the doctrine of 'non-resistance' to the King. Sunderland ousted not only Halifax but even Rochester from the forefront of the King's counsels and the Duke of York became a central figure.

The King was able to carry on without the assistance of Parliament, partly because of the expansion in the Customs revenue, partly because of an improved yield from the excise. In the autumn of 1681 King Louis XIV had seized the imperial free city of Strasbourg, attacked the Duchy of Luxembourg which belonged to Spain, and occupied the town of Casale which was under the sovereignty of the Duke of Mantua. This had caused the Swedes and Dutch to enter into a defensive treaty, and William of Orange came over to England to try to persuade his wife's uncle to join them, but King Charles refused. Yet for a moment that autumn it had seemed as if the blatant aggression of the French would compel some action by England. But King Charles II was promised a *douceur* of a million *livres* by the French ambassador in London and his face was saved by an offer from the French King to accept him as an arbitrator. There were chops and changes in policy in the following months, but the discreditable secret diplomacy of the English King – unknown to the public and even to his more moderate advisers – froze the Concert of Europe and helped Louis XIV to make many acquisitions in which he was confirmed for twenty years by the Truce of Ratisbon of 1684.

Thus, after all the ups and downs of his reign, King Charles II attained a position of commanding authority never touched by his Stuart predecessors. Behind him stood the loyal Tories, glorying in the survival of a patriarchal monarchy, sustained by a loyal Church; the Whigs were shattered and dispersed. He preferred to manage without a legislature, although Halifax had advised him to summon a friendly parliament after the dissolution of the abortive Oxford assembly. His personal friend, Louis XIV, overawed Europe. He had a standing army and capable fleet. The succession of his bigoted Roman Catholic brother, for which he had risked his throne, was assured. Under these circumstances Nemesis overtook the Merry Monarch. On 1 February 1685 he was suddenly taken ill. When he was known to be dying, an aged Roman Catholic priest, who had helped him escape from Oliver Cromwell after the battle of Worcester thirty-four years earlier, was smuggled into the bedchamber by the King's agreement to administer extreme unction. King Charles II passed away on 6 February and King James II, the accredited heir and the first Catholic ruler of England since 'Bloody Mary', mounted the throne.

CHAPTER XI

The Age of Experiment

1660–89

HISTORICAL generalizations are always properly introduced with words of caution: no year or even group of years can ever be safely selected as marking the dividing line between one age and another. Having poured out this libation to Clio, let us venture upon the opinion that the reign of King Charles II witnessed the fag-end of the Middle Ages in England and set a pattern for the world in which we now live. This is true not only of the Church and the State, but in scientific thought, the drama, and music. In the Church the idea of a single exclusive body to which all Christians had willy-nilly to belong was abandoned as the nonconformist preachers were expelled from their parishes, and before the century was out, in tune with the general trend in Protestant Europe, the case for religious toleration, first put forward authoritatively by Oliver Cromwell and later sponsored by Halifax and Locke, was accepted. At the same time, after the Puritan rebellion the old order and outlook could not be reinstated. Puritanism might be persecuted and driven underground, but it was never destroyed. The groundswell was always there. And indeed as doubts began to be thrown upon the miraculous side of Christianity, emphasis shifted more and more to its ethical aspects and men, whether they believed they were the chosen of God or not, were conscious of the need to live a virtuous life. In the State the Restoration era saw the rise of party – whether called Court and Country or Tory and Whig. Since that time the two-party system has gradually evolved, though modern historians still argue whether it was a party or group system in the early eighteenth century. Since then, too, we have been governed by a limited monarchy, though the powers of the King were only slowly eaten away. Henceforward the King had to work through parliament. He could never work without it. In the last years of King Charles II's reign and in the short reign of King James II the swan-song of absolute monarchy was sung.

In the realm of thought an era of science, mathematics, and physical experiment had arrived. That is not to imply that there were no worthy English scientists or experimentalists before 1660. On the contrary, men like William Gilbert, the expert on magnetism, and Francis Bacon had flourished at the beginning of the century. But it had taken time for the plea for free inquiry put forward by Bacon and the questioning spirit of the French philosopher, Descartes, to have their full impact on English thinkers. Now, however, the death blows were dealt at medieval scholasticism. Robert Boyle, for instance, disposed of Aristotle's idea that chemistry had to be based on four elements. The echoes of old scholastic controversies were heard, but dispersed in the work of Isaac Newton. Francis Bacon, who had opened a clearing through the scholastic forest, had nevertheless been in many ways medieval in outlook himself. It was only late in the century that 'the resort to experiments' was 'tamed and harnessed'. (Butterfield.)

This change was naturally gradual. Superstition and dilettantism were mixed up almost inextricably with serious scientific research. Men like the second Duke of Buckingham, who dabbled in all sides of life, the bad as well as the good, boasted their private laboratories. King Charles II, who also had his own laboratory, was as fascinated by astrology as by astronomy. Research in chemistry might come out of the age-old pursuit of alchemy, the elusive art of manufacturing precious out of base metals. Unquestionably it was the teaching of Bacon that stimulated scientific investigation as distinct from haphazard experimenting. Bishop Spratt, the author of the first *History of the Royal Society* (as well as of that of the Rye House Plot) observed that no other preface was necessary than some of Bacon's writings, and H. B. Wheatley, a later historian of the Society, considered that Bacon inspired the early history of the

Society as much as Newton commanded the second phase.

Although the origin of the Royal Society had been traced back to 1645 when certain philosophers formed an 'Invisible College' and meetings of savants took place at Oxford during the Interregnum, it was not until the Restoration that a more settled political situation permitted a scheme for an enduring and central scientific association to be drawn up. The atmosphere was favourable to scientific inquiry. The year 1659 had seen numerous original and ingenious minds at work. Unlike James Harrington's 'Rota Club', which had contained many eminent thinkers who used to meet at a City coffee-house, the 'Invisible College', which also met in a London tavern in 1659, survived and indeed benefited from the Restoration. In November 1660, after Christopher Wren had delivered a lecture at Gresham College in London, some members of his audience discussed a scheme for founding a permanent institution to promote experiments in physics and mathematics. A Society was then established, and on 15 July 1662 obtained a royal charter. The Society met every Wednesday or Thursday afternoon under the presidency of Lord Brouncker, the mathematician. One is particularly struck by the versatility of the members of the Royal Society. They included John Aubrey, the author of the *Brief Lives* of his contemporaries, that delightful lucky dip for seventeenth century biographers; John Evelyn, botanist and numismatist, and Samuel Pepys, the naval administrator, who live in their diaries; John Locke, metaphysician, educationist, political philosopher, theologian, physician, and man of affairs; Sir William Petty, who contends with Captain John Graunt for the distinction of being the first English statistician or 'political arithmetician'; Dr John Wallis, who wrote books on arithmetic as well as English grammar; John Dryden, the poet; Wren, the architect; Dr John Wilkins, the bishop who was Oliver Cromwell's brother-in-law; Joseph Williamson, the politician; the Duke of Buckingham and the Earl of Sandwich; Sir Kenelm Digby, the Roman Catholic, who collected book bindings and invented the 'powder of sympathy' to heal wounds; and even the Moroccan ambassador who was admitted an honorary member. Besides them stood scientists whose names are still universally honoured: Robert Boyle, the 'father of modern chemistry' and inventor of 'Boyle's law'; Isaac Barrow, the mathematician and clergyman; Robert Hooke, city surveyor, mathematician, physicist, and a great inventive genius; and Jonathan Goddard, one of the first English makers of telescopes. The motto of the Royal Society was taken from one of Horace's letters where he says: 'The words are the words of a master, but we are not forced to swear by them. Instead we are to be borne wherever experiment drives us.' The subscription to the Society was a shilling a week and the annual general meeting was held on St Andrew's Day. Aubrey records how Sir William Petty expressed the opinion that St Thomas's Day might have been more suitable, for St Thomas 'would not believe till he had seen and put his finger in the holes'. The investigations of the Society were carried out by a series of committees which did not confine themselves entirely to scientific matters. One committee in 1664, for example, concerned itself with histories of trade and was presided over by Thomas Povey, the colonial merchant, and another concentrated on improving the English language, particularly for philosophical purposes.

The early days of the Society were therefore filled with eclectic experiments of a Baconian kind. It was not in reality until 1684, when the Senior Secretary of the Royal Society, Dr Edmund Halley, went to Cambridge to consult Isaac Newton on the subject of the elliptic motion of planets, that the purely scientific history of the Society began. Newton, who was born in 1642, succeeded Barrow as Lucasian Professor of Mathematics at Cambridge when he was only twenty-seven and was to be President of the Royal Society for 24 years. Newton discovered gravitation and proved that the force of the gravitational pull decreases as the square of the distance. When in 1685 he showed that 'a sphere of gravitating matters attracts bodies outside it as though all its mass was concentrated at the centre. . . . It was now in his power to apply mathematical analysis with absolute precision to the problems of astronomy.' (Dampier.) In his *Principia* (1687) he formulated dynamical principles that held good for 200 years. He established the binomial theorem, developed the theory of equations, introduced literal indices, founded tidal theory, wrote on optics, made a telescope, contributed to the invention of the infinitesimal calculus, and created hydrodynamics. Finally, he argued that the structure of light is essentially atomic. He was in fact one of the greatest and most versatile mathematicians in history, even if he did believe in absolute time and space. His epoch, when mechanics and astronomy were linked, was that which saw the first notable synthesis of scientific knowledge. Although his *Principia* did not appear until 1687, many of his theories were formulated by 1665 and by the end of the century science was fully cooperative in its approach and internationally-minded (Newton, for example, made good use of French calculations about the distance of Mars). Thus, except for those who still regard history as the bare story of past politics, the second half of the seventeenth century need not be regarded as consisting of the inglorious reigns of King Charles II and King James II, but as the wonderful age of Newton.

Although Isaac Newton and some of the other thinkers in this able and inventive generation lived and worked in the universities, this was not a specially lively period at Oxford and Cambridge, although they had not yet sunk into the torpor of the eighteenth century. 'Neither Oxford nor Cambridge', writes Mr David Ogg, 'was contributing to the intellectual life of the nation in a measure proportionate to the endowments and opportunities enjoyed by them; and both were outstripped by the Royal Society, to which Oxford was at first somewhat antagonistic.' The nonconformists were, of course, excluded from the universities, and rank and wealth meant more to the undergraduate than learning. Degrees were not hard to come by (though a recent piece of American research suggests that the ancient universities were not as backward as was once supposed) and Fellows of Colleges found it more profitable to become a tutor in a nobleman's household than to write a Latin grammar in the library. At Oxford the dons were still in the reign of King Charles II solving such ancient riddles as 'Can love be induced by philtres?' or 'Did Duns Scotus write better Latin than Cicero?' but it has recently been shown that the extra-curricular studies were more liberal.

The educational situation in schools was less lively after the Restoration than at the beginning of the century. Grammar schools, which had been the nurseries of Puritan leaders, declined in quality somewhat after the Restoration, although new schools were being founded throughout the century. The grammar schools, for the most part, were still wholly absorbed by the study of the classics; Eton and Winchester kept up a higher standard, but these aristocratic institutions were of an exceptional character. Various experimental schools were started, nonconformist academies were opened, and charity schools began to save the poor from ignorance, but not to give them ideas above their station. And by the time of Queen Anne school education was again on the upgrade. An impulse for educational reform came from a number of earnest men. Samuel Hartlib, the German, opened a school at Chichester in the sixteen-thirties. John Milton and John Aubrey put forward their own schemes; Comenius, the Bohemian educationist, was invited to England. But John Dury, another educationist, who was the friend of Hartlib and Comenius, noted severely that 'children are not taught to pronounce and write accurately their own language before learning other languages; are not taught to draw pictures when being taught to write; are not taught the rudiments of arithmetic at the same time as writing; are not taught the Holy Scripture'. Thus it may be said that progress in scientific discovery and learning came from the top rather than the foot of the educational ladder; an insatiable itch for knowledge, stimulated by ideas of foreign scholars, like Descartes, Spinoza, and Leibniz, wafting across from France and Holland, helped to incite the fine work of the pundits of the Royal Society. The scientific and mathematical discoveries of Newton and his friends did not at first undermine religion. Newton himself is said to have spent as much time on theology (and chemistry) as he did on mathematics. Like Henry More, a queer fish among the Cambridge Platonists, many of them repudiated the teaching of Descartes as being damaging to the Christian faith, even though Descartes's doubts led them safely back to the existence of God. Newton and Boyle both emphatically believed that their scientific work served the cause of religion and both of them held that God was immanent in nature and not simply the power that wound up the clock to make it tick. Nevertheless, the Christian religion had been forced on to the defensive before the end of the century. The Cambridge Platonists laboured to reconcile the teachings of Descartes and Francis Bacon with a reasonable theology; Sir Thomas Browne expounded his religion as a doctor to convince doubters; and the numerous pleas for toleration, culminating in the writing of John Locke, witnessed the shifting temper of the times.

Just as in science the Restoration may be taken as a turning point on the road from medievalism to modernity, so in music there was a change of direction. 'By the end of the Commonwealth,' wrote Sir Hubert Parry, 'the secularization of musical art in England was complete.' Although there was naturally a revival in church music when the bishops came back into their own in 1660, the King himself did not care for devotional music and sent Pelham Humfrey, a promising young composer, to study in Paris under the Italian Lully, defraying the expense out of the secret service funds. Before the civil wars English music, apart from religious music, consisted mainly of madrigals. Afterwards a significant change came. The first public concerts date from the Restoration; the violin was introduced; Purcell wrote the first one-man English operas (although *The Siege of Rhodes*, a cooperative venture, had been performed in 1656). Henry Purcell was an outstanding genius among English-born composers, but his works, of extraordinary versatility, vary much in quality. Nevertheless, 'he wrote masterpieces in every department of music practised in his time'

(Ernest Walker). Besides operas and masques, he composed church music, music for fifty-four plays, secular songs, sonatas for strings and the harpsichord, and much other music, some of which still remains unpublished. Like Mozart and his own contemporary, Pelham Humfrey, Purcell died young, and after his death in 1695 English music in its most characteristic forms progressed no further. With the arrival of Handel in London in 1710 English music again altered course.

The reign of King Charles II also saw a change in the character of English drama and literature. During the Interregnum the drama came to a full stop as the Puritans did not approve of the theatre. Afterwards it was confined to a somewhat narrow circle concentrated on the Court. There were only two theatres in London at the beginning of the new reign, and they were not usually full. Outside London plays were almost unknown except at Oxford and Cambridge. But on the stage a new phase was reached. Scenery was introduced; the 'apron' stage, with the audience crowded round it, was abandoned for its modern successor; actresses took part in plays more or less for the first time, replacing the boy actors who played female parts in the age of Shakespeare; and 'stars' like Thomas Betterton and Mrs Barry had their devoted following. The peculiar nature of theatre audiences, consisting for a large part of courtiers and hangers-on of the Court, reflected itself in the character of the plays. There was a vogue for heroic tragedies, which were put on frequently by Sir William Davenant, the owner of the principal theatre. Many of the tragedies or melodramas were 'historical', tales of love and passion written in heroic couplets accompanied by goodly flourishes of trumpets and drums. A typical example was *The Conquest of Granada* by John Dryden. Many of the Restoration dramatists wrote both tragedies and comedies, including Dryden, Thomas Otway, and William Congreve. Others, like Sedley, Shadwell, and Wycherley, offered comedies of manners, while the second Duke of Buckingham wrote a brilliant piece called *The Rehearsal* satirizing the kind of dull historical tragedies that Dryden wrote (Dryden had his revenge in some immortal lines in *Absalom and Achitophel*). The sixteen-seventies were a notable period for comedies, such plays as *Love in a Wood*, *The Country Wife*, *The Plain Dealer*, *The Man of Mode*, and *Love for Love* being performed. It is only in very recent times that these comedies have come to be appreciated again. Professor Allardyce Nicoll, writing in 1923, was more than censorious about these Restoration comedies which in their outspokenness and cynicism illustrated a reaction after the puritan interlude. But since 1923 these plays have been revived on the London stage and elsewhere with success.

As in the theatre the Restoration was best represented by the comedy of manners, so in literature – apart from Milton and Bunyan, survivors from an earlier period – the most marked characteristic was satire. The vehicle of poetic satire was the heroic couplet which, as with English music and, to a lesser extent, the English plays of the time, was deeply influenced by French models. The first of the satirical Restoration poets was Samuel Butler, whose unheroic hero, Hudibras, a fat and cowardly presbyterian, is said to have been based upon Sir Samuel Luke in whose house he lived during the Interregnum. But the most famous of the satirical poets was Dryden, a younger man, whose long poems, *Absalom and Achitophel* and *The Medal*, with their caustic witty lines upon the Whig heroes, Shaftesbury, Buckingham, and Monmouth, contributed in no small measure to the Tory triumph at the end of King Charles II's reign. Dryden began his life by trimming his sails to the prevailing winds, writing an elegy in praise of Oliver Cromwell before hailing the Restoration in verse. His work, which was prolific, was by no means confined to satire. He wrote a great deal of excellent prose, but above all he was a poet of his times, writing of the Dutch wars, the Plague, the Fire, the Anglican Church, and, when he became a Roman Catholic, of that persecuted body. It was appropriate enough that in 1670 he should have become the first Poet Laureate. He became a Catholic in the reign of King James II, but refused to renounce his new faith when William and Mary came to the throne, and though inevitably he ceased to be Laureate, he lived on unmolested and admired until 1700. Dryden has been called the critics' poet and has certainly been praised by many of them from Dr Samuel Johnson to Dr T. S. Eliot. Johnson wrote of him that he found English poetry 'brick and left it marble'. One modern critic has claimed that *Absalom and Achitophel* is more than a satire and is a heroic poem. Others, while not going so far as this, would claim sublimity for the poems of his Catholic period, notably *The Hind and the Panther*. Matthew Arnold and Sir Herbert Grierson, on the other hand, expressed the opinion that Dryden lacked a soul. That is up to them. No other poets who wrote in the reign of King Charles II touched Dryden's genius. Andrew Marvell was the opposite number of Samuel Butler and in some of his satires (which often had to be published anonymously) punched the Royalists as hard as Dryden struck the Whigs. Abraham Cowley, a lyrical poet, whom Dryden admired, died in 1667 and was buried in Westminster Abbey. Aristocrats like Buckingham, Dorset, and Rochester tried their hands at verse, sometimes with success, but 'John Dryden overshadows the last half of the seventeenth century as Ben Jonson did the Jacobean age'. (C. V. Wedgwood.)

In English prose this age was, on the whole, utilitarian. Since most authors were passionately interested in politics or religion much of their prose was expended on these topics. The newspaper, or rather the newsletter, had by now become well established. It had become an accepted means of reporting events and spreading propaganda during the civil wars and afterwards Roger Lestrange edited a semi-official weekly paper called *The Intelligencer*. Later this was superseded by the *London Gazette*. But the modern newspaper, as we shall show, originated in the reign of Queen Anne. It is to be remembered that many of the books which are most familiar to students of the seventeenth century like Clarendon's *History of the Rebellion*, Burnet's *History of My Own Time*, Samuel Pepys's *Diary*, and John Aubrey's *Brief Lives* were not published contemporaneously. But if we add them to the works of Dryden, Marvell, Sir Thomas Browne, John Bunyan, Jeremy Taylor, and Isaak Walton, who wrote his *Compleat Angler* in the middle of the century and afterwards published various *Lives*, we can surely say that the second half of the seventeenth century was remarkable in the history of English prose. In conclusion we should doff our hats to a lady who demands a passing reference. Mrs Aphra Behn, who also tried her hand at spying and compiling plays, was perhaps the first English novelist, a somewhat thin and feeble shadow of her French contemporaries who regaled the Court of King Louis XIV with their long romances. Her *Oroonoko*, set in Surinam, is said to be the great-grandmother of all the modern horrors that bespangle our bookstalls.

The reign of King Charles II was lavish in political theory if not in political philosophy, and might have been more so had it not been for the censorship. The champion of the Tory faith was Sir Robert Filmer, whose book, *Patriarcha* or *A Defence of the Natural Power of Kings against the Unnatural Liberty of the People*, written before 1640, was published in 1680. His work used to be underestimated, but modern historians have shown how and why he exerted considerable influences in the reign of Charles II, especially on the 'non-resisters'. Filmer rested his case chiefly on the Old Testament and the supposed monarchical power conferred by God on Adam in the Garden of Eden, which had passed down by way of Noah and the Ark until it safely ended up with the Stuarts. The nub of his argument therefore was that government was based on status and not on consent, and historically there was more to be said for it than appeared on the surface. At any rate, the theory was much preferred by keen royalists to the materialistic and logical notions of Thomas Hobbes, which in any case suited a Cromwellian dictatorship just as well as Stuart absolutism. Indeed, it is only in our own time that Hobbes's arguments, much less easily disposed of than the dubious history of the simple Filmer, have entered into the swim of political thought. Sidney answered Filmer's biblical arguments at enormous length, and in his *Discourses Concerning Government* (published posthumously in 1698), the book for which he perished on the scaffold, but which was to become a gospel in New England, he went on to argue that the best form of government varies according to the conditions of the country. Real democracy, as in Greece, he said, was suited only to a small town. But in every nation there is a natural aristocracy who should advise the executive and carry out the laws promulgated by the legislature. What Sidney aimed at was a mixed monarchy, 'regulated by the law and directed to the public good'. At about the same time that Sidney was writing and Filmer was published, Henry Nevile, a disciple of James Harrington, published his *Plato Redivivus*. This was Harrington's *Oceana*, adapted to meet the situation of King Charles II. Nevile argued that King Charles's powers were excessive – his right to make peace and war was, he claimed, for instance, a usurpation. Moreover, he thought that the King's control of the militia, the revenue, and officers of state ought to be taken away from him as such far-reaching powers were damaging to efficient government and were improper in an age when property had become more and more concentrated in the hands of the upper and middle classes and not of the king. Although Nevile asserted that he was against revolution and in favour of a limited monarchy, he wanted to leave the king with virtually no powers, rights, or duties. If we consider the writings of Sidney and Nevile in conjunction with the earlier republican or semi-republican writings of Milton and Marvell, we can see how a political theory of aristocracy was being built up which was to bear fruit both in England and in America in the eighteenth century.

The sixteen-eighties, the period following the spurious Popish and Rye House plots, was, then, rich in political writing. At the end of 1684 George Savile, Marquis of Halifax, circulated anonymously his *Character of a Trimmer*, in which he expounded his own original doctrines. His was the philosophy of the golden mean, and in it he drew a famous comparison between the state and a boat at sea in which the balance of safety is preserved by the passengers keeping towards the middle. Halifax had fought the Exclusion Bill to keep James II off the throne, but had wanted to impose statutory limitations on a Roman Catholic monarch. He had accepted the outlawing of Roman Catholics from parliamentary life, but soon ceased to believe in the reality of the Popish Plot. He was against a pro-French foreign policy, but did not wish to deprive the King of his right to make decisions on international affairs. So firmly did he plant his feet in the middle that he has been hailed as a seer by many different parties. Some compare him to Bolingbroke, author of *The Patriot King*, others to Edmund Burke, who refuted Bolingbroke. He has been classed as a republican because of the limitations he was prepared to put upon the monarchy. Finally, it has been said that he 'was the first Utilitarian in the history of English political thinkers' since he did not believe in the social contract and had no unalterable principles except to maintain the safety of the people and the sanctity of property. The value of his political thought has been rather exaggerated, but he was a lively apologist for the concept of a 'limited' or constitutional monarchy, which Charles II had to some extent attempted to embody. On the whole, however, it can be said that the differences in outlook between Halifax, Sidney, and John Locke, whose writings we shall consider in a later chapter, were not enormous. They all sought after liberty of the subject in their own particular way, believed in religious equality except for 'papists', distrusted democracy in our modern sense, and regarded the first duty of the state as the protection of property. When King James II attempted to put back the clock by reviving the doctrines of the divine right of kingship propounded by Filmer, this Whig political philosophy stood ready at hand to justify and explain the Glorious Revolution of 1688.

CHAPTER XII

King James II and the Glorious Revolution
1685–9

UNLIKE his brother, King James II was not by any means a congenial or attractive figure. Impatient, bigoted, vain, and haughty, he exacted the last ounce out of the privileges of his office. He received foreign diplomatists not, as King Charles II had done, standing bareheaded in his bedchamber, but seated in a special room with his hat on. His personal conduct was no more restrained than his brother's had been, but his choice of mistresses showed inferior taste: indeed, King Charles II had been wont to maintain that they were imposed upon him by his priests as penances. Be that as it may, his latest biographer is of the opinion that when King James came to the throne at the age of fifty-three he had already been weakened by his excesses and that his peculiar arrogance and blindness to the consequences of his actions were evidence of a premature mental decline. For in so far as training went he had ample experience, he was a qualified soldier, sailor, and administrator. During the last years of the previous reign he had been at the centre of affairs. In Rochester, Sunderland, Godolphin, and Halifax he had capable Ministers not overburdened with scruples, ready to do his will if he did not go too far.

Nevertheless there seemed to be good reason for surprise that he, an avowed Roman Catholic, should have come in such a calm to the throne of a Protestant realm. A few years earlier when a majority in the House of Commons voted to exclude him from the throne it was assumed that he could only attain the crown through a sea of blood. But the Whigs lay broken. On the very morrow of his accession the King had hastened to tell his Privy Council that he would 'make it his endeavour to preserve this government in Church and

State as it is now by law established' and this speech was at once commended and published. Somewhat paradoxically King James relied confidently upon the passive loyalty of the members of the Church of England to sustain the high prerogatives of one who did not share their faith. The Anglicans, for their part, were willing to wait and see. Moreover they were aware that they had a tough character with whom to contend. 'They knew well', wrote the Yorkshire royalist, Sir John Reresby, 'the difference that there was between the spirits of the late and the present King, and thought the first would sooner be induced for peace's sake to relinquish his brother, than that the latter would tamely renounce his just possession of three kingdoms out of fear of a war.'

The King decided immediately to call a parliament, which met soon after the Coronation that had taken place on St George's Day with all the customary rites performed by the Archbishop of Canterbury, the aged Sancroft, except for the Communion service. The King took the Mass openly in Whitehall, but this was scarcely a matter for comment and was acceptable to his more powerful subjects so long as he left them and their religion alone. The general election was a triumph for the Court. Not only the boroughs, whose charters had been remodelled in the King's interest in the previous reign, but many of the counties were persuaded to return enthusiastic royalists. 'Such a landed parliament was never seen,' announced one of them, and King James II himself observed that 'there were not above forty members but such as he himself wished for'. Before the English Parliament met, a Scottish Parliament had already demonstrated subservience, among other things prescribing severe penalties against all preachers and congregations at conventicles, 'the nurseries and rendezvouses of rebellion'. The English Parliament, which met in May 1685, after hearing another short discourse from the King in which he demanded supplies rather curtly, granted him a generous revenue. Sir Edward Seymour, a west country Tory, who complained about the 'tampering' with elections, failed even to find a seconder. And when a committee on religion resolved to ask the King to enforce the existing laws against Roman Catholics and the King as a Roman Catholic expressed understandable annoyance, the Commons rejected the resolution. In the midst of these harmonies it was learned that a double invasion of Great Britain had been undertaken by rebels from abroad. In the first week of May the ninth Earl of Argyll landed in the Western Isles and on 11 June the Duke of Monmouth arrived with 150 followers at Lyme Regis. Parliament voted the King an additional £400,000 to pay for suppressing these rebellions. Argyll's forces were soon rounded up and their leader sent to Edinburgh to be executed. Monmouth managed to collect a fair-sized but ill-equipped army which after vainly knocking at the gates of Bristol was finally defeated at the night battle of Sedgemoor on 5 July. Monmouth, after he had been taken prisoner, tried to save his life in an interview with the King, but in the end died like a man. His supporters in Dorset, Somerset, and the neighbouring counties were severely punished even judging by the standards of those days; the Lord Chief Justice Jeffreys 'made a campaign in the west' after Lord Churchill, once the King's page, had obtained the military decision, and condemned men to death or banishment at the 'Bloody Assizes'. 'The country looks, as one passes, already like a shambles,' wrote a loyal Tory from Taunton.

It has sometimes been said that the lack of success of these rebellions organized by the English and Scottish Protestant heroes of the former reign was remarkable. But the reason for their failure is not hard to discover. Though Monmouth and Argyll had made an alliance, the purposes of their joint invasion, whether to establish a republic or make Monmouth King, were never agreed and their military movements were poorly planned and worse concerted. Republican sympathizers in London backed out and lost their nerve and no effective rising took place in Cheshire or the other Whig centres. Moreover it can be argued that the undertaking was wrongly timed. King James was still proclaiming his kindly intentions towards the Church of England and had not yet disclosed any other aims. But what was extraordinary was not really the failure of the rebellion but how near it came to success. Thousands of poor simple men flocked to join Monmouth's colour and twice – even at Sedgemoor itself – he was within an ace of victory. The rebellion had been described as 'the last popular rising in the old England' and a 'last flash' from the Good Old Cause of 1642. But was it indeed a 'last flash'? Was not the Monmouth rebellion, like the so-called Rye House conspiracy, in fact a link between the movement of opinion that brought King Charles I to the scaffold and that which was to thrust King James II into exile for ever?

After the execution of Monmouth, King James hardened his heart and went his way. The very ease with which the rebellion had been put down appeared to him a good augury. Parliament had voted him impressive sums. European Powers were competing for his friendship. He had at his disposal a strong army and navy. His enemies were dead or disarmed. Henceforward he was determined to be the unquestioned ruler of his lands and to revive the pristine glories of the divine right of Kings. Looking across the Channel he saw King Louis XIV at the full height of his achievement employing all his resources in shaping his subjects into an unsullied Roman Catholic block. In October 1685 the French monarch had revoked the Edict of Nantes, thus depriving the French Protestants of their charter for freedom of worship. The English King was at first pleased at this blow on behalf of his own faith, but when he learned of the harsh methods used he was less enthusiastic. James stood for religious equality. He therefore granted numerous commissions in his army to Roman Catholics in defiance of the statute law and aimed at the repeal both of the Test Acts and the Habeas Corpus Act. He met some opposition in his Privy Council and proceeded to purge it of all critical elements. On 21 October Halifax was dismissed and was later succeeded by the greedy and hypocritical Sunderland as President of the Council. Jeffreys, fresh from the Bloody Assizes, was appointed Lord Chancellor. Leading Roman Catholic peers, including some who had only barely escaped with their lives from the furies of the Popish Plot, were admitted into the Privy Council. And Rochester and his brother Clarendon hung on disregarded, only to lose office at the beginning of 1687 and to mark the final victory of the 'Roman Catholic Cabal'.

Long before this the loyal Anglican Parliament was no more. When it had reassembled in November 1685, it protested against the employment of Roman Catholic officers and resisted the plan for a standing army and the repeal of the Test Acts. On a crucial occasion the ministerial side was beaten by one vote. Among the chief opponents of the Crown was Henry Compton, the militant Bishop of London, who represented his Church more effectively than the feeble Primate. On 20 November the King had prorogued Parliament and it was never to meet again.

The infatuated King now devoted all his energies to his policy of equality. Throughout 1686 in fanatical enthusiasm and with a magnificent disregard for worldly advice he promoted Roman Catholics to key positions everywhere. Not only did many Roman Catholics officer the army, a Roman Catholic was put in command of the fleet, a leading Roman Catholic became Lord Lieutenant of Ireland and another Master of the Ordnance. An ecclesiastical commission was set up to silence Anglican critics, presided over by Jeffreys, which succeeded in depriving the Bishop of London of his functions, and an appeal was made to Nonconformists by the publication of a Declaration of Indulgence invoking the royal power to 'dispense' with all statute law so as to secure liberty of conscience for all. A coalition of Nonconformists, renegade Tories, and resurgent Catholics was envisaged as a combat team with which to assault the citadel of Anglican exclusiveness. The constitutional basis for the King's action was provided by the Hales case, a test case in which eleven out of twelve judges found that the King was entitled to exercise the power he claimed to dispense with the laws.

But the King drove too fast and furiously. In our later days of religious toleration plans for liberty of conscience may or should be admired. But then by his extreme methods he created opposition first because he too plainly weighted the scale in favour of his <u>fellow religionists</u>, who were certainly a minority, and secondly because his procedure was too blatant and his methods too blunt. When a Papal Nuncio was accorded a public reception in the summer of 1687 and the King's Jesuit adviser, Father Petre, was introduced into the Privy Council this was to throw out a challenge to public opinion. When a Roman Catholic head was forced upon an Oxford College, the Anglican Tories were touched where their hearts beat most strongly. By preferring to smother discontent instead of removing its causes and by making such unscrupulous use of his prerogative powers King James not only alienated the normally ruling aristocracy but even excited the voteless mob. His most trusted advisers saw that he was blowing the lid off the stove. Sunderland said that there was no leading the King but 'by a woman, a priest or both'; 'all was naught,' the profane Jeffreys declared later, 'the Virgin Mary was to do all'.

The King omitted no method in his attempt to create a wave of opinion favourable to his policy. He had buttonholed the influential; he had 'purged' the boroughs; he had ordered many changes in the Lords Lieutenant and the Commissioners of Peace. He now used the machinery of local government to see if it were possible to obtain a new parliament which would do his will. In the autumn of 1687 the Lords Lieutenant were ordered to go down to their counties, summon together all the important officials and local magnates and inquire whether (1) if they should be chosen members of parliament, they would favour the repeal of the Test Acts, (2) whether they would assist in the election of members pledged to the repeal of the Tests, (3) whether they would actively support the King's Declaration of Indulgence. The documents concerning this inquiry are now in the Bodleian Library at Oxford. Most of the Lords Lieutenant refused even to put the three questions and accepted dismissal. In some counties the local gentry would not come to a meeting. But wherever the questions were put, the answers showed that the majority of leaders of local opinion throughout the land were opposed to the royal programme. The largest minority was in Westmorland and Cumberland. The Lancashire records do not survive, but it appears that even this, the most Roman Catholic area in England, did not approve the King's policy. In several counties the Justices of Peace and others agreed together to give a uniformly evasive reply; in others many boldly announced that they were against the repeal of the Tests or would agree to it only if it did not hurt the Church of England. King James's apologists have sometimes argued as if his enlightened policy of religious toleration was sabotaged by a few very wealthy men. But these records prove – if any documentary evidence can be trusted – that a great many of the gentlemen of England were overwhelmingly against the Crown. In a recent book Professor J. R. Jones argues that, despite the unfavourable response to the three questions, James II during 1688 concentrated upon a campaign to pack a parliament ready to repeal the Test Acts using in particular the influence of former Whigs and Dissenters in urban areas to create an atmosphere conducive to religious toleration. But in spite of pressures the most the King could have hoped for was a substantial minority of supporters in the new parliament. This campaign did not really get going until James had despaired of help from the Tories.

In April 1688 he published a second Declaration of Indulgence and required that it should be read on successive Sundays from the pulpits of all the churches. Archbishop Sancroft and six other bishops petitioned King James asking him to withdraw this order because they considered that his power to dispense with the penal laws was illegal. The King retorted that this was the standard of rebellion and had the Bishops put into the Tower of London to await a prosecution for seditious libel. It was significant that while they were in the Tower the Bishops were visited by leading Nonconformists. On 30 June after the judges had been divided and the jury had disagreed the seven Bishops were found not guilty. Even the King's army encamped at Hounslow to overawe the capital could not forbear to cheer.

King James II's two daughters had not approved their father's conduct. The elder, Mary, was married to William of Orange and attempts had been made to induce her husband to support King James in return for a promise that his succession to the English throne should be ensured. Up to 1687 William had behaved with exact and discreet propriety. But in February of that year he had dispatched a special envoy to London who, since he was unable to make any impression on Court circles, had entered into communication with discontented politicians of whom by far the busiest was Danby, who had been released from the Tower at the beginning of the reign. Meanwhile Princess Anne, the King's younger daughter, married to the oafish Prince George of Denmark, had fallen under the influence of Sarah Churchill, the fierce but attractive wife of one of the King's few Protestant favourites. Hating her step-mother and doting on her religion of High Church Anglicanism, Princess Anne became alienated from her father. And John Churchill sent a letter to William of Orange by the special Dutch envoy assuring him that the Princess was ready to suffer death rather than change her religion; he added modestly that he himself, though he could not live the life of a saint, was ready 'if there ever be occasion for it to show the resolution of a martyr'.

The fate of England was now entangled in the affairs of Europe. King Louis XIV of France had become neither satisfied nor pacific after the Truce of Ratisbon in 1684, but had tried to fortify his country by extending its power into Western Germany. He laid claim to the Palatinate which lay between Strasbourg and Mainz and attempted to secure control of another Electorate, that of Cologne. These French graspings, together with a tariff war started by the French Government, made the Dutch again anxious as to their future safety. The Emperor and some of the more important German princes were also provoked by the encroachments of the French King and thus the lines of war were once more being drawn across Europe. King James II's obstinacy and haughtiness had prevented him from becoming as deferential to the French King as his brother had been, for he was proud of his independence. Indeed at the beginning of his reign King James II had renewed a defensive treaty with the Dutch. But now as the fog of war descended and all became obscure, William of Orange, the lifelong opponent of King Louis XIV, grew increasingly concerned about the side on which the English would range themselves. We do not know when he finally made up his mind to move against his father-in-law. But when in January 1688 King James II demanded the recall of six English and Scottish regiments which were serving in Holland under Prince William's command the crux was reached. A Whig grandee, Edward Russell, who was in Holland in April, was informed by Prince William that he was ready to lead an armed force to England if he should receive a suitable invitation to do so from men of influence.

On 10 June before the trial of the Seven Bishops King James II entirely unexpectedly became the father of a son. There was no particular expectation that the baby would survive the grave hazards of seventeenth-century childhood – Queen Mary was now thirty and all her other children had died. But here was a battle cry for the King's enemies: an unending Roman Catholic dynasty was envisaged. A number of Whigs and Tories entered into secret alliance and a letter signed by seven of them was carried to Holland by Admiral William Herbert, disguised as a common sailor. This invitation was sent on 30 June 1688, and soon King James II was being warned from a dozen sources that naval preparations were being undertaken in the Dutch ports, watched with satisfaction by a crowd of English and Scottish political exiles, and that these preparations were intended against England. James abandoned his attempt to pack Parliament and concentrated on preventing invasion.

It was a strange interlude that now occurred, marked on King James's side by a policy of concessions to public opinion, on Prince William's by nervousness over the situation in Europe. Then suddenly all was settled. In the middle of September the Dutch States General gave their consent to William of Orange's plans and King James finally realized that the invasion of England was imminent. Actually on 15 September the main French army, engaged in war against the Emperor, had begun the siege of Philippsburg, 200 miles from the Dutch frontier, and free from anxiety William then told the States General in secret session that he proposed to land in England with an armed force to secure the rights of the Protestant religion and vindicate his wife's right to the succession. On 24 September King James saw Clarendon, one of the Tory chiefs he had dismissed from office, told him of the Dutch intentions and observed 'Now, my lord, I shall see what the Church of England men will do'. Clarendon answered sourly that they would do their duty. By this time the King had published a proclamation in which he promised to uphold the laws in Church and State and that he would summon a fresh parliament. He had taken off the suspension of the Bishop of London, abolished the ecclesiastical commission, restored the forfeited charters of London and other cities, and allowed the return of the Fellows he had expelled from Magdalen College, Oxford. He had also assured the Dutch that he had no secret treaty with France and earlier refused an offer of help from the French King. But he had not promised to remove the Roman Catholic officers from his army nor ceased to make use of the dispensing power, the cause of his quarrel with the bishops. All his concessions were in vain. For the die had been cast. The Dutch military preparations were completed. The conspirators were committed. Prince William had made up his mind. But the invading fleet lay weather-bound in the Dutch ports. In a brief moment of confidence King James dismissed the last of his competent Ministers, the Earl of Sunderland, who had completely lost his nerve. On 1 November the wind changed and Prince William with his motley horde of Dutchmen, English and Scottish exiles, and all sorts reached Torbay on the fifth. Thence he moved to Exeter where he struck camp and waited to see if the English people would rally to his side.

What were the causes of the revolution of 1688? There is

no need to look for any subtle explanation. Many people had been fully convinced (though wrongly) that King James II was determined to impose on his kingdoms a Roman Catholic despotism similar to that exercised by King Louis XIV in France. A nation which had already been transformed in outlook and in spirit by the Puritan rebellion and the great civil wars would not acquiesce in any such policy even though it was sustained by a standing army and fortified by the popular Anglican doctrine of non-resistance to an anointed King. There are three pieces of evidence that opposition to the Crown was wide. The first is the surprising number of the common people who had joined Monmouth during his premature rebellion of 1685. The second is the evidence afforded by the replies to King James's Three Questions of 1687. The third is that once William of Orange landed, although King James had an unbeaten fleet in being (merely rendered temporarily ineffective by the prevailing winds) and an army at least twice the size of that of his enemy he nevertheless conceded a bloodless victory in England. Sir John Reresby, who was loyal to the King to the end, notes that 'it was very strange, and a certain forerunner of the mischiefs that ensued upon this invasion, that neither the gentry nor the common people seemed much afeared or concerned at it, saying "the Prince comes only to maintain the Protestant religion; he will do England no harm".'

William of Orange had played a curious part. He had planned his operation before the birth of the Prince of Wales and had none the less sent a special envoy to congratulate his father-in-law on the happy event. In his proclamation issued before he left Holland, he had hinted that the birth was an imposture, thus accepting the unfounded slander put about by the Whigs. In this proclamation he adopted a formula, originally employed, ironically enough, by King Charles II, that all disputed questions in Church and State would be referred to a free parliament. William was not sure of his ground nor entirely clear as to his mission. But what seems certain is that he wanted first to range the kingdom alongside the Dutch in the coming war with France and secondly to protect his wife's hereditary rights. At the end of 1687 Dr Burnet, one of the Whig exiles in Holland and a confidant of William and Mary, had noted 'The Prince may find himself eventually compelled to interfere in the affairs of England; since a rebellion of which he should not retain the command would certainly entail a commonwealth.' A number of men who had links with the Commonwealth extremists were still alive, such as Wildman, the friend of John Lilburne who had been dead for thirty years, and Sir William Waller, the son of the parliamentary general of the same name. Republicanism still claimed its adherents, but the fact that some, though not all, of the leaders of the Tory party supported William of Orange's expedition was a guarantee that no such startling consequences would follow the new revolution as those which had followed the civil wars of the sixteen-forties. Because a prince, married to a Stuart princess, took charge, it was lent an air of respectability agreeable to the possessing classes and the rising merchants and financiers of the late seventeenth century.

King James moved hesitantly to meet the threat to his throne. For he was oppressed by the memories of his youth. He was reluctant to leave his capital when he thought of what had happened when his father had done so, and slow to put himself at the head of his large army at Salisbury. Soon he found the two pillars of his sovereignty, the loyal Tory gentlemen and the army officers, were being undermined. From the north he received news of towns being surrendered almost without a shot, at camp desertion began, and from Whitehall he heard that his own daughter, Princess Anne, had hurried to join the enemy. Consumed by sickness and absorbed in prayer, he withdrew from Salisbury, and having talked of calling parliament and having sent out a commission headed by Rochester and Halifax to treat with Prince William as a smokescreen, he fled to Faversham and tried unsuccessfully to escape to France, whence he had already dispatched his wife and child. Crestfallen, he crept back to London, only to leave again and for the last time the week before Christmas. On 18 December William of Orange entered a capital distracted by anti-Popish rioting and was invited by a representative gathering of Whigs and Tories to call a Convention Parliament. The convention met on 22 January 1689.

When the two houses sat they were inevitably divided over the future government of the country. The House of Commons had perhaps a two-thirds majority of Whigs, but the Lords contained a majority of Tories. The Commons voted that King James II had 'endeavoured to subvert the constitution by breaking the original contract between king and people' and had therefore 'abdicated' the throne. They also resolved that it was 'inconsistent with the safety and welfare of this Protestant kingdom to be governed by a popish prince'. The Lords, while ready to agree to the second resolution, were unwilling to swallow the first, which suggested that the monarchy was elective and violated their cherished doctrine of hereditary right. What the Tories, headed by Nottingham, would have liked was a regency, but this proposal was defeated by two votes. Eventually, after Princess Mary had let it be known that she would not accept a position superior to that of her husband, the Lords assented to the theory that James by abandoning the country had 'abdicated' (which he had not done in fact) and that the throne was therefore vacant. On 6 February 1689 William and Mary were declared King and Queen: in that declaration all parties – except the supporters of King James, henceforward known as 'Jacobites' – now agreed, the erstwhile republicans being pleased enough that a precedent had been established that rulers were elected by the people and could be deposed if they misgoverned.

The crown had not been offered to its joint wearers unconditionally. Its transfer was accompanied by a Declaration of Rights (afterwards converted into a Bill) which deprived the monarch of the power, exercised by King James II, to suspend the law of the land and the right to maintain a standing army in time of peace; it also condemned the use of the dispensing power and asserted that parliaments should be called frequently. Finally the succession was prescribed, though no provision was made if William, Mary, and Mary's sister, Anne, should die without heirs. This Declaration was followed by the passing of a toleration act which freed dissenters from penalties for failing to go to church and remitted many of the other punishments inflicted by the 'Clarendon Code'. But a plan for a comprehension bill fell to the ground; the Nonconformists continued to be shut out from public offices, both civil and military; and the acts against Roman Catholics remained in full force, though some relaxations were allowed later. Clergy of the Church of England who refused to take the oaths of allegiance to the new sovereigns were liable to fine or imprisonment. A considerable number – about four hundred – refused to do so and became known as 'Non-jurors'. The revolutionary settlement was completed by a mutiny act which ensured the discipline of the army.

On 15 April King James II, having recovered his nerve and found generous succour in France, returned to Ireland, home of many of his fellow religionists, to begin in earnest the fight to regain the throne he had abandoned so pusillanimously. He was accompanied on his mission by French officers, and the Commons naturally voted the new King supplies so that he might take measures against France on whom war was declared in May. In November 1688 King Louis XIV had declared war against the Dutch and on 12 May 1689 the Dutch and the Emperor had entered into a defensive and offensive alliance. By September King William III was able to bring in England, and thus complete the second Grand Alliance against France. King William's lifelong enmity to France had been the chief motive which had induced him to invade England under the Protestant banner and it was logical that one of his first acts should thus be to carry over the kingdoms of England and Scotland into the combination against his ancient foe. Thus King William III (as the Marquis of Halifax suggested) 'took England only in his way to France', and a diplomatic revolution followed.

CHAPTER XIII

King William III and Queen Mary II
1689–1702

THE early days of the new reign were overshadowed by two facts, the war against France and the uncertain tenure of the English throne by its new occupants. While Queen Mary held the title jointly with her husband, the executive power lay entirely in his hands. He would not allow parliament to meet when he was out of the country, as he frequently had to be, and left specially selected Lords Justices as effective governors to advise the Queen in his absence. She, poor woman, doted on her husband (though she had found compensation for a loveless life in writing from Holland fulsome letters to one of her girlhood friends of the English Court) and did as she was told. William himself, though he, too, had his personal favourites, was not a man who radiated love. Henry Sidney, younger brother of the dead republican, Algernon, and Keppel, a handsome Dutchman, were among his men intimates, while Elizabeth Villiers, Countess of Orkney, was reputed to be his mistress: as George Villiers, first Duke of Buckingham, had been the favourite of James I and Charles I, and Barbara Villiers, Duchess of Cleveland, had been the mistress of Charles II, Elizabeth Villiers maintained a tradition stretching almost beyond dynasties. But William's life was warmed by hate rather than love. He resented alike his early treatment at the hands of the Dutch burghers and the attacks of the French King not only on his beloved Holland, but on his own principality of Orange, which French troops had occupied in the previous reign. An asthmatic, a cripple, and with a tubercular lung, a passionate fire ever glowed within him. Everything – wealth, health, and happiness – was subordinated to this desire to destroy the menacing power of the French monarchy. Hence English party politics were anathema to him. He never trusted any English statesman or general: at best he used them. It was significant that among those he found most serviceable were not ardent revolutionaries, but Halifax the Trimmer who had stayed in James II's camp until it broke up, and Sunderland, the once avowed 'papist', and James II's chief Minister, who had fled abroad, was brought back, forgiven, and finally restored to office.

The war against France was one of the first revealing examples in modern times of the influence of sea power on history. At first, owing to the earlier exertions of Louis XIV's Minister, Colbert, the French navy was able to offer a challenge to two of the strongest naval powers, England and Holland. It was because the French navy won a temporary supremacy in the Channel in 1689 that King James II landed safely in Ireland and a dangerous threat had been imposed on King William's flank. On the other hand, in the long run King Louis XIV was obliged to make peace not so much because of the weight of the armed land coalition against him, which embraced Spain and Savoy as well as England, Holland, the Emperor, and a number of German princes, as because the French fleet could not command both the Channel and the Mediterranean. But to begin with, the French had some success. A defensive policy was deliberately adopted on the continental mainland, while if King William III could be pulled off his throne again the coalition might be disrupted. King William, for his part, found the Irish side-show most distasteful. He wanted to hasten to Flanders and come to grips with his enemy. However, by 1690 danger in Ireland had been removed. Though the English and Dutch fleets were beaten at the battle of Beachy Head on 30 June, on the following day James II was defeated by William III at the battle of the Boyne, and later in the same year John Churchill, now created Earl of Marlborough, captured Cork and Kinsale in a masterly campaign lasting only twenty-three days. Two years later English naval supremacy was reaffirmed at the battle of La Hogue and French military supremacy was reasserted at the battle of Steenkerke. The war continued much according to that pattern. The allied armies suffered defeat in 1693 at the battle of Neerwinden, and though in 1694 King William himself retook Namur, which belonged to Spain, in 1697 the French captured Barcelona on the other side of Europe. Although the war of siege and counter-siege in Flanders led practically nowhere, the final result was determined by the sea power of England – her fleet entering the Mediterranean and staying there throughout 1694 and 1695 – and by the resilient financial resources that fed the allied armies everywhere in continental Europe in spite of their frequent defeats.

But while King William III thus successfully pursued with English aid the task to which he had dedicated himself, his seat on the throne was precarious. The Whigs regarded their chosen ruler as ungrateful because he first governed by means of a coalition containing the Tory Danby (now made Marquis of Carmarthen and later Duke of Leeds), as President of the Council, the Earl of Nottingham, another Tory, as Secretary of State, and the Trimmer, Halifax, as Lord Privy Seal. They strove to increase the powers of the House of Commons (where they had a majority), to reduce the remaining prerogatives of the Crown, and to push their way into all available offices. King William, who was utterly determined not to be a mere Venetian Doge or figurehead, resisted the Whig pressure, but he was obliged to accept a Triennial Bill (to which he gave his assent in December 1694), which laid it down that parliaments must meet every three years and not sit for more than three years, and a Treason Bill which in 1696 established that two witnesses as to fact were required in every trial. On the other hand, he stopped the enactment of a Place Bill which, by preventing M.P.s from holding office, would have severed the executive from the legislature, as in the United States today.

For the six years from 1690 to 1695, during which there was no general election, Ministers were constantly changing, but it was not until 1694 that a mainly Whig Ministry was forced upon the King. The Tories, for their part, though they were originally preferred by the King because they were less inclined to attack his prerogatives, had palled upon him when they opposed the war with France, tried to restrict the size of his army, were critical of his propensity for foreign favourites, and for the most part kept in touch with King James II, 'the king across the water'. Such was the maelstrom of intrigue and so thick the political fog in the first months of the new reign and so intense was the unpopularity of the new King in high society that it was universally admitted that if (and it was in fact an impossible condition) King James II had been willing to change his religion, he would at once had been brought back amid general acclamation. For not only were the majority of the Tories, the non-Jurors, and the Jacobites friendly to their former monarch, but a number of the more moderate Whigs or non-party men told each other frankly that they dared not identify themselves too heartily with the regime lest a counter-revolution should leave them stranded. Halifax, who was at first much with the King, said to his friend, Sir John Reresby: 'Come, Sir John, we have wives and children, and we must consider them and not venture too far.'

Shrewsbury, a neurotic Whig magnifico, who became Secretary of State in 1689, resigned office, and then resumed it again in succession to Nottingham in 1694, was in constant touch with King James II, housed in the Palace of St Germain; so, too, was the Earl of Marlborough, who even induced Princess Anne (who had quarrelled with her elder sister, Queen Mary) to write a contrite letter to her father, and many others. King William III knew all about this secret passing of polite but non-committal messages across the lines, but ignored it except in moments of crisis. He reckoned that no English statesman or general deserved to be trusted, but that they could be held to his interests as long as the war against France was won. Indeed, he was even lenient to avowed Jacobites and allowed them to make their peace with him if they wished. This imperviousness to treachery is but one example of the genius of his statesmanship.

The war against France was sustained by a number of financial expedients novel in the history of England, many of them blossoming in the fertile mind of Charles Montagu, a Lord of the Treasury and later Chancellor of the Exchequer, who was created Lord Halifax after the death of the Trimmer. Though the unpopular hearth tax introduced in 1662 was abolished, it was later replaced by the window tax, and in 1692 an effective land tax of four shillings in the pound was introduced, based on a re-assessment of property to yield £2,000,000 a year. In 1694 a lottery loan was devised to raise £1,000,000, the money being borrowed by offering annuities on single lives at the rate of 14 per cent as well as prizes. This Lottery Act was the first instance of the Government borrowing money directly from the public on a long-term basis and not as a mere anticipation of revenue from a few rich men (as Cromwell and Charles II had borrowed from the London goldsmiths). In 1694 the Bank of England was founded: this institution undertook to raise £1,200,000 from the public – and did so in twelve days – and to lend it to the Government at 8 per cent. In return it was incorporated as the first English joint-stock bank and allowed to issue notes (which did not, however, rank as legal tender) and discount bills. This loan from the Bank to the Government did not have ever to be fully repaid so long as the interest was forthcoming, and thus is the origin of the present funded national debt. In 1698 a new East India Company was founded with statutory privileges in rivalry to the old East India Company which had existed since the days of Queen Elizabeth, and this also undertook to lend the Government money at 8 per cent. Both these institutions were in fact Whig finance companies, and by persuading people to invest in them they not only helped King William III to make war, but also ensured the permanence of the revolution of 1688. Finally, since the Bank and the new East India Company owed their powers to parliament and might not lend to the Crown without parliament's consent, the hold of the Commons upon the Crown was sensibly strengthened. Another big financial transaction carried through chiefly by Montagu was the re-coinage of January 1696, in which he had the advice of two eminent savants, Sir Isaac

Newton, who became Master of the Mint in 1699, and John Locke. The silver coinage had become so clipped and therefore reduced in value as to upset the exchange as well as to raise internal prices. The desperate decision was taken to introduce in time of war a new and better coinage without debasing it at a cost to the Exchequer of at least £1,200,000. This had adverse consequences for the Bank. For as the demand for the new coins was prodigious and the Bank had issued notes in excess of its deposits, a run on it developed (encouraged by rival bankers), and it was only saved by a fortnight's moratorium. However, when the peace was signed the Bank was justified, was able to declare a dividend of 20 per cent, and was rewarded with additional privileges. And the national debt which had been created with its foundation, though it stood at £14,000,000 was small compared with the national income. However the political parties might quarrel, the Bank had helped to win the war and to seal the peace.

The Bank of England was attacked by the Tories on both political and commercial grounds. And in 1696 a rival Land Bank (which offered to lend money to the Government at 7 per cent instead of 8 per cent) was set up to meet these criticisms. This institution failed to weather the storm of the times, as the Bank of England did. When it failed, Montagu employed another device for raising money for the State, an issue of exchequer bonds valued at £5 and £10 as a means of obtaining short-term loans from the public.

Not only Whig merchants but Tory gentlefolk, such as the Earl of Marlborough, invested in the Bank of England: and where their treasure was, there were their hearts also. The constitution and survival of the Bank is therefore an outstanding event in the reign of King William III. It both reflected and assisted the growth of national wealth and ultimately enabled the English Government to defeat the more populous France of Louis XIV. Moreover, as Sir George Clark has said, 'England was becoming not only a business nation, but a nation with a growing capitalist class and a growing class of wage-earners who owned nothing except their labour power.'

The Peace of Ryswick, product of England's financial strength, the persistence of King William III (who, like George Washington, never knew that he was beaten), and the influence of sea power, was concluded in September 1697. King Louis XIV gave up all his conquests except Strasbourg and the town of Landau. Lorraine, which had been occupied by French troops, was restored to its Duke; the French candidates to the Electoral thrones of Cologne and the Palatinate were abandoned; the French agreed to the Dutch garrisoning border fortresses in the Spanish Netherlands; and finally their monarch recognized William III as King of England. These were substantial concessions made in part because France was worn down by the long war, but mainly because the French King was now eagerly awaiting the long expected demise of the King of Spain, Charles the Sufferer, and hoped to draw large benefits from this eventuality. But to the English subjects of King William III the gains from the war did not appear remarkable. The war had cost them £40,000,000 and had required an army of 90,000 men. Once the treaty was signed they looked for peace and retrenchment.

From 1694 to 1698 the domestic affairs of England had been virtually run by a Whig 'Junto' of five with the able and attractive Somers as Lord Keeper (afterwards Lord Chancellor), Edward Russell (later Lord Orford) at the Admiralty, and Thomas Wharton as a vigorous party organizer: in the background hovered Shrewsbury and Sunderland, grandees of wide experience and mysterious character. These statesmen, whose position was built upon a Whig majority in the House of Commons, tended to adapt their work to the benefit of themselves and their friends. (An instance of this was the creation of the new East India Company and the attempt to destroy the old one.) The Whigs with a cheeky virtue lashed the Tories with the accusation of being Jacobites, although some of their own members were not above flirting with the king across the water. A number of real or imaginary plots were unravelled. At one time Marlborough had been dismissed from office, at another (wrongfully) put under arrest and sent to the Tower.

The death of Queen Mary on 28 December 1694 had left the King as the conspicuous target of Jacobite wrath, and in February 1696 he himself had told Parliament of a plan to assassinate him at Turnham Green. King James II sat at Calais and optimistically awaited his recall to England, as his brother had awaited it forty years earlier. The Whigs wanted to introduce a form of 'association' to defend King William's person and to make the taking of an oath of association a test for holding offices and membership of parliament. Although this plan was not fully carried through, the Habeas Corpus Act was suspended in those doubtful days, and when that spring a certain Sir John Fenwick was arrested for alleged complicity in the Turnham Green assassination plot and in a scheme for rebellion he was put to death not by judgement in the High Court, but, as Strafford had been, by act of attainder. Before Fenwick perished he made accusations of Jacobitism against a number of leading Whigs and men of the middle like Godolphin and Shrewsbury. These embarrassing accusations (which had some foundation) contributed to the break-up of the Junto: Shrewsbury again resigned; Sunderland retired; and Montagu gave up his brilliant handling of the national finances to ensconce himself in a well-prepared sinecure.

Thus the Whig Party's stock had sunk low when the second general election under the Triennial Act, following the peace, was held in 1698. This, which has been called a Jingo election because of its nationalist and anti-foreign tone, meant some gains for the Tories, but the parties were so fluid and confused at the time that it was difficult to judge the meaning of the result except by the subsequent behaviour of Parliament. In the new House of Commons a lead was taken by Robert Harley – 'Robin the Trickster', a courageous, hard-drinking politician with a nonconformist background – who headed a group called indifferently the 'Old Whigs' or 'new Country Party'. Now that the war was over, Harley represented a great deal of articulate political feeling when he sought to reduce the national expenditure, to abolish the standing army (declared by the Bill of

Rights to be illegal in time of peace), and to end the King's gifts to his foreign favourites: King William III had made lavish grants out of lands forfeited in Ireland to the eldest son of his able adviser, the Earl of Portland, to Keppel, and to others. An Irish forfeitures bill was introduced into the Commons providing that all these lands should be vested in trustees and grants made since 1689 annulled. Although the two Houses quarrelled over the Bill, it finally became law in April 1700. Before that Harley had managed to compel the reduction of the army from 15,000 to 7,000 and taken from the King his beloved Dutch Guards. The King was disgusted by what he considered to be the ingratitude of the English. Had he not won a war for them, established a tolerant and merciful form of rule, tried his best to unite the contending groups, and selected Ministers purely for their capabilities in the nation's service? He could not be expected to understand completely the intricacies of party politics, the pride and independence of the Commons burnished in two revolutions, or the natural desire of ordinary citizens to rid themselves of redcoats and high taxes once the continental war had come to an end. He threatened to leave so graceless a people for ever and return to Holland, where his worth was appreciated. But he was persuaded to remain. And lacking the diplomatic strength which a strong army and a united people afford to international negotiators, he tried to reach a European settlement with the King of France which would prevent the outbreak of another war.

The Treaty of Ryswick had not looked like a permanent settlement, since the future was clouded by the problem of the Spanish succession. The Spanish Empire consisted not only of Spain itself and more than half of Italy, but modern Belgium, Mexico, and the whole of Central and South America except Brazil, part of the West Indies, the Philippines, Morocco, and the Canary Islands. When its ruler, the childless Charles the Sufferer, should at last die – and he had been reported to have been dying for thirty years – this magnificent empire would distintegrate. The French King's wife had been the eldest daughter of King Philip IV of Spain and half-sister of Charles the Sufferer and therefore the French dynasty, represented in the person of King Louis XIV's eldest son, the fat and idle Dauphin, had wide claims to be interested in spite of the renunciation of their rights by all the princesses concerned. Among other claimants to the throne was the Emperor Leopold, who was a grandson of King Philip III of Spain and had married as his first wife a daughter of King Philip IV. A daughter by this last marriage was married to the Elector of Bavaria and had a son by him, Prince Joseph Ferdinand. King William III was fully aware that the French King was determined to obtain a great deal of the Spanish inheritance, whoever might succeed to the Spanish throne. But he was most perturbed lest the Spanish Netherlands should fall to the French and thereby menace the strategic security of both England and Holland. His last years were therefore devoted to perfecting an arrangement that would maintain the balance of power in Europe and prevent the destruction of his life's work of restraining the might of France.

King Louis XIV, whose kingdom was exhausted after a hundred years of incessant war, was willing to concede something; for at first he failed to see how he could scoop the pool except at the cost of yet another European conflagration. By the first Partition Treaty concluded between these two great antagonists, signed in October 1698, it was agreed that Prince Joseph Ferdinand of Bavaria, the weakest candidate, should become the actual King of Spain, but that the Dauphin should take Sicily and Sardinia and certain smaller territories as his share, while the Emperor should be allotted the Duchy of Milan. Neither the King of Spain nor the Emperor was consulted about this distribution of prizes, but in any case it came to nothing, for in February 1699 the Electoral Prince, the child on whom so many hopes were hinged, died, and the negotiations had to start all over again. By the second Partition Treaty, completed in February 1700, the Emperor Leopold's second son, Archduke Charles, was to obtain the throne of Spain as well as the Spanish Netherlands and the far-flung possessions of Spain, while the Dauphin was to add to his share Lorraine (exchanged for Milan with its Duke). On the face of it the treaty was a wise compromise and a triumph for King William III, who had few bargaining weapons in his armoury. But its weakness lay in the fact that, like the first treaty, it had not been accepted by either Spain or the Emperor. Moreover, the King's English Ministers were not taken into the confidence of William III until the last possible moment, when its principles had been virtually agreed. It was signed by Portland, the chief negotiator, a Dutchman, and by Edward Villiers, Earl of Jersey, a brother of the King's mistress. Although since the time of Queen Elizabeth I the control of foreign policy had always been the recognized privilege of the executive, when it became known that these far-reaching negotiations had been secretly carried through by Dutchmen acting on behalf of England a storm broke in parliament. The Tory majority in the Commons threatened to impeach not only Jersey and Somers, who had affixed the Great Seal to the second Partition Treaty, but almost the entire Cabinet. They deeply resented such huge commitments being undertaken without their being consulted; they did not much care who was the King of Spain; and they thought that the terms of the Treaty would convert the Mediterranean into a French lake and ruin British commerce. Moreover, they were isolationist in outlook and tired of Europe:

> Enough [wrote Dryden] for Europe has our Albion fought;
> Let us enjoy the peace our blood has bought.

A general election held at the close of 1700 had ended in a big Tory victory. The first question that the new parliament had to consider was not the Spanish succession, but the English, for in July the sole surviving child of Princess Anne, the Duke of Gloucester, the cynosure, like the young Joseph Ferdinand, of so many political aspirations, had died of smallpox at Cambridge. An Act of Settlement was passed whereby in the event of King William (who had contemplated but not ventured upon re-marriage) and Princess Anne dying without issue the throne should go to the

Protestant Electress Sophia of Hanover, a granddaughter of King James I, and her heirs. The same Act laid down that every future sovereign should be a member of the Church of England; that no foreign-born monarch should engage in war in defence of his continental territories without the consent of the English parliament; that he might not go abroad without its consent; that no foreigner should be allowed to sit in parliament or in the Privy Council; and that the judges should not be removed from office by the Crown except on an address from both Houses of Parliament. Except for the last clause, the Act of Settlement was therefore a critical commentary on the behaviour of King William III.

Meanwhile party squabbles had temporarily died down in face of the increasing gravity of the international situation. The half-lunatic King of Spain had finally passed away in November 1700, but before he died he had been persuaded to write a will bequeathing his throne to Prince Philip of Anjou, a grandson of the French King, in order that the unity of the Spanish empire might be preserved. After a momentary hesitation King Louis XIV embraced the splendid opportunity, repudiated the second Partition Treaty so laboriously negotiated with the Maritime Powers, and accepted the will. There seemed sound realistic reasons why he should do so; neither the English nor the Dutch were in a bellicose mood; moreover, a war with the Emperor appeared certain whether the will or the treaty was adhered to. King William was exceedingly upset. 'I am perfectly persuaded', he said, 'that if this will be executed England and the Dutch Republic are in the utmost danger of being totally lost and ruined.' He therefore urged the Dutch 'to oppose so great an evil', and promised 'to engage people here, by prudent conduct, by degrees and without perceiving it'. Both the English and Dutch Governments at first recognized the validity of the will, so reluctant were the maritime peoples to fight again. But King Louis XIV now made two tactical errors. He expelled the Dutch garrisons from Belgium and replaced them by French troops (a step only to be justified if he thought that war was coming) and later when King James II died, he recognized his son James Edward, known to history as the Old Pretender, as the rightful King of England, a gesture as romantic as it was provocative. Before the second occurrence, however, both the opposition parties in Holland and England, aroused to the peril of the times, were urging King William to prepare for war. In this crisis he turned to John Churchill, Earl of Marlborough.

John Churchill is one of the most inscrutable figures in our history. If one reads through the hundreds of letters and dispatches which he left behind him, one sometimes asks oneself: 'Was this indeed a being of flesh and blood or just the perfect courteous official?' He spent his whole life at Court or at war. Page and servant to King James II before his accession, Churchill had followed his master into exile in the reign of King Charles II. When James became King he concealed his misgivings with the rest and deserted his master's cause at the last critical moment. Having done this, he thought during the first part of King William's reign that he had been insufficiently rewarded for his services at the Revolution, even if he had obtained an earldom and several commands, and he entered into correspondence with the Jacobites, although the accusation that he betrayed vital military secrets to them cannot be proved. His wife, Sarah, was ambitious and avaricious and exercised a strange fascination over Princess Anne. It was thus obvious that as soon as she succeeded to the throne Marlborough would be among her chief advisers and Marlborough had done what he could to stir up trouble for King William and hasten the happy day when that should be. Marlborough was now over fifty and while he had never held a major command on the Continent, he had already done more than enough to prove to William that he possessed military genius. Because of that and of his friendship with Princess Anne, King William, forgetting all past insults, now made him commander-in-chief and selected him to negotiate a second Grand Alliance against France. This was concluded on 7 September 1701, nine days before the death of King James II. King Louis

XIV's foolish action in recognizing the Old Pretender rallied England to another war. While a new general election at the end of the year made for an equality of Whig and Tory parties in the House of Commons that almost amounted to stalemate, there was no serious division over foreign policy. As ever in times of crisis, the British people closed their ranks. Thus when on 9 March 1702 King William III died, the nation stood ready once more to do battle with France, this time under the guidance of Good Queen Anne and her commander-in-chief, the incomparable Marlborough.

CHAPTER XIV

Queen Anne and the War against France

1702–13

THE reign of Queen Anne was filled by the war against France which began two months after she came to the throne and did not end until a year before she died. She had inherited the war from King William III. The Treaty of Grand Alliance which Marlborough had signed on behalf of England in 1701 bound the allies to offer terms to France and Spain and to make war on those states if they did not agree to them. The Allies were willing to see the French monarch's grandson on the throne of Spain provided that the crowns of the two kingdoms were never united, that the House of Austria should receive the Spanish Netherlands (Belgium) and the Spanish possessions in Italy, and that a 'barrier' should be erected to separate France from the United Netherlands (Holland). Certain trade privileges were also sought for the English and Dutch merchants. The terms of the Grand Alliance were kept secret; but King Louis XIV's recognition of the Old Pretender, the occupation of Belgium by French troops, the conferring by the Spaniards of a trade monopoly in South America on a French company, and the shutting out of English commerce from the Mediterranean exasperated British feelings against France. In the last two general elections of King William's reign there was a Tory majority, but though the Tories were bitter about the King, distrusting his diplomacy and his management of the former war, the House of Commons had accepted the need to fight again and voted in October 1701 to raise a large number of men for the army and navy. In May 1701 a petition drawn up in Maidstone, Kent, had been presented to the House of Commons asking that supplies should be voted to enable the King to assist his Allies 'before it is too late'. Though this Kentish Petition disgusted the Tories as savouring of Whig gerrymandering, it indicated a climate of opinion in favour of rearmament.

Thus when King William died in a unique odour of unpopularity the country was ready for war, but relieved that it was to be waged not under the distasteful Dutchman but under an English Queen and directed by an English general.

In accordance with an Act of 1697 Parliament at once met and continued in being for six months after the accession. In her first speech to the two Houses on 11 March the Queen laid emphasis on her 'English heart'. This back-kick at the dead monarch was well received, and after the first campaign was over the Tory majority in the Commons completed the insult to the dead Whig hero by voting that the Earl of Marlborough had 'retrieved the honour of England'. On 18 March the Earl hastened to Holland to reassure the Dutch that the new ruler would honour the terms of the Grand Alliance, and when King Louis XIV showed that he had no intention of accepting its terms war was proclaimed in front of St James's Palace on 4 May. To wage the war the Queen selected, as King William had done, a coalition Ministry, though her own predilections and its bias lay toward the Tories who in the first election of the reign, held in July 1702, gained at least fifty seats. It must be remembered that party labels were less precise than they afterwards became and a fair number of members of parliament were always 'Queen's servants' who supported whatever government was in power.

The Queen herself could be called a Tory because she was a faithful daughter of the Church of England – and particularly of the High Church. As to her character Sarah Marlborough, who knew her well, recorded privately the opinion that 'she certainly meant well and was not a fool, but nobody can maintain that she was wise or entertaining in conversation.' She was slow-witted, but could be obstinate. She was devoted to her sottish husband and had homely virtues. Between 1684 and 1700 she gave birth or had miscarriages seventeen times. She had all the Stuart characteristics including a passionate loyalty to her favourites until they lost favour, and extreme love of her Church. Her only hobby was eating. Her gout and general ill health made administration and politics a nightmare for her, but she bore herself bravely and occasionally showed glimpses of common sense, for which the country had cause to be grateful. Apart from Marlborough, who was made Captain General and Master of the Ordnance, her first Ministry included as Lord Treasurer Sidney Godolphin, a kind of highly competent Civil Servant who had equally served King Charles II and King James II and was 'never in the way and never out of it'; Nottingham, the Tory Secretary of State; Rochester, her uncle, a perfervid Tory; Robert Harley, now a moderate Tory, who was Speaker of the House of Commons; Somers and Halifax of the Whig 'Junto'; and the Duke of Buckinghamshire and the Earl of Jersey, both High Tories. Though the Tories had a majority in the Commons, the Whig party was more united and better disciplined and controlled the House of Lords. The most energetic Whig leaders were not members of the Government; but one of them, the third Earl of Sunderland, who succeeded his father in 1702, was married to Marlborough's daughter and was a favourite of Marlborough's wife; this was a source of future trouble. But at first the Queen looked benignly upon the group with whom she had been friendly in the previous reign, to help her through her duties. 'We four', she wrote to Sarah Marlborough in 1703 of herself, the Marlboroughs, and Godolphin, 'must never part till death mows us down with his impartial hand.' But an immediate cause of political crisis was the determination of Rochester and the extreme Tories to draw profit from their strong position. In the autumn of 1702 they introduced an Occasional Conformity Bill aimed at preventing dissenters from qualifying for offices simply by once taking the Communion according to the rites of the Church of England. Since such dissenters were Whigs, this was a party measure and it failed of success only because of obstruction in the House of Lords. This was a difference over domestic policy, but there was also division over strategy between Marlborough and Godolphin, on the one side, and Nottingham and Rochester, on the other. Marlborough's idea, novel in an age which was inured to polite sieges on an approved pattern, was to get to grips with his enemy in a pitched battle on the plains of Flanders or wherever else was convenient. But the Tories thought, as later generations also imagined, that wars can be won simply by the pressure of sea power and economic sanctions without losing men on the battlefield.

The war had not started well in 1702. True, Marlborough had at once proved his genius as a commander by clearing the French from the line of the Meuse and capturing Liège, while in October the Tory admiral, Sir George Rooke, had seized a Spanish treasure fleet off Vigo. But the Elector of Bavaria, one of the most powerful princes in Germany, had declared for the French and surprised Ulm on the Danube. Rooke had failed to seize a Mediterranean base and another English fleet was beaten near the West Indies. Marlborough was made a Duke for his services and granted £5,000 a year out of the Post Office revenue (though the Commons then refused to make the grant to him and his heirs in perpetuity). Rochester, who was jealous of Marlborough and opposed to his methods of continental warfare, was dismissed from office in February 1703; and after the next campaign in May 1704 Nottingham resigned and was succeeded by Harley as Secretary of State. These two events eased the political situation at home, but the war had still to be won.

In 1703 Marlborough was early in the field and hoped to relieve pressure on the Emperor in Austria by at once invading Belgium. But the Dutch, still extremely cautious after the initial French aggression, maintained a veto on battles, which they had exercised through their field deputies attached to the Allied armies in the previous campaign – even though they had accepted Marlborough as their supreme commander. The Duke, therefore, at the Dutch request, first took Bonn on the Rhine, thereby clearing communications with Germany. He then planned an ingenious but complicated operation which should have resulted in the capture of either Ostend or Antwerp or both. But one of his Dutch subordinates was defeated in a minor battle at a critical moment and the only other consequence of the season's campaign was the acquisition of two more petty fortresses. Meanwhile Marlborough urged the importance of obtaining a naval base in the Mediterranean; for, like King William III, he understood that the exercise of sea power there would offset the advantage possessed by France in holding the inner lines on the continental battle ground. During the course of 1703 both Savoy and Portugal joined the Allies, thus improving the chances of such a Mediterranean strategy. The alliance with Savoy shifted the balance of power in Italy and facilitated a threat to the French port of Toulon: the Portuguese treaty provided a naval base at Lisbon, a door into the Mediterranean. However the terms of the Portuguese treaty were ominous and meaningful. The King of Portugal insisted that the Allies should now put forward a candidate for the Spanish throne who could show himself in Portugal and, sustained by an Allied army, thrust into Spain. This stretched the Allies' military resources and extended their war aims: for it was laid down in the Portuguese Treaty that 'no peace shall be made till the House of Austria be in possession of the whole monarchy of Spain'. The Dutch disliked the clause, for it seemed to them to mean that the war would be prolonged indefinitely while it rallied the Spanish people more strongly to the cause of their new French King. It was, however, accepted by the English Coalition Government apparently without much thought – as large promises often are in times of war, though they may prove embarrassing when peace comes.

The High Tories joined with the extreme Whigs in censuring Marlborough for his failure to achieve more than he had done in the campaign of 1703. Dutch obstructiveness, the deep French penetration into the heart of Germany, which even menaced Vienna, and the lack of success by the English navy made it look as if the war was being lost.

Godolphin believed that the Government might fall and Marlborough talked of resigning his supreme command. But next year the sun shone. And at home there was at least the consolation for these two Ministers that the Queen had been alienated from the High Tories who were most critical of their policies.

In May 1704, after Nottingham had resigned, the executive was in fact chiefly in the hands of Marlborough, Godolphin, and Harley, who were popularly known as the Triumvirate. At this time an able young man of twenty-five, as famous for his oratory as his debaucheries, became Secretary at War; his name was Henry St John, better known in history as Viscount Bolingbroke, though he did not obtain that title until 1712. During the early part of the year Marlborough worked out a plan to separate the English and Dutch armies of which he held the joint, but restricted, command, and move those in English pay into Germany so as to relieve the Emperor. His original intention had been to invade France by way of Lorraine from the Moselle, but when he realized that even this threat might not save Vienna, he decided upon the bold hazard of a six-hundred-mile flank march to the Danube to knock out the Elector of Bavaria and rescue Austria. This large operation was planned in response to appeals from Vienna, but, so far as we know, the detailed conception was all his own, although he may have been encouraged by the success of the French Marshal Villars' similar long march into Austria. It was not until the beginning of May that Marlborough disclosed his great plan to Godolphin, who was virtually the Prime Minister. Marlborough's march with an army of 50,000 began on 19 May. He created a fog of war by persuading the French at first that he was really going to invade Lorraine or Alsace; but when he reached Heidelberg he turned sharply eastward and on 10 June he met the Austrian commander, Prince Eugene, and the Margrave of Baden, who was at the head of another German army, at Gross-Heppach on the road to the Danube in order to concert operations. It was arranged that Prince Eugene should station himself on the Rhine to watch the French Marshals Tallard and Villeroi (who had moved south, thus reducing pressure on Holland), while Marlborough and the Margrave should move towards Ulm. On 2 July they met and defeated the Elector of Bavaria at the hard-fought battle of the Schellenberg and afterwards crossed the Danube and laid waste Bavaria. The Elector of Bavaria, however, refused to submit to them and on 7 August Tallard, who had managed to escape the attentions of Prince Eugene, joined the Elector south of the Danube. Four days later Prince Eugene came up with part of his forces and joined Marlborough, while the Marquis of Baden, who had not proved an agreeable colleague, went off to lay siege to Ingolstadt, the sole fortress then remaining in French hands on the Danube. The French and Bavarian forces who were superior in numbers and artillery to the Allies and occupied a position of textbook excellence by the Danube did not expect to be attacked; but they were, and were beaten on 13 August 1704 at Blenheim – one of the decisive battles of history. The Allies took some 15,000 prisoners and inflicted about 23,000 casualties. It was the first time that the French had suffered defeat for over two generations. The victory saved Vienna and conquered Bavaria. It assured the ultimate aggrandizement of the House of Austria and imposed a final check on the territorial ambitions of Louis XIV beyond the Rhine. It was also a blow to the Jacobites and enabled Godolphin's and Marlborough's Coalition Ministry to stay in office in England for another four years.

At about the same time as Blenheim the Rock of Gibraltar was taken by an amphibious operation and the French fleet in the Mediterranean was defeated by Admiral Rooke at the battle of Malaga (24 August). Though Gibraltar was besieged throughout the winter, it managed to hold out against a Spanish attack from the land side and investment from the sea and in March was relieved by a British naval reinforcement. While the French and Spanish were being defeated abroad, the High Tories experienced a further setback at home. They vainly tried to minimize Blenheim by crying up the victory of Rooke. Their Occasional Conformity Bill was once again lost in the House of Lords, and both Marlborough and Godolphin, who previously, with their tongues in their cheeks, had voted for the Bill, so as not to give offence to their Tory colleagues or annoy the Queen, now voted against it. The House of Lords, which still carried much weight in the constitution, also resisted the claim of the Commons (arising out of the cases known as 'Ashby *v.* White' and 'the Aylesbury Men') to determine who the parliamentary electors were as well as who might be elected. After many quarrels between the two Houses the issue was not decided because the Queen in March 1705 prorogued and subsequently dissolved Parliament in accordance with the Triennial Act. In the general election that spring the High Tories lost a number of seats to the profit of the Whigs; their election programme of ignoring the French war and asserting that the Church of England was 'in danger' was ineffective. The Ministerial Tories, headed by Harley, and the Whigs thus held a majority in the new House and Ministerial changes now reflected its altered composition. The Queen dismissed two more High Tories and Admiral Rooke lost his command, and as a sop to the Whigs Marlborough's son-in-law, the Earl of Sunderland, was appointed to the important post of ambassador in Vienna. A moderate Whig named Lord Cowper was made Lord Keeper. St John thought that in the new Ministry and Parliament 'the real foundations of difference between the two parties' was 'removed' and the Queen 'seems to throw herself on the gentlemen of England'. It was not long, however, before this happy condition evaporated and the Triumvirate were assailed by the Whig Junto greedy for office and backed in Marlborough's bedchamber and the Queen's closet by that eager woman politician, the Duchess of Marlborough.

After his successes on the Danube Marlborough planned to undertake the operation which he had previously contemplated at the beginning of 1704, the invasion of France by way of the Moselle valley. When he returned from the Danube in the autumn of that year he had surprised Trèves (or Trier) and arranged for the capture of Trarbach, which gave him a starting point for this operation. Although he had not reached home until the middle of December, after a visit to Berlin to persuade the Elector of Brandenburg, who was one of England's allies in Germany, not to withdraw his troops from Western Europe, he was back in Holland in April ready to give effect to his plan. But he soon met with disappointment from his other allies. The Dutch, although in the end they had sent a portion of their army to the Danube in 1704, were reluctant similarly to cooperate on the Moselle and had not furnished the supplies he needed at Trèves. The Austrians were lethargic and confused by the death of their emperor, Leopold, who was succeeded by his son Joseph in June 1705. Thus he was unable to collect the forces and resources which he needed. But he refused to be discouraged and confronted France's best general, Villars, with an inferior army in the hope of tempting him to battle. But Villars, who, like the other French generals on the western front, had orders to act defensively in 1705, was too wily to be caught and in Marlborough's absence from Flanders Marshal Villeroi retook Huy and Liège, fruit of Marlborough's previous campaigns. Marlborough returned to Flanders and took Huy once again in July outmanoeuvred Villeroi and broke through his lines with negligible loss of men. In the following month he again outmanoeuvred Villeroi and had the opportunity to fight him on favourable terms on the future battlefield of Waterloo. But the Dutch field deputies once more forbade the contest. Thus his campaign was a comparative failure.

But there was compensation for the Allies in Spain where the eccentric Earl of Peterborough captured the valuable port of Barcelona in Catalonia by siege after landing from the sea. The French and Spaniards tried desperately to retake it, but in the spring of 1706 it was relieved. Indeed the early summer of 1706 found the Allies at the peak of their military fortunes. In May Marlborough inflicted another severe defeat on the French under Villeroi at the battle of Ramillies. As a consequence of the battle the chief Belgian towns including Brussels, Antwerp, Bruges, and Ostend surrendered almost without resistance. By August Marlborough had reached the French frontier and laid siege to Menin in France, which he took on 22 August. By the end of the campaigning season the whole of Belgium was in Allied hands. Meanwhile another Allied force under Lord Galway, a one-armed Protestant Frenchman (such were the curiosities of the time that throughout most of the Peninsular campaign the English were commanded by a Frenchman and the French by an Englishman) who, advancing from Portugal, entered Madrid, and in September the Austrian general Prince Eugene relieved Turin in Savoy which the French were besieging. For a moment it seemed as if the war were nearing its end. But the Allied invasion of Castile aroused the nationalist ardour of the Spaniards, and they rallied to King Philip who was still in Burgos while his rival, the Archduke Charles, delayed fatally in coming forward 'to pick up his crown'. (Trevelyan.) Although there were interminable quarrels between the soldiers and statesmen of the many nationalities concerned, it appears probable that the real reason for the subsequent Allied military setback was that their communications in Spain were overstretched and Galway soon had to withdraw and allow the French to reoccupy the Spanish capital.

The French King was not over-elated by this one gain in a year of disaster and in the autumn of 1706 he put forward his first serious peace feelers. The skilled French diplomatists failed to detach the English or the Dutch from the Grand Alliance, whatever their differences may have been. But dissensions developed between the Dutch and the Austrians, the Dutch seeking to fortify the Belgian towns conquered by Marlborough as a permanent barrier against French aggression, the Austrians claiming to rule Belgium as part of the heritage of Archduke Charles, who had now been acknowledged by the Allies as the sole heir to the Spanish throne. Marlborough was anxious to hold the alliance together, but the Austrians threw in an apple of discord by offering the English commander-in-chief the Governor-

Generalship of the Spanish Netherlands in the name of the Archduke Charles, a post with a salary of £60,000. Though the offer was ultimately and reluctantly refused, it created a cleavage between Marlborough and the Dutch Government. And in 1707 the French armies recovered some of their tarnished military prestige.

In the first place the French were able to strengthen their position in Spain and on their western frontiers by obtaining the neutralization of Italy. For the new Emperor agreed to this, without consulting his Allies, in the Treaty of Milan concluded in March 1707. In April the Duke of Berwick, an illegitimate son of King James II (oddly enough, by Marlborough's own sister) inflicted a big defeat on Galway at the battle of Almanza. Marlborough was obliged to keep on the defensive because his forces had been reduced in order that the main Allied effort could be concentrated on the unsuccessful siege of Toulon. The Archduke Charles, driven from Castile, held out in Catalonia and the Austrians occupied Naples, but that was the sum of the Allies' achievements in a year which brought them no nearer the defeat of France and of Spain. But if 1707 was a year of failure, 1708 was one of hope. Though the French retook Ghent and Bruges in Belgium and threatened Ostend, on 11 July Marlborough again defeated a French army, which was only saved from annihilation by the coming of dark, at the battle of Oudenarde. Afterwards Marlborough wanted to mask the French frontier fortresses and strike straight for Paris. But that scheme was too bold even for Prince Eugene, who had shown himself to be a good and loyal colleague. So instead the Allies laid siege to Lille which with its citadel finally surrendered at the end of the year. In the same year British naval forces occupied Sardinia and Minorca thus assuring British supremacy in the western Mediterranean, while an attempted Jacobite invasion of Scotland supported by French arms was repelled. And again the war seemed near its end.

While Marlborough was winning victories abroad, his colleague, Lord Godolphin, was having his difficulties at home. The Whig Junto was far from content with the small concessions exacted for their group in 1705. The Queen, through the agency of the Duchess of Marlborough, who was her husband's rival rather than his helpmeet in the sphere of domestic politics, was submitting to incessant demands for more Whigs to be taken into the Ministry. Looked at from the eighteenth-century point of view this appeared like blackmail, though we should regard it merely as the recognition of parliamentary facts. In December 1706 Sarah Marlborough's son-in-law, Sunderland, a member of the Junto, at last obtained the post of Secretary of State in place of the colourless administrator Sir Charles Hedges and thus became the unwelcome colleague of the moderate Tory, Harley. In that same month five more leading Tories were removed from the Privy Council.

Queen Anne had given way to the Whig insistence with the deepest reluctance and distaste and allowed herself the consoling luxury, also subject to Whig criticism, of appointing a couple of Tory bishops. She was now beginning to tire of the hectoring ways of Sarah Marlborough and in 1707 another woman favourite, the red-nosed but ingratiating Abigail Masham, began to insinuate herself into the Stuart favour. She was a relative and friend of Robert Harley and exercised her growing influence on his behalf. At the same time the Queen was alienated from Godolphin and if the choice had rested with her free will she would have preferred Harley as first Minister in his place. But the Whigs had the majority – or at any rate the largest group – in the House of Commons and Queen Anne soon discovered that to dispense with Godolphin might also mean the loss of the services of her friend, the Duke of Marlborough, with the laurels of Blenheim, Ramillies, and Oudenarde still fresh upon his brow. Eventually after long and tedious intrigues, accusations, and squabbles, Harley was bested and compelled to give up office in April 1708, when Marlborough threatened to resign if he did not. And some time after the election of May 1708, in which the 'Junto' Whigs further increased their majority in the Commons, the Queen was obliged to admit more Whigs into high office including Somers, one of the Junto, who became President of the Council, and Wharton, the Whig party manager, who took the Lord Lieutenancy of Ireland. But the Queen had been temporarily disarmed by the death of her husband and by the attempted Jacobite invasion when she was proclaimed a usurper by her half-brother, the Old Pretender, and yielded to 'the five tyrannizing lords' of the Junto, as she called them, under a constant pressure she resented and never forgave.

The Godolphin–Marlborough Coalition which had virtually won the long and world-wide war with France and Spain now began to collapse. Between Godolphin and the original members of the war-winning Coalition on the one side and the office-seeking members of the Whig Junto on the other no love was lost. The Duke of Marlborough, being abroad on active service most of the time, was chiefly concerned to have a united government at home: 'England can't be safe', he wrote to Godolphin, 'but by a right understanding between the Queen and the Whigs.' But Godolphin, closer to the party realities, felt mournful about it all. 'The life of a slave in the galleys', he wrote to Marlborough in January 1709, 'is paradise in comparison with mine.' During 1709 the Junto concentrated much of its energies on getting its nominee, Lord Orford, into the office of Lord High Admiral which carried the huge salary for those days of £7,000 a year. By November Orford had exacted his desire. On the other hand, the Duke of Marlborough had refused to take another member of the Junto, Lord Halifax, with him to negotiate as a plenipotentiary and had selected instead a younger Whig, Lord Townshend.

The Whigs were rabid, largely for commercial reasons, for having the Spanish empire in the hands of a weak naval power like Austria; they therefore resisted to the uttermost any suggestion that a peace treaty should be made which left King Louis XIV's grandson on the throne of Spain. At the same time they sought to carry the Dutch along with them and to obtain a Dutch guarantee of the Hanoverian succession to the throne of England. To exact these commitments from the Dutch they had to give them what they wanted in return. What the Dutch sought was a treaty which would assure to them complete control of a barrier of strong fortresses in Belgium. Their wishes were understandable. Three times in fifty years they had been assaulted by the French, as the French themselves were to be assaulted by the Germans two hundred years later. Thus in March 1709 Marlborough and Townshend went to The Hague to negotiate a Barrier Treaty with Holland. Marlborough, however, was unwilling to make big concessions to the Dutch, partly because he wished to hold the Grand Alliance together in order to win the war, partly because he still hankered after the Governor-Generalship of the Spanish Netherlands which the Austrians had once offered him. Because he was afraid that once the Dutch had obtained what they wanted, they would make peace, he at first procrastinated and then washed his hands of the whole affair and left it to Townshend. But Marlborough was mistaken in his judgement. When the Barrier Treaty was at last signed on 29 October 1709, the Dutch Republic was in fact bound to the chariot wheels of England.

At the same time that the Barrier was under discussion the French, reeling under their defeats and exhausted by their exertions, were seeking peace, and their Foreign Minister, Torcy, came, cap in hand, to Holland to see what could be saved from the wreck of his master's hopes. In May the three main allies agreed on what were euphemistically called the 'Preliminaries' of a peace treaty, but were in fact the terms of an ultimatum to France. France was asked to surrender the entire Spanish Empire as well as Strasbourg and most of Alsace to the Emperor, a group of fortresses to the Dutch, and substantial trading concessions and oversea rights to England. If Philip of Anjou failed to evacuate Spain within two months of the signature of the peace treaty, the Allies were to keep all their gains and then renew the war with French help. Marlborough thought that the French were so thoroughly beaten that they would be obliged to consent to these humiliating demands. But King Louis XIV would not agree to the clauses which in

effect obliged him to make immediate war on his own grandson, and the Allies' ultimatum was rejected. Marlborough
was staggered by the news. 'Are there, then, no counter-
proposals?' he inquired. Negotiations were continued for a
time; a scheme was mooted whereby the French should be
required to compel the Spaniards to hand over three key
towns to the Allies as a guarantee of good behaviour; but
this was tantamount to unconditional surrender; and so the
war continued. On 11 September, after taking Tournai,
Marlborough faced at Malplaquet France's last big army
under the able Villars. Gaunt and haggard soldiers manned
the trenches, but the spirit of the French nation was there
also. Marlborough had to attack well-sited and prepared
positions, and though he drove the French back he suffered
heavy losses in the process. Judged by the larger issues, Malplaquet was a French victory. It is true that the French had
to abandon their lines and leave the town of Mons to its fate.
But Villars had restored the honour of his army and staved
off the invasion of France. Not only could the Allies no
longer really hope to impose their burdensome terms on the
Kings of France and Spain, but the English Government
was placed in jeopardy. For England was tiring of the war.
In the autumn of that year Marlborough made an unwise
request to Queen Anne that she should secure his personal
position by appointing him Captain-General for life. His unprecedented petition was refused and the Queen's refusal
marked the last breach between the 'four who should never
part'.

During 1710, while little was achieved on the field of
battle except the re-occupation and subsequent re-evacua-
tion of Madrid by the Allies, the Godolphin Ministry gradually broke up. Apart from war weariness that was felt by
the Queen, there were domestic reasons for this, too. On
5 November 1709 (anniversary of the day when William of
Orange had landed at Torbay), a High Church clergyman
named Dr Sacheverell had preached a sermon in St Paul's
Cathedral in which he had by implication attacked both the
existing Government and the hallowed principles of the

Glorious Revolution. Godolphin, provoked beyond endurance, had pressed for his impeachment; and although the Whig majority in the Lords sufficed to secure the condemnation of Dr Sacheverell, he was punished in March 1710 only by being suspended from further preaching for three years, and the attack had merely served to raise the stock of the High Church party to which in principle the Queen herself was attached. In January, Marlborough had refused to give a regiment to Colonel Hill, brother of the Queen's new favourite, Mrs Masham, and when he vainly tried to induce the whole Cabinet to make this a matter of confidence with the Queen, he found how deep had gone the fissures within the Ministry – even if this had appeared to be a strange and perhaps trivial matter on which to undertake a trial of strength with the sovereign. In April the Duchess of Marlborough finally left the Queen's service after a heated and unpleasant scene. The Duke had pleaded with Queen Anne to spare his wife from humiliation, but in vain. Urged on by Mrs Masham and by Robert Harley, who came up the backstairs to the Court and was now determined to overthrow the Government, the Queen in April appointed the Duke of Shrewsbury, veteran man of mystery, as Lord Chamberlain, in June removed Sunderland, her *bête noire* in the Ministry, from his office of Secretary of State, and lastly in August dismissed the Earl of Godolphin himself. Thus the great Godolphin–Marlborough Ministry, that had been first a coalition and then a Whig Government and had forced King Louis XIV to his knees, came to an ignominious end. Its Whig Ministers, uttering the cry '*sauve qui peut*', did not attempt to protect Godolphin, who was now replaced in effect if not at once in name by Harley. Even Marlborough, Godolphin's closest friend, though he had been ready to resign over the appointment of Colonel Hill to a regiment, stayed in office, though he disinterested himself from domestic affairs and merely continued to run the war.

In those times when the Queen was still personally responsible for the administration and, at any rate in theory, presided over Cabinet meetings, it was entirely legitimate for her to remove Ministers who no longer possessed her confidence, as a Prime Minister does today. She did not even have to take into consideration the wishes of the Ministry as a whole, since there was then no accepted principle of collective responsibility. On the other hand, ever since the Revolution the Government in fact was dependent on the support of the House of Commons, where the Whigs still commanded a majority. Thus Queen Anne could not have sustained her choice of Ministers unless her decisions reflected the feeling among the electorate as a whole. And in fact she undoubtedly was then acting in accordance with the wishes of the politically conscious people of that time.

The reaction to the Sacheverell trial showed that many people were convinced that the Church really was in danger from the predominance of the Whigs; but far more important than that was the fact that the country was sick of a war that had dragged on for so long, was costing so much, requiring such heavy taxation, and involved recruiting by a press-gang system. The 'murdering' battle of Malplaquet, as Marlborough himself called it, and the refusal of reasonable terms to the enemy now suing for peace had but underlined the public resolution against the continuation of a war that had lost all reason for its existence. The old idea, deriving from a Whig interpretation of history, that the political changes of 1710 were owing to a palace intrigue has now gone by the board. When at the end of that year after the dismissal of Godolphin a general election was held it resulted in one of the biggest Tory victories in British history. To the passion for the Church and the general anxiety for peace was added 'the glamour of the Queen's name now on the popular side'. (Trevelyan.) Nothing that Marlborough could do – though he was still a victorious hero – could change the trend of anti-war feeling throughout the nation. He stayed at his post of commander-in-chief for another year, but then he, like Godolphin, was unceremoniously dismissed by the Queen whom he had served so well – after the Tories had blackened with false charges of corruption the name of one of the greatest soldiers in British history. While he remained in command abroad, the reconstructed Government, headed by Harley, had secretly set about negotiating a separate peace with France. And since Marlborough openly avowed that he did not approve of the peace proposals, the Queen had little option but to dismiss him. But only personal and party rancour could explain the manner in which it was done. It is curious that Robert Harley, who is usually considered to be the first leader of a specific Tory party should have thought of himself as a non-party man. His conduct was so devious and his letters so convoluted that it is only in recent times that he has found biographers. One biographer called him 'the backstairs dragon', another a 'puritan politician'. It is doubtful if either title is exact. Professor Plumb says he was 'a Whig *manqué*'. The argument is that he thought Marlborough and Godolphin were prisoners of the Whigs, while he himself aimed at non-party government. But what the Tories wanted above all was to put an end to the war and here Harley agreed with them.

In April 1711 a series of new proposals (outcome of earlier and more clandestine talks) that were particularly generous to British trade had been officially put forward by the French, and in July a poet, Matthew Prior, representing Henry St John, now Secretary of State, had gone to Paris as the delegate of the Tory Government. On 27 September terms were agreed to and signed in London. After Marlborough, who had been dismissed on 31 December 1711, was replaced by the Tory Duke of Ormonde with secret orders not to fight, the negotiations dragged on and the Dutch and Austrians, left in the lurch, were compelled to accept Britain's virtual withdrawal from the alliance. To assure the Government's authority in Parliament, the Queen created twelve Tory peers so that there should be a Tory majority in the House of Lords, and a stamp tax was imposed on newspapers that had the effect of restricting public criticism of the peace terms. In July 1712 Prince Eugene, bereft of British help, was defeated by Villars at the battle of Denain. And in April 1713 the Peace of Utrecht brought the long war to an end so far as Great Britain was concerned.

CHAPTER XV

The Peace of Utrecht and the Growth of the First British Empire

WHEN on 9 April 1713 Queen Anne announced in Parliament that Peace had been concluded at Utrecht 'in the churches the bells, in the streets the bonfires, and in the windows the illuminations, proclaimed the joy of the people'. This Peace, of which the chief engineer was Lord Bolingbroke, though forced upon Britain's allies in a dishonourable way, compares as a European settlement quite favourably with the Treaty of Vienna which crowned the war against Napoleon or that of Versailles that ended the first world war against Germany. The immediate gains for Britain were manifold. Dunkirk, so long a nest of privateers preying upon British commerce, had its fortifications destroyed under the supervision of British troops, a signal humiliation for the proud French monarch. Queen Anne's rights and the prescribed Hanoverian succession were recognized and the Pretender was to be expelled from France. Hudson's Bay, Newfoundland, Nova Scotia (which had been successfully invaded from Massachusetts in 1710), and the island of St Christopher (or St Kitts) in the West Indies were to become British, although the French were allowed to retain certain fishing rights off Newfoundland, the subject of subsequent disputes. By the treaty with Spain, Britain kept her conquests of Minorca and Gibraltar, confirming her command of the Western Mediterranean, and obtained the Asiento or monopoly contract for supplying slaves to South America. She was also allowed to send one ship a year to trade at Puerto Bello on the Isthmus of Panama. Finally a commercial treaty was concluded between England and France which would have put an end to the long tariff war between the two countries. This, however, was rejected in the British

Parliament and the trade war between the two nations continued long in the eighteenth century, to the detriment of both countries.

So far as the general settlement at Utrecht was concerned, the English Tory negotiators agreed to the Bourbon King Philip's staying upon the throne of Spain and the Indies, the conditions which to the Whigs had been an irremovable obstacle to peace. In April 1711 the Emperor Joseph had died and his brother, the Archduke Charles, the Austrian candidate to the Spanish throne, had unexpectedly succeeded as Emperor. If he had acquired the throne of Spain too this would have recreated the Habsburg Empire of Charles V, a huge power sprawling across the face of Europe, and have upset the balance as gravely as if the crowns of France and Spain had been united. So the case for allowing King Philip to stay in Spain, although he was King Louis XIV's grandson, was strengthened, provided that he solemnly renounced all claim to the succession in France. This he was obliged to do by the terms of the peace treaty. The Dutch did not object; what they did resent was the substantial colonial and commercial concessions that Bolingbroke had exacted in his separate negotiations with France. They would have liked, for example, to possess joint rights in Gibraltar and Minorca, a share in the Asiento, and so on. All this was denied them. Moreover, the Tory Government repudiated the Barrier Treaty of 1709 signed by Townshend as the price for keeping the Dutch loyal to the alliance. Although they still obtained a fair barrier of fortresses, including Menin, Tournai, Mons, and Namur and equal trading rights with England in the Spanish Netherlands (which went to Austria) this was far less than they hoped for. Only the exhaustion both of their soldiers and their finances, and the base British withdrawal from the battlefield in 1712 compelled them to agree. The Austrians went on fighting on the Rhine for another year, but they finally acquiesced in the general settlement in 1714, when the French gave up their conquests on the right bank of the Rhine, but kept Strasbourg and Landau.

It is arguable – and was argued at the time – that this not unreasonable peace settlement could only have been obtained in the way that it was, by separate and secret negotiations between England and France and by the British troops' ceasing to fight in the west. King William III had set a precedent for separate negotiations and the Emperor Joseph by concluding the Treaty of Milan put a beam in the Austrian eye. After wars end allies always fall out; yet dishonourable courses are seldom to be convincingly defended by appeals to self-interest. It was a shocking fact that in 1712 the British Government not only left Prince Eugene to his fate, but betrayed his military plans to the French. The treaty also delivered the Catalans who had fought with the Allies in Spain over to the vengeance of the proud Castilians. The means by which Bolingbroke concluded the Peace of Utrecht left a nasty taste in the mouths of decent Englishmen.

The Peace of Utrecht was a milestone on the road that led to the first British Empire. The forceful acquisition of Hudson's Bay, Nova Scotia, and Newfoundland from France extended English supremacy in North America and opened a door into Canada. When fifty years later Chatham and Wolfe conquered Canada from the French, this event (by removing the last foreign threat to the independence of the American colonists) led to the establishment of the United States and the building of the later Commonwealth. But the Empire of the early eighteenth century was a very different entity. Its origins date from the reign of King James I.

Although in 1583 Sir Humphrey Gilbert had taken possession of Newfoundland in the Queen's name and in the following year Sir Walter Ralegh had received a patent to colonize Virginia, the history of British colonization really begins in the seventeenth century. The Tudor age, as Dr J. A. Williamson has written, 'grouped uncertainly towards an oceanic empire', but the Stuarts 'founded and developed it'. Although we may like to think of colonization in terms of the peaceable pilgrims aboard the *Mayflower*, it would be foolish to deny that the first British Empire, like all empires, was acquired chiefly by the exercise of military and naval strength. At the close of the seventeenth century the only colonial empire in the world was that of the Spaniards who then also ruled over Portugal. Where the Spaniards had made permanent settlements, for example, in Mexico, their empire remained intact throughout the century. But in areas where they or the Portuguese had merely blazed the trails of trade they were subjected to the pressure of the great sea powers, England, France, and Holland. And gradually the English adventurers pressed to the fore. In a famous generalization written by the American Admiral Mahan about the position at the end of the Spanish Succession War he said: 'Before that war England was one of the sea powers. After it, she was *the* sea power, without any second.' The French lost ground partly because of relative weakness at sea, partly because of their defeats on land in the war of the Spanish Succession. The Dutch, who throughout the century had been the very successful rivals to the English in commerce, the fisheries, the carrying trade, and in colonization, were seriously exhausted by their efforts in that and their previous European wars. (Indeed, in some ways the story of Anglo-Dutch rivalries dominates English seventeenth-century history in its international aspect. The contests between the two sets of Protestant adventurers, merchants, and seamen were heroic.) Thus in the eighteenth century the British Empire became the busiest colonial empire in the world. As to military power, apart from the fact that Marlborough anticipated Chatham in 'conquering America in Germany', the superior weapons with which the English traders were equipped enabled them to establish and maintain themselves amid hostile native populations in tropical countries and in North America.

What were the causes that led to English colonial settlement at this time? Unquestionably the primary motive was economic. English rulers and statesmen had long enviously watched the arrival of treasure ships from South America and the happiest moments in the wars of Oliver Cromwell and Queen Anne against Spain, as in those of Queen Elizabeth, were when a treasure ship was impounded by the

English navy. But apart from men's eternal quest for precious metals, there was a constant demand for naval stores, of which the Baltic countries then had a virtual monopoly, and for spices from the East: pepper was particularly valuable. It was long hoped that the American colonists would replace the Baltic States as suppliers of timber and naval stores, but in fact the chief crops that came from the early settlements were tobacco and sugar. Military and religious arguments were also used for establishing colonies especially under the Long Parliament and Cromwell. Cromwell, indeed, regarded it as a religious duty to deprive the Spaniards of as much of their empire as possible – although, as in the Baltic, Cromwell was not regardless of realistic economic considerations in his foreign policy. But it would be a mistake to imagine that Protestant missionary zeal was an important cause of colonization in the seventeenth century. It was not until the Society for Promoting Christian Knowledge and the Society for the Propagation of the Gospel in Foreign Parts were set up in the reign of King William III that organized missionary endeavours began. It is, however, true that a desire to escape from the restrictions put upon the exercise of their particular form of Christianity was a motive for colonization among Puritans and Roman Catholics at different periods in the seventeenth century. But they did not sail the Atlantic to promote religious freedom. For example, 'the early political history of Massachusetts' was 'that of a close and intolerant oligarchy'. (Williamson.)

One other cause may perhaps be ascribed for the first wave of colonization in the seventeenth century. It was widely argued in the early part of the century that the nation was over-populated. The argument may have been an interested one, but unemployment was rife and some enterprising families thought, as they still do today, that they had a better chance of raising their standard of living overseas. After the Restoration, however, opinion changed and the pamphleteers who wrote about such matters expressed the view that the country was in fact under-populated. Cromwell's forceful foreign policy gave an impulse to an expansion of foreign trade, and although the reign of King Charles II has not yet been subjected to full economic investigation, all the indications are that it was a time of rising national prosperity. Thus the economic and political uncertainty of the early part of the century encouraged colonization and, once it was shown to be profitable and could be made to flourish under the protection of naval power, it was pressed forward as a means to greater wealth.

If in the reign of King Charles II an informed statesman had been asked which were the most valuable colonies acknowledging allegiance to the King, he would probably have answered first Bermuda and the West Indies, secondly Newfoundland, thirdly the trading posts in India, fourthly the North American colonies, and lastly Africa. The first English settlement in the Atlantic arose from an accidental cause. In 1609 Sir George Somers and other leaders of an expedition on the way to Virginia were wrecked by a hurricane and thrown ashore on the uninhabited Bermuda Islands. The next Virginia charter was therefore made to include the Bermudas (called the Somers Islands after Sir George), which were first prized for their wild hogs. In 1615 a number of investors, mostly members of the Virginia Company, acquired a separate royal charter and planters settled there to cultivate tobacco. In 1625 another London merchant sent a small expedition to claim Barbados, which at first produced tobacco and cotton, and afterwards sugar. Later the Leeward Islands were occupied. Though a Puritan attempt to colonize the island of Providence partly for the purposes of privateering failed by 1641, when it was recaptured by the Spaniards, in 1654 a naval expedition sent by Cromwell took Jamaica after it had failed to throw the Spaniards out of San Domingo. Jamaica did not originally look a very promising conquest, but as it was the first overseas possession deliberately seized by an English Government, Cromwell determined that it should be successfully colonized, and even proposed to transplant to it the population of New England. To begin with, buccaneering was its most paying industry, but by the end of the century it had been successfully developed and replaced Barbados, which was much smaller, as the richest island. Barbados, however, was reckoned a 'pearl in the English Crown' throughout most of the century. In the middle of King Charles II's reign it had a white population of 20,000 and twice that number of Negro slaves. Some of the aristocratic planters became fabulously rich on the sugar trade. The Bahamas were settled in the reign of Charles II. Other islands, such as St Christopher and Tobago, were partly occupied by English planters, and though all of them were fought over, at the end of the century a roaring trade was being done throughout the group in sugar, tobacco, molasses, indigo, ginger, and cotton. The West Indian 'interest' was to colour much of the political and social history in the eighteenth century.

If in the West Indies fortunes were made out of sugar, in Newfoundland they came from fish. Discovered by John Cabot as early as the fifteenth century, this colony was valued first for the amount of cod that was caught off its coasts, and secondly as a training ground for fishermen. Fishermen crossed the Atlantic at the beginning of the season in March and returned by October of each year. They sailed chiefly from Devon and the west of England, and the Government deliberately discouraged a permanent settlement for fear that the full benefits of this area would then be lost to the Englishmen. In the first half of the century ten thousand men earned a living there and in the second half twenty thousand; but it did not even contain one sizeable village. Its chief product was dried cod, the gastronomic delight of the Portuguese and Spaniards, which was in great demand throughout the Mediterranean. However, there were conflicting claims between the west country fishermen, the handful of settlers, and the French, and in 1680 the Lords of Trade in England at last decided upon the appointment of a governor and the fortification of St John's, the largest of the very small settlements. But in spite of the definition of its status in the Treaty of Utrecht no regular governor was appointed until 1728. It remained a lonely and precarious but profitable outpost of the first British Empire.

When King James I made his treaty of peace with Spain in 1604 no recognition was given to the Spanish claim to prior rights in North America. Here possession was at least nine-tenths of the law, and soon English adventurers moved in. The first land to be permanently colonized by English settlers in the seventeenth century was the rich alluvial soil of Virginia, so named by Ralegh after Queen Elizabeth in 1584. A Virginia company was formed in 1606 as a semi-public undertaking that hoped to find gold. A first expedition sailed from London in December 1606, and Jamestown was founded in May 1607. The colonists themselves soon grew discouraged – no gold was discoverable – but there was surprising enthusiasm for the project in London and relief missions were sent out. Nevertheless, the colony was nearly abandoned owing to threat of starvation, but under a strong Governor, Sir Thomas Dale, the settlers managed to overcome all the hazards of pioneering, and in 1612 a first cargo of tobacco, which proved to be its most valuable crop, was dispatched to England. When in 1623 the company was on the verge of bankruptcy the King decided to abrogate the charter and the Crown took over control of a colony now consisting of 1,200 persons. Thenceforward it made steady progress. The output of tobacco increased and Negroes were imported as slaves. In 1623 Sir George Calvert (Lord Baltimore) who had been associated with the Virginia project, received a patent to establish a new colony north of Virginia, and thus Maryland, the first permanent proprietary colony, came into being in 1634. Here not only Roman Catholicism, the religion of the proprietor, but all other Christian beliefs were tolerated, and in spite of quarrels with its neighbour it soon became an economic success.

Meanwhile, in August 1620 the famous ship *Mayflower* had sailed from Plymouth with its load of dissenting emi-grants. These dissenters had originally fled from England to seek freedom for their Calvinist religion in Holland. But a grant of land was obtained for them from the Virginia Company, and in November 1620 they landed safely in Cape

Cod in New England (charted and named by Captain John Smith in 1614). Later, in March 1629, a group of wealthier Puritans received a royal charter for the Massachusetts Bay Company into which New Plymouth was ultimately absorbed. As in Virginia, these early settlers had a desperate struggle to survive the rigours of their first winters. But by 1642 there were 3,000 settlers in the area of New Plymouth and 16,000 in Massachusetts. From these colonies offshoots were established in New Hampshire and Maine in 1635, in Connecticut in 1636 and Rhode Island in 1638. Populated by the Puritan exodus during the period of Archbishop Laud's supremacy, they were always somewhat independent in spirit and were not reckoned profitable settlements in London. During the reign of King Charles II the Carolinas were founded (1663) and Pennsylvania, the Quaker colony, received its charter in 1682. During the second Dutch war New Amsterdam was conquered from the Dutch and renamed New York after the future King James II, and New Jersey and Delaware were also acquired by the peace treaty. Thus by the end of the seventeenth century twelve out of the original thirteen American colonies had been founded. With the exception of Maryland, Pennsylvania, Connecticut, and Rhode Island, all these were or had become crown colonies and a plan was put on foot in the reign of King Charles II to consolidate the five colonies in New England under one rule; but nothing came of this urge for administrative tidiness. However, an empire had definitely been established in North America; by the Treaty of Breda in 1667 the Dutch withdrew and the French only kept their settlements in Canada by the Peace of Utrecht, although they were to push down the Mississippi and were not to be thrust out of the centre of the Continent until the nineteenth century.

Meanwhile the English and Dutch had been fighting it out on the other side of the world. At first the traders of the East India Company which had been founded in 1600 hoped to rival the Dutch in the Far Eastern islands where they exchanged manufactures and bullion for spices and pepper. But under the ruthless direction of Jan Coen the Dutch drove out the English merchants who suffered a decisive defeat; this culminated in the torturing of the English community in the main East Indian entrepôt of Amboyna in 1623, said to have constituted 'one of the blackest deeds in history'. Be that as it may, the crime was successful and henceforward British trading efforts in Asia were concentrated on continental India where the Portuguese proved less dangerous competitors than the Dutch. By a local agreement of 1635 the Portuguese conceded English rights to trade in all Indian ports. A factory at Surat became the centre of British trade until the headquarters of the East India Company were in 1687 transferred to Bombay (acquired by the Crown in the Portuguese marriage treaty of 1661). Madras was occupied by English merchants in 1639, and by 1658 had become the largest factory on the east coast of India. The principal exports from India consisted of indigo and calicoes, but in 1700 the import of Indian printed calicoes was forbidden. The East India Company went through three phases in the seventeenth century. During the first it raised capital for each separate voyage; during the second it raised a 'terminable joint stock' for a period of years; during the third it became one of the first joint-stock companies in English history, but without practising the principle of limited liability. Sometimes it made high dividends and at other times it scarcely paid its way. It was much dependent on royal whims. King Charles I, for example, licensed 'interlopers' in the trade in 1635. Oliver Cromwell left the trade open to all comers in the first years of his Protectorate, but later granted the company a new charter. Then under King William III a rival company was set up, but in 1708 the two companies coalesced and remained the dominating body in India until the nineteenth century. The old company always had the advantage that it possessed many assets in the way of fixed capital in its forts, its guns and trading stations. The mere threat to put these up to auction was sufficient to compel rival merchants in the profitable trade to come to heel. The company not only suffered from jealous rivals and from wars with the natives and from

kings who hoped to acquire benefits by threatening to withdraw its charter, but also from critics who complained that
it violated the principles of good economic statesmanship by
exporting bullion. One of the earliest English economists,
Thomas Mun, who was a servant of the Company, defended
its policy in two brilliant pamphlets, the best known of
which is called *England's Treasure by Forraign Trade*, published posthumously in 1664. This pointed out that many
of the imports from India were re-exported and therefore
brought back the bullion originally risked. But his arguments did not carry complete conviction, and the East
Indian merchants, like the West Indian, were objects of
suspicion in the eighteenth century.

The African trade in the seventeenth century consisted
mainly of the export of slaves, punctuated by bankruptcies.
After three companies had gone bankrupt, the Royal Africa
Company was set up in 1672 and took over various forts and
produced various dividends. But ultimately it went the way
of the rest chiefly because it was unable to enforce its monopoly.

Just as the Duke of York was made Governor of the Royal
Africa Company which dealt in slaves, so in 1670 Prince
Rupert had been created first Governor of the Hudson's
Bay Company, which made money out of furs. Unlike the
other Stuart ventures into business, it has survived into our
own times.

Although many modern historians, notably American
scholars, have painstakingly investigated the question, one
cannot say with confidence that any clear picture of colonial
administration or political ideas emerges in the seventeenth
century. Most of the colonial constitutions provided for a
Governor, his Assistants, and a local assembly. Colonies were
freed from taxes and made their own laws (but broadly following the Common Law), and in return paid to the English Crown 5 per cent of the value of their exports and 5 per
cent of any precious metals found. At home various bodies
tried their hand at supervising the scattered, not to say haphazard, empire. In 1606 a Royal Council of Virginia was

set up; in 1634 King Charles I appointed a special colonial commission, including the two Archbishops. In 1660 an unwieldy advisory Council for Foreign Plantations was set up, but after five years colonial affairs reverted to the control of a committee of the Privy Council. In 1670 the Council for Foreign Plantations was born again, coalescing with the parallel Council for Trade, but after another five years a committee of the Privy Council again took charge, and for twenty years this body, now known as the Lords of Trade, conducted the business of colonial administration with some degree of success. On 15 May 1696, partly to protect himself from the clamours of Parliament ever eager for new spheres of influence, King William III formed a separate Board of Trade and Plantations which survived for many years. Through all these vicissitudes it was more or less accepted that the colonies were primarily the concern of the Crown or executive, and not of parliament. King James I and King Charles I were determined not to allow parliament to interfere in colonial affairs, and up till the Civil Wars parliament passed no act directly affecting the colonies. When the Parliamentarians triumphed over the King parliament appointed a Commission for Plantations which took control of all colonial matters for a time. In 1651 the Long Parliament passed the Navigation Act which confined the colonial export trade to English ships and was enforced sporadically against the Dutch carriers at whom it was chiefly aimed, while an earlier act of 1650 prohibited all commercial intercourse with the pro-Royalist colonies. But there was even during the Interregnum little intervention in the local affairs of the colonies, and after the Restoration the monarchy reasserted its prerogative of colonial administration. It is true that a second Navigation Act was passed in 1660, but it was promoted by the executive itself. The Act of 1660 tried to stop loopholes in that of 1651 and laid it down (broadly) that no goods might be imported from or exported to the colonies except in English-built and English-owned ships, and that certain 'enumerated' colonial products, such as sugar and tobacco, might only be shipped direct to England or to other

English colonies. This Act was supplemented by the Frauds Act of 1662, the Staple Act of 1663, and the Plantation Duties Act of 1673, known collectively as the Navigation Acts. These Acts were evaded by the colonists wherever possible (and it was particularly possible in war time) and though they might have been justified in so far as the security of the colonies depended ultimately on a vigorous mercantile marine, and in so far as the 'enumerated' commodities were given preference in the English market, the fact remains that they were excessively unpopular throughout the New World and ultimately contributed to the break-up of the first British empire. Yet they stood within the logic of the ideas of the century which regarded foreign plantations mainly as suppliers of goods that were needed and could not be produced at home or might be re-sold profitably abroad. These Navigation Acts were the only important instance of parliamentary concern with the colonies in the seventeenth century, for even after the Revolution King William III accepted the dependence of the colonies on the Crown.

As to the character of the administration, both King James I and King Charles I sought to promote some sort of centralized political control. But the confusion of the Interregnum facilitated decentralization, even though the Royalist colonies, such as Barbados and Virginia, were awed into submission. The English statesmen of the Restoration era set out to make the country rich as the centre of a trading empire, and nearly all the councils and committees that flourished under the later Stuarts worked hard and earnestly to promote this end. Dr J. A. Williamson is of the opinion that 'during this period the administration of the old empire reached its highest peak of efficiency'; yet general principles of colonial administration could not in fact be imposed on the heterogeneous possessions which constituted that empire and indeed when the late-seventeenth-century statesmen attempted to do so, as in the case of Jamaica under King Charles II or Massachusetts under King James II, they usually failed. Moreover, with advisory committees lacking executive power managing affairs in the first fifteen years of King Charles II's reign and the French war distracting attention under King William III and Queen Anne it was impossible for a centralized colonial administration to sustain any consistent policy other than that of safeguarding the economic interests of the homeland. Governors might be pestered with innumerable questionnaires and even inspections by roving commissions, but when they were three thousand miles away from Whitehall they had to pay more attention to the wishes of men on the spot than to the vague and variegated desires of a changing Crown. So, on the whole, seventeenth-century England rested content with an expanding and profitable field of foreign trade and did not raise – or at any rate wisely left unsettled – those constitutional problems that were to perplex many generations yet to come.

But England's principal colony in the seventeenth century was neither a West Indian sugar plantation nor an Indian fort struggling with the vagaries of the central administration thousands of miles from the capital, but an old English conquest across the St George's Channel, war-swept Ireland. Although Ireland had been conquered in the time of King Henry II and visited by King John and King Richard II, it had not been until the Reformation that a King of England, Henry VIII, also assumed the title of King of Ireland. Up to the Reformation the wars in Ireland had been of little more than local significance, but now religious complications supervened since the majority of the native Irish and the English lords who in earlier times had occupied the 'Pale' round Dublin still remained loyal to the old religion. In 1607 King James I struck the gong by publishing a proclamation against Jesuits, and when in 1609, because of the flight of two earls who had rebelled against the Crown, he decided to plant Ulster with English and Scottish colonists, this was to introduce a new Protestant colony amid a predominantly Roman Catholic community. The Lord Deputy of this time, Chichester, criticized the Ulster project as making too small a provision for native freeholders and the scheme was never fully carried out. Nevertheless, many

Scottish Presbyterians (fleeing before the attack on their own country) came to Ireland and were the source of much future trouble. After the retirement of Chichester in 1615 nothing much happened in Ireland until Sir Thomas Wentworth arrived to take up his post as Lord Deputy in 1633. While his period of rule benefited the country in some ways, for example, by the suppression of pirates and the promotion of the linen industry, his attempt to thrust the Thirty-Nine Articles down the throats of the Irish Catholics and Ulster Presbyterians was highly provocative, as was also his plan forcibly to plant large parts of Connaught with settlers. When he left to face his tragic death in England the Irish rebellion burst forth as a bolt from the blue; to begin with, there was 'a rising of a mob of unarmed peasants chiefly bent on plunder'; but soon the Anglo-Irish Lords of the Pale joined in confederation with the northern rebels and the insurrection then spread to all parts of the country. Though eventually King Charles I made a treaty with the confederate Irish against the English Parliamentarians, the Irish suffered for their temerity when they were defeated by Michael Jones and Oliver Cromwell. The arrival of a Papal envoy, Rinuccini, in 1645, to bring Ireland under the Pope had made the Puritans all the more determined to reconquer Ireland.

While Ireland was incorporated with England under the terms of the Instrument of Government (1653), the Irish Catholics were unrepresented in the English Parliament, many lost their lands and were told in effect to go 'to hell or Connaught', and others were transplanted to the West Indies. Nor did these loyal allies of the Stuarts receive much compensation at the Restoration. An Act of Settlement of 1665 was a compromise between the demands of the loyalists and the claims of the thousands of English Cromwellians and others who had been settled there during the Interregnum. It is possible that in the reign of King Charles II two-thirds of the land in Ireland belonged to the Protestant minority. And it was not until King James II came to the throne that hope of redress rose in Irish hearts. Nevertheless, a proposal by Lord Tyrconnel, King James's

Roman Catholic Lord Lieutenant, to upset the Act of Settlement was rejected by the Privy Council in 1688, and once again Irish Catholics marched to defeat under the Stuart banner at the battle of the Boyne. Promises held out by King William III of good terms for the Catholics at the peace of Limerick of 1691 were finally in 1697 broken by the Irish Parliament itself which now consisted entirely of Protestants. (Members of the Irish Parliament were compelled by an Act of 1691 to renounce the Catholic doctrine of transubstantiation.) From that point forward dated the period of Protestant ascendancy in Ireland. Ireland suffered every political, economic, and religious handicap. By espousing the cause of the Stuart Kings the Irish Catholics had not preserved their power, but merely sealed their doom for years to come. So the misery of Ireland and the Irish hatred of the English dated very largely from the seventeenth century.

If Ireland was treated as a colony throughout the seventeenth century and, whatever her political treatment, derived some material benefits from English trade, Scotland, in spite of the Stuart succession to the English Crown in 1603, was excluded from most of the advantages of English economic progress. And while the country remained extremely poor with little industry (even the capital, Edinburgh, had only some 20,000 inhabitants) it was torn, like Ireland, by religious conflicts. After abolishing the Roman Catholic religion without the consent of the reigning sovereign in 1560, the General Assembly of the Scottish Church had declared for Presbyterianism when King James VI (King James I of England) was still a minor. King James resented this, and by rupturing the alliance of the Scottish nobles with the Presbyterian Ministry by means of their wholesale bribery with Church lands he obtained the reintroduction of episcopacy and the imposition of a number of non-Presbyterian practices – such as kneeling at Communion – in the Five Articles of Perth. But, as in England, King James drove less furiously than did his son, King Charles I. King Charles alienated the Scottish nobility by the Act of Revocation (aimed to take lands from them) and in 1637 vainly tried to force Archbishop Laud's prayer-book on the Kirk, thus causing the Covenanters to spring from the earth in an incredible ardour of religious nationalism. Thenceforward Scottish and English history intertwined, the Scots going over to the offensive by trying to compel the Long Parliament to establish Presbyterianism in England as well as in Scotland. As with Ireland, Scotland entered into a legislative union with England under the Instrument of Government of 1653, but lost all her newly acquired rights at the Restoration.

The Navigation Act of 1660 excluded Scottish traders and shipping from the English colonies; the Recissory Act made null and void all legislation affecting Scotland passed since 1636. The Scottish bishops were again restored and after 1663 Scotland was largely governed by the Privy Council in which from 1669 Lauderdale was the presiding genius. Lauderdale himself had been a Presbyterian, and ruled with some sensibility. But both in 1666 and in 1679 the extreme Covenanters rose in arms and in 1685 the Earl of Argyll, who had already been condemned to death in the English Courts, invaded Scotland from Holland. There was a paradoxical situation throughout this century in that the majority of Scotsmen were keen monarchists – the Covenanters had fought well for King Charles II against Cromwell – but constant attacks on their Presbyterian religion had given rise to a republican movement in the Lowlands.

This republican feeling was reflected in the 'Claim of Right' put forward by the Scottish Convention after the Revolution of 1688, which maintained that the Scottish Estates had the right to depose any king who violated the laws of the land. The Revolution however more or less pacified the Lowlands, for episcopacy was again abolished as the national religion and for the last time a Calvinist ruled in London. In the Highlands the Roman Catholic clans were loyal to the exiled King James II and bloody battles had to be fought and the so-called 'massacre' of the MacDonald clan at Glencoe take place before they were reduced or suppressed.

So long as there was discontent in Scotland, she remained a threat to English security, a possible base for French invasion. On the other side, the Scots were firmly shut out from the benefits of English commerce and colonies and they burned their fingers badly when they tried to set up a colony of their own at Darien in Colombia. Thus both sides had reasons for wanting a legislative union.

Commissioners to negotiate the terms of such a union between the two countries were appointed soon after Queen Anne came to the throne, but on the English side there was an unwillingness to let the Scots share in their now expanding commercial and colonial advantages, and the Scots did not believe the English were in earnest. Meanwhile in Scotland there was an outburst of nationalism, stimulated by the political and religious freedom bestowed upon the country under William and Mary. The first Scottish Parliament of the new reign had a Whig majority – a striking contrast with the Tory majority in the English Parliament. Moreover, in spite of that Whig majority the Scottish Parliament demonstrated its independence by refusing to pass an act abjuring the old Pretender. They followed up this gesture of defiance by passing an Act of Security: this laid it down that if Queen Anne were to die without issue the Estates should not name the same sovereign to succeed to the throne of Scotland as to the throne of England unless 'there be such conditions of government settled and enacted as may secure the honour and sovereignty of this Crown and kingdom, the freedom, frequency and power of parliaments, the religion, freedom, and trade of the nation, from English or any foreign influence'. The Queen refused to give her assent to the Act, but later did so under a Scottish threat to withhold supplies. The revelation by the Queen's Commissioner in Scotland of a Jacobite plot there in 1704 underlined the dangers of a future separation of the two Crowns. The English Parliament of 1705 therefore retorted upon the Scots with an Aliens Act which would have imposed a complete embargo on all trade between Scotland and England if the Scots still refused to name the same successor to the two Crowns. The

Act also provided for the nomination of fresh Commissioners for Union. The Scottish leaders now realized that the game was up and even agreed to the Queen nominating the new commissioners. These commissioners set to work with a good will. Concessions were offered on both sides. The English showed financial generosity in granting a large sum to Scotland as compensation for her assuming a share of the English national debt. Henceforward Scotland was to be represented both in the English House of Lords and House of Commons and Scottish members were given the right to vote on all questions whether of domestic concern or not. In return the Scots at last agreed to the Hanoverian succession and gave up their own separate parliament. It is this last feature in the Act of Union, completed on 1 May 1707, that has always caused discontent among Scots. For their Parliament of 1702 was the freest and strongest they had ever known. After 1707, while they retained their own laws and their own Church, they were painfully conscious of being governed from London. Though they were not averse from driving along it, they reckoned that the road to England should not contain one-way traffic. Thus in many parishes of Scotland 1 May 1707 was observed as a day of fasting and humiliation. On the north shores of the Firth of Forth thirty-one whales were found dead, an ominous occurrence, and modern Scottish historians look back on that day with mixed feelings. One thing, however, is certain: the political unity conferred upon the British Isles by the Act of Union and the Scottish genius for statesmanship and business enterprise that was thus given a wider scope helped to complete the first British Empire, to construct the second, and to adorn the Commonwealth of later times.

CHAPTER XVI

England Under Queen Anne; the Augustan Age

ENGLAND was described by Daniel Defoe, the superb and knowledgeable reporter who toured the country in the reign of Queen Anne, as 'the most flourishing and opulent country in the world'. He was writing of the epoch after the Treaty of Utrecht had been signed, for during the war prices were high, taxation was stiff, and foreign trade was interrupted. Though at least one-quarter of the country was still uncultivated, though farmers were innocent of inventiveness, and though half of what was under the plough was still subject to the old wasteful 'open field' system, in the early eighteenth century there was considerable prosperity whenever the weather smiled – at any rate among those who owned their land. And throughout the countryside and in market places and the growing towns the daily affairs of life seemed a little more tolerable. If the poor were still badly off and a startling contrast with the very rich – who were richer then than they are today – real wages were higher than at any time since the reign of King Henry VI; fresh meat and wheaten bread were more generally eaten; poor rates were low; the kingdom had begun to bask in the warmth of a long and victorious peace.

While agriculture remained the chief national pursuit, the rising material well-being upon which Daniel Defoe remarked and most contemporary observers agreed, and which is confirmed by such fragmentary statistics as we now possess, came largely from commerce and industry. In the previous chapter we sketched the blooming of trade in what was to become the first British Empire, nurtured by sea power, military victories over England's main rivals, the French and the Dutch, and a thriving mercantile marine, blessed or at least protected by the Navigation Acts. Besides the profitable business in tobacco, sugar, furs, spices, and pepper, carried on within the Empire by the East India Company, the Hudson's Bay Company, and the independent merchants, a number of other companies and individuals were earning satisfactory profits elsewhere in the world. It has been roughly estimated that the value of British foreign trade increased threefold between the opening of the seventeenth century and the reign of Queen Anne, and if this estimate errs it is probably on the low side. British woollen cloth continued to be the principal article of export (its value was computed by a contemporary statistician at £2,000,000 a year at the time of the Revolution) and English merchants reaped rich returns for it in Northern and Central Europe. Up till 1689 the once famous Merchant Adventurers Company had monopolistic rights in the foreign trade of Central Europe; but its monopoly had been constantly challenged inside and outside parliament and after 1689 the export of cloth was thrown open to all except in the Levant, the Baltic, Russia, and Africa.

The Baltic trade had long been carried on by the Eastland Company which was particularly valued by statesmen because it not only exported cloth, but in exchange acquired stores that were essential to the British fleets. As in the case of the Merchant Adventurers, the Company's privileges were reduced towards the end of the seventeenth century, but it kept its exclusive rights in the Eastern Baltic. Its activities did not extend to Russia which was the province of a separate Muscovy Company. But business in Russia came almost to a standstill during the English Civil Wars since the Tsar disapproved of a people who cut off their sovereign's head, and while there was some revival in the reign of King Charles II, by the end of the century the trade had fallen into the hands of a small group. In 1699, however, the entrance fee into the Company was lowered from £50 to £5 and certain restrictions on membership removed. The change appears to have given an impulse to commerce with Muscovy and in 1762 the English were said to be 'entire masters' of the trade with Russia. The Levant trade was far less the property of the few and the members of the Company traded vigorously with the Turkish Empire and with Persia throughout the seventeenth and eighteenth centuries. As a price for its privileges the Company had to maintain an ambassador at Constantinople and consuls elsewhere, but its monopoly does not seem seriously to have hindered English trade in the Near East. After the middle of the century the growing import trade in currants from Greece was in separate hands. Up till the reign of Queen Anne commerce with our nearest neighbours, France, Spain, and Portugal, was not the perquisite of any exclusive company. With France we were invariably at war of some kind, but a substantial cloth export trade was done with Spain, and our business relations with Portugal improved after a treaty concluded by Cromwell's Government in 1654 and another signed by John Methuen in 1703 which brought about the exchange of cloth and port wine. In 1710 Robert Harley as Lord Treasurer thought up a wonderful scheme for prising benefits out of the coming peace settlement. The holders of the floating debt were incorporated under an act of parliament passed in that year into a joint-stock company to which was given the monopoly of trade with the Spanish possessions in South America. Thus the creditors of the State were guaranteed their rate of interest out of the profits which would supposedly be obtained from an exclusive trade in the 'South Sea'. Fundamentally it was a political scheme aimed against the Whigs, as the Land Bank had been before it. Harley became Governor of the Company and when the Administration exacted at the peace of Utrecht the monopolistic right to export slaves to South America, it appeared as if the fortunes of the shareholders would be made. But they were to be unmade in the catastrophe known as the 'South Sea Bubble' in 1720.

With the exceptions of the South Sea Company and the East India Company most of the seventeenth-century trading companies were what were known as 'regulated companies'; that is to say, they obtained complete control of a particular foreign market, but any merchant who cared to join the company, pay its dues, and obey its regulations, might share in the benefits of its monopoly. The companies generally laid down minute regulations and confined the trade to men who were primarily merchants and not shop-keepers. But any genuine merchant might stake his capital and enter the trade. Thus foreign commerce was by no means as exclusive as the casual reader of seventeenth-century parliamentary debates and controversial pamphlets might imagine. Moreover wars and political disturbances at home frequently enabled enterprising free-lances to break into foreign trade without in fact joining the companies. The companies for their part were burdened with heavy obligations; they were often compelled to pay dues and lend money to the government and to be responsible for the up-keep of diplomatic offices and military posts. But by the end of the century the voices of envy aroused by their commercial successes had swollen to a clamour, and the word 'monopoly' was ugly in seventeenth-century ears, familiar with the financial devices of Queen Elizabeth I and King James I. In the reign of William and Mary a number of trading monopolies were destroyed and complaints were even put forward in the House of Commons when the Levant Company sought to confine its membership to recognized merchants. On the whole, in those days it was the Whigs, sitting on the throne of commercial power, who were the protectionists and the Tories who were free traders, but the underprivileged merchants were scarcely galvanized by those theoretical principles that were erected into a phil-osophy by Adam Smith and Richard Cobden. And it may be questioned whether an 'open trade' at an earlier date would have added materially to the wealth of England, more especially as (apart from cloth) a good many exports ap-pear to have consisted of goods brought to London under the protection of the Navigation Acts and thence resold to overseas markets. One thing at least is certain as we reach the peaceable close of a century of fierce energy in every direction – that commerce was already becoming the life's blood of the island. Differences between town and country were becoming less marked. The squires had become business men; and the successful business men became squires. It was significant that a Tory Government, which represented the gentry rather than the merchant class, should have laboured so unscrupulously to secure a peace conspicuously beneficial to British oversea trade.

If British foreign trade was expanding fast in the reign of Queen Anne, it was because it was solidly founded on industrial progress. The general character of that progress, amounting to a minor industrial revolution in the seventeenth century, has already been outlined. The cloth industry was saved from stagnation by the trade in the 'new' lighter 'draperies' and the opening of fresh markets, while the existence of the now established coal industry permitted the development of other promising industries. Travellers to Newcastle noted, for example, how the glass and salt works were assisted by the burning of coal. The silk industry, hitherto chiefly a French or Italian speciality, began to take root here through the enterprise of French Protestant immigrants who arrived in search of political asylum. Great capitalists, equally interested in commerce and industry, such as Sir John Winter and Sir Josiah Child, had appeared and business was no longer looked down upon as a pursuit unfit for a gentleman. As early as the Restoration three thousand merchants were counted at the Royal Exchange. Later the reform of the coinage and the Bank of England had given buoyancy to industrial enterprise. 'Behind and underlying the world of Pope and Addison', wrote Professor G. D. H. Cole of the reign of Queen Anne, 'was a new world of bourgeois habits and culture, which, still insignificant politically even after 1688, was swiftly building itself up into the most powerful force in the nation.' The considerable degree of industrialization was not confined to the 'domestic' or 'commission' system of work. Though yarn might still be spun in country cottages, weaving was increasingly done in workshops. Thus small capitalists began to flourish, as well as their bigger brethren whose investments were necessary to the coal and iron industries and to large-scale foreign trade. Progress was somewhat restricted by the poor condition of the roads which handicapped transport. But many goods were moved along the rivers or by coastal shipping. Defoe remarked upon the activity in the ports, especially at Liverpool, centre of the colonial trade, 'one of the wonders of Britain' – contrasting with a still modest Manchester which he called the 'greatest mere village in England'. But London kept its astonishing pre-eminence.

The London of Queen Anne's day impressed every contemporary with its enormous size and population. It was perhaps fifteen or twenty times the size of any other British town and Defoe remarked on the prodigious increase in its buildings within his own memory. Still it had not yet subdued the country. It was still possible to shoot woodcock in Regent Street. And as at the start of the seventeenth century it was a town of deep contrasts. On the one side was the Mall filled with lovely ladies and the houses of the great in St James's Square. On the other side were the brutalized criminals of Bridewell and Bedlam and an underworld described in all its horror by Ned Ward in *The London Spy*. Sir Christopher Wren had fashioned a handsome city after the Great Fire of 1666, but not as handsome as he would have wished. St Paul's Cathedral was a long time rebuilding: its dome was completed in 1710, but the whole was not finished until 1717. Around the immense new structure were to be found picture sellers offering smutty prints, blind ballad singers, and numerous stalls of nuts and gingerbread. The river was a grand highway, London Bridge was embellished with new buildings, and the Tower was a zoo as well as a prison. London was not only the seat of government, but a busy market place and the liveliest port in the world. Sir Christopher Wren, Nicholas Hawksmoor, and Sir John Vanbrugh, playwright as well as architect, were glorifying English architecture and compensated for a lack of distinguished native-born musicians and painters. Sir Godfrey Kneller, one of the long line of British portrait painters of this age, was, it is true, depicting courtiers and leading members of society – as William Dobson, John Greenhill, Samuel

Cooper, Robert Walker, John Riley, Mary Beale, and others did in the seventeenth century. But poetry and architecture were the outstanding native arts. The 'Queen Anne' style of architecture was enhanced by elegant furniture, by the carvings of the Dutchman, Grinling Gibbons, and by grand-father clocks of oriental design that still survive. For the well-to-do it was a world worth living in.

It is difficult to determine how far this increase in material prosperity affected the religious life of the community. But it is certain that the relative degree of domestic peace and of toleration that existed after the accession of William and Mary somewhat reduced passions inside and outside the Church of England. The teachings of the Cambridge Platon-ists and other moderate theologians on the one hand, and the natural reaction against the excesses of Puritanism on the other had already created a powerful Broad or Low Church movement in the reign of King Charles II. These were Christians who set more store upon a decent life than on the sacraments and ritual. And though there were High Churchmen both before and after the revolution of 1688 who had a different point of view they stood far less near to Roman Catholicism than Laud had done before or Keble was to do later. Indeed the High Church attitude of mind manifested itself not so much in its dogma and ritualistic demands as, at its best, in the behaviour of the Non-jurors, who could not reconcile their consciences to abandoning their sworn loyalty to King James II and, at its worst, in attacks upon those who remained outside the State Church. In 1700 another act against Roman Catholics was passed to cap the penal code and throughout the whole of Queen Anne's reign the assault was continued against the practice of occasional conformity for political reasons. When the Act against Occasional Conformity was finally passed in 1710 it was supplemented by the Schism Act aimed at Noncon-formist schools. Between the High Church majority in the House of Commons and the Whig majority in the House of Lords long fights were waged over questions of religious toleration and discipline, while similar contests took place between the Lower House of Convocation, containing the representatives of the clergy, and the Upper House with its platoon of Whig bishops. But restrictions on freedom of worship were often ignored or avoided. And when Dr Sacheverell preached his sermon at St Paul's Cathedral condemning as iniquitous the principles of the Revolution this was the last fling of High Anglican intolerance in a losing battle within the Church that lasted all through the reign of Queen Anne.

But in spite of the excitement aroused by the sermons and the trial of Dr Sacheverell, passions over religious questions were not nearly so strong as they had been a hundred years earlier. The Church was now less vulnerable and more closely allied with society. The clergy were becoming more respectable and better class. Whereas at the beginning of the seventeenth century most of the parish clergy were scarcely distinguishable from their parishioners (as in Ireland in modern times), they 'now stood midway between the low social position they had occupied in the Middle Ages and the high social position to which they attained under the House of Hanover'. (Trevelyan.) As a result of the institution of Queen Anne's Bounty in 1704 – a fund for improving the pay of poorer clergy – and the introduction of certain other clerical privileges their economic position was bettered and in the late eighteenth century the parson came to rank after the squire in the village hierarchy. But the squire set the tone. Sir Roger de Coverley was represented as suffering nobody to sleep in church except himself. The good examples given by such worthy bishops as Stillingfleet, Tenison, Tillotson, and Burnet afforded a pattern of reasonable Christianity; the Book of Common Prayer, restored like the bench of Bishops after the turmoil of the Civil War, was the accepted guide to unfanatical worship.

Outside the Church the Nonconformists no longer agitated violently, but were content to remain on the defensive. Now that they were allowed to meet in their own chapels all they wanted to ensure was that their right to conduct their own services and to bring up their own children in their own religion was not interfered with; they did not desire to be 'comprehended' in any way within the Church of England. To safeguard the sanctity of their meeting houses, they even preferred to sacrifice their political rights. If, as the cynics said, the Madonna of the Church of England was now Queen Elizabeth of blessed memory, the Nonconformists found their saints in the eloquent preachers in their own congregations. So Christians became content with things as they were. And religion gradually sank into a torpor from which it was to be shaken first by the clarion call of Wesley and Whitfield and later by the Oxford Apostles of the early nineteenth century.

But something more happened than that. As sacramental religion was pushed into the background, so the importance of moral precepts became more widely appreciated. The outrageous behaviour of the leaders of society at the Courts of King Charles II and King James II was frowned upon at the Court of Queen Anne. And following the example of the Queen popular writers and teachers inculcated the virtues of decent and charitable conduct and the 'reformation of manners'. The banners of the S.P.C.K. and the S.P.G. were lifted over the home counties as well as the Empire. London and the ports had their underworlds, as they always have; and the rich and powerful were always liable to prescribe their own moral codes in private life, as they have done from King Charles II to King Edward VII. Yet if the Puritans had on the surface suffered defeat at the Restoration and the Church of England had survived the heaviest onslaught in its history, nevertheless Puritanism as an attitude of mind had gained a resounding victory. Though the dissenters in Queen Anne's reign might still have to fight as best they could to preserve the inviolability of their congregations, they no longer needed to battle for their faith. For, by and large, the active religious life of the whole of England, as of most of Scotland and Wales, had become Puritan.

The spirit of toleration which differentiated the eighteenth from the seventeenth century owed not a little to the writings of John Locke which influenced his contemporaries in the realm of philosophy as profoundly as did the discoveries of Newton in the schools of science. Locke, the son of a Puritan, enjoyed an Oxford education and found a patron in the first Earl of Shaftesbury, the Whig leader. After Shaftesbury's fall Locke fled to Holland and returned to England with King William III. Most of his books were published in the five years after the Glorious Revolution, and when he died in 1704 his political, philosophical, and religious theories had been absorbed by the English educated classes in an astonishing manner. In many ways Locke was a typical English philosopher, for he had neither the logical precision of the French nor did he draw the ponderous conclusions of the Germans. He rejoiced in common sense, distrusted metaphysics, and has been called the father of empiricism, that is to say, of the doctrine that all knowledge comes from experience. In his view propositions have probability rather than certainty and the grounds of probability are their conformity with one's own experience or the testimony of the experience of others. Though he was a Christian of sorts, he observed that 'revelation must be judged by reason' and condemned the 'enthusiasm' of the extreme Puritan sects as contrary to that love of truth which he prized so highly. That is why the late Professor Laski called him the first secular philosopher. In his teaching on ethics Locke was a utilitarian': 'things are good or evil,' he wrote, 'only in relation to pleasure or pain. That we call "good" which is apt to cause or increase pleasure, or diminish pain in us.' But his common sense told him that this doctrine would soon lead him into difficulties if it were pressed too far.

Locke's philosophical and ethical ideas were published in his *Essay Concerning Human Understanding* (1690) and his case for freedom of thought in three *Letters on Toleration*. His political philosophy was expounded in two *Treatises on Government* (1690). The *Treatises on Government* are generally held to have furnished the theoretical or scientific apology for the Revolution of 1688, although they were certainly written much earlier under the influence of Shaftesbury. Locke refuted the accepted Tory view of an absolutist monarchy deriving from a patriarchal view of society. The first part of his two *Treatises of Government* was, like the posthumously published work of Algernon Sidney, devoted to answering the arguments of Sir Robert Filmer's *Patriarcha*. Locke denied that men were born into political subjection because they were born into subjection to their parents. On the contrary, Locke believed that men were born free and equal and that God had not put any one man above any other. He was deeply concerned to overthrow the doctrine that hereditary monarchy belonged to the natural order of things. For above all he was the friend of Shaftesbury who had aimed to prevent the succession of the Roman Catholic James II to the English throne. He was little interested in Hobbes's theories (though he seems to have read *Leviathan*) for at the time when he was writing his *Treatises* 'at the level of practical politics Hobbes had not then a fraction of the importance of Filmer'. (Cranston.)

What Locke set out to prove was that governments are not supreme and untrammelled authorities and may be overthrown by society if they violate the principles for which they are established. There was nothing startlingly novel about this argument. From the time when the great emperors and popes had struggled against each other in Western Europe, publicists had been found to argue that human government, unlike the divine, was based upon a 'contract' and evil rulers could justifiably be overthrown if they broke it. In the sixteenth century, after the Reformation, both Calvinist and Jesuitical authors had occasion to express this opinion so as to encourage the assassination of sovereigns of whose religion they disapproved. By the mid seventeenth century it was common form among the opponents of King Charles I to maintain the King was 'a King by contract' – the contract being proved by the terms of his coronation oath – and that he might be deposed because he had not kept it. But Locke went much further than that. He claimed that men had certain inalienable rights that no government could touch and illustrated this by drawing a picture of a 'state of nature' before governments existed, in which men were free and equal and no one was bound by other than moral obligations. In addition he described a 'law of nature' or 'reason' which taught all mankind that 'no one ought to harm another in his life, health, property or possessions'. The difficulty was, however, that in a 'state of nature' every man had himself to be the judge in his own cause and enforce the 'law of nature' or 'reason' as best he could. The characteristic therefore of the 'state of nature' was 'want of a common judge'. Thus in fact, although Locke argued against it, the state of nature he thought about could easily have degenerated into the 'state of war' which Hobbes for his part had seen as the natural condition of mankind before governments came into being. All these imaginary pictures of a state of nature have, of course, no historical validity – they were used both by Hobbes and by Locke to give substance and clarity to their arguments.

'The great and chief end of men uniting in common-wealths', wrote Locke, 'and putting themselves under government, is the preservation of their property; to which in the state of nature there are many things wanting.' Government is therefore created as a trusteeship to protect life, liberty, and property – and, above all, property. But governments must be careful not to trespass over the boundaries for which they have been constituted; and to prevent abuse of power the legislature, the most important branch, the executive, and the judiciary must be kept separate. The State, in fact, preserved from degenerating into tyranny by checks and balances, was a 'gigantic limited liability company' (Laski), and if it overstepped the mark the citizens could destroy it by force, as they did in 1688. Hobbes would have argued that this is not a system of government at all, but of anarchy; but Locke would have answered that the Glorious Revolution proved his point – that civil society could survive the destruction of the government. Locke's political ideas spread like wildfire. They were taken to France by Voltaire and by Montesquieu (who misunderstood them). They are embedded, along with those of Algernon Sidney, in the venerated and venerable American Constitution, though the Founding Fathers 'took him up in a sense which he cannot be said to have contemplated'. (Laslett.) His ideas endured as the characteristic political philosophy of the governing classes of Great Britain for about two hundred years.

Though the name of the atheistical philosopher of Malmesbury, the timid Hobbes, was rarely mentioned in polite society, Tory or Whig, even the most extreme Tories paid lip service to John Locke, the Whig Aristotle. His empirical, rationalist, utilitarian, and liberal approach to life was reflected in many of the writings and speeches of his contemporaries. But it must be remembered that he was regarded (wrongly) as the apologist for the Revolution of 1688 rather than as a pure theorist, and most of them had been through the same experiences together and had learned the same lessons. Daniel Defoe, for example, the finest journalist – or at any rate industrial correspondent – of his time, had, like Locke, been born into a dissenting family and was educated at a nonconformist academy. He, too, had been a keen supporter of King William III and an active apologist for religious liberty. But he went too far when in 1702 he published his *Shortest Way with the Dissenters*, a study in irony which was mistaken for the real thing and brought him to prison and the pillory. However, Harley procured his release and thus this former Whig pamphleteer and shopkeeper temporarily found himself ranged on the Tory side. Defoe's ability to mix fact with fiction and view his principles with an eye to the main chance makes his work a little difficult to assess objectively; for his reporting is sometimes too imaginative and his fiction occasionally too matter-of-fact. But in *Robinson Crusoe*, published in the next reign, his genius found its right vehicle. Richard Steele (1672–1729), like Defoe, had some unfortunate business experiences before he found a livelihood in journalism. He planned *The Tatler* as a thrice-weekly periodical, blending the services of a newspaper and a society magazine. He and Joseph Addison (1672–1719) interpreted to their readers 'the new enlightened religion of the middle classes', the religion of John Locke. Their public was the serious, progressive-minded citizenry which frequented the coffee-houses of Queen Anne's time. *The Tatler*, started in April, 1709, was succeeded by *The Spectator*, which owed more to Addison as *The Tatler* owed most to Steele. Daniel Defoe also had his paper, *The Review*, which was more satirical and economic than *The Tatler* and *The Spectator* and survived the changing fashions in demand better than they did.

Defoe, Steele, and Addison are the three leading literary figures in the so-called 'Augustan Age' of Queen Anne. Two greater authors, Jonathan Swift and Alexander Pope, belong more to a later time, though Swift published his *Tale of a Tub* in 1704 and Pope his two long poems *Essay on Criticism* and *The Rape of the Lock* towards the end of Queen Anne's reign. Neither of them was a simple character: Swift, a clergyman despite himself, moved sardonically and rather unhappily through a world in which he was determined not to be snubbed; Pope, a dwarf with a Roman Catholic upbringing, glorified with his wit and genius the Lockian approach to life.

It was in the reign of Queen Anne that the real origins of the modern newspaper and periodical may be discovered, though shadowy prototypes, for which excessive claims are often made, are scattered over the history of the whole seventeenth century. The first daily newspaper, *The Daily Courant*, was published in the opening months of Queen Anne's reign and seven daily newspapers existed when she died. A provincial press also came into being in the reign. Robert Harley, a statesman who patronized authors, understood the value of newspapers as organs of propaganda, and also contributed to the study of English history by means of a fine collection of manuscripts, now in the British Museum, employed Swift (who began as a Whig), Defoe, Matthew Prior, and Dr John Arbuthnot in justifying his peace policy of 1710–13. Dean Swift contributed a masterly pamphlet, *The Conduct of the Allies*. Sarah, Duchess of Marlborough, retorted by inducing the Whigs to hire Steele and Addison, but Harley got in first and his pamphleteers won the battle of words.

But amid all the true wit and calculated vituperation lavished upon the reading public in the reign of Queen Anne one fact stands out: the whole atmosphere differed markedly from that of the reigns of King Charles II and King James II. If the force of the Puritan rebellion against the monarchy had spent itself, so, too, had the Royalist revenge. Harley was influenced by a Presbyterian father. Steele had been the author of *The Christian Hero* and in *The Tatler* had stated that he was 'of the Society for the Reformation of Manners'. *The Spectator* was said to consist of 'literary pamphlets concerned with morals and manners'. Steele once wrote that 'to love Lady Elizabeth Hastings was a liberal education', a proper sentiment, no doubt, but a very different tone from that used by the literary figures of Dryden's age. The theatre, too, was much more respectable, warned by Jeremy Collier's *Short View of the Immorality and Profaneness of the English Stage* (1698) – a successor to William Prynne's *Histrio-mastrix*, which scarified the theatre before it fell at the blast of the Puritan trumpets. Dryden had died in 1700 and Congreve ceased to write plays; *King Lear* was given a happy ending, Addison's *Cato* was reckoned the peak of polite drama, and over Queen Anne's stage Colley Cibber, actor, author, and impresario, breathed the lukewarm air of the new morality. Beside this new morality, stemming from the Puritans, the seedy side of life throbbed on still. One can read about it, if one wants to, in the outspoken reports of Ned Ward, a talented rogue out of his time. Moreover, some of the practitioners of the new manners and morals might come in for some rough cross-examination at a Puritan Seat of Judgement. But these cross-currents and contrasts, these pious overtones and unscrupulous methods of public and private conduct, are part and parcel of the history of modern England, conferring on us more often than we care to realize it the name of 'Perfide Albion' and a reputation for hypocrisy. The fascination of seventeenth-century history in fact is that as we move from Tudor absolutism, through the great divide of the Civil Wars, past the Royalist reaction when the last remnant of a medieval public economy vanished, and over the Glorious

Revolution, sanctified by the Christian rationalist, John Locke, we realize that we are coming forward towards the kind of country and society into which we ourselves were born.

Yet as we gaze back over the huge seventeenth-century landscape we must never overlook two important differences between then and now, the one in politics, the other in economic life. When we remark on the triumph of the House of Commons, the rise of party, and the beginnings of Cabinet government, we must also observe that the vast majority of the English people had no vote at general elections and no say in local affairs. And while we may take note that there were no such fences between the social classes as then existed elsewhere in Europe and that an apprentice might become an earl, we should recall that the gulf between rich and poor was far wider and deeper than it is now. It is a pardonable exaggeration to say, as Disraeli did more than a hundred years afterwards, that England was for the few – and the very few.

CHAPTER XVII

Epilogue: The Death of Queen Anne

CHARLES TALBOT, first Duke of Shrewsbury, is one of the odder figures in English history. With an established reputation for timidity he yet all his life assumed principal parts at times of crisis without possessing anything much more than an inherited position and a compelling charm of manner to sustain them. When he was very young his father had died soon after fighting a duel with the second Duke of Buckingham over his mother's dishonour: at the age of nine Charles Talbot was a wealthy earl; at the age of twenty-eight he was an architect of the Glorious Revolution, having signed the letter of invitation to William of Orange; when he was forty-two he boasted of having been offered and having refused nearly all the 'great places' in the kingdom. After his late marriage to an eccentric Italian countess he became almost amenable to the temptations and responsibilities of high office and temporarily forgot his customary hypochondria. His entry into Godolphin's Ministry as Lord Chamberlain in 1710 had been the first indication that the Queen was tiring of her famous war-winning administration. Suddenly, in 1713, after taking part in the final negotiations for the Treaty of Utrecht with his new Tory colleagues, Shrewsbury disappeared into Ireland as Lord Lieutenant. His return to London in June 1714 was, as it proved, the signal for the last political crisis in the reign of Queen Anne.

After the Peace of Utrecht the two chief Tory Ministers, Robert Harley, Earl of Oxford, the Lord Treasurer, and Henry St John, Viscount Bolingbroke, the principal Secretary of State, had fallen foul of each other. They had both enjoyed the Queen's confidence and behind them pranced a Tory majority in both House of Parliament, which had been confirmed, if not strengthened, in the general election of September 1713. But the future stretched mistily ahead. In December 1713 the widowed Queen, long racked by her gout, was taken more seriously ill and the question at once arose whether the Tory Government should remain loyal to the Act of Settlement and prepare for the accession of the statutory heir, the eighty-four-year-old Sophia, Electress of Hanover, or attempt to place the son of King James II, the Old Pretender, on the throne. The Queen was known to have a warm spot for her half-brother; Bolingbroke and his agents had flirted with the Jacobites during the early stages of the peace negotiations; and although perhaps half the Tory party, known colloquially as the Whimsicals, were ready to welcome the Protestant Succession, the Cavalier ghosts still walked and many country squires would have preferred to see, instead of an aged German princess, the grandson of King Charles the Martyr back in an English palace – provided he would change his religion. So in February 1714 Oxford informed the Pretender that if he would renounce Roman Catholicism the Government would try to persuade the Queen to name him as her successor and ask Parliament to repudiate the Act of Settlement. But the Pretender, a chip of the old block, preferred the Mass to London. It was a rebuff from which Oxford's divided Government never recovered. Meanwhile the Electress Sophia, whose ambition was to die Queen of England, was energetic in her own interest. She asked that her grandson (the future King George II), who had been made Duke of Cambridge in 1711, should be allowed to take his seat in the House of Lords. Queen Anne, who hated all talk of, let alone the sight of, her Hanoverian successors, was exceptionally annoyed, and Bolingbroke wrote sharply to the Electress about her request. Thereupon on 28 May the Electress expired, according to some, in distress at the rebuke she had received.

After that accomplishment Bolingbroke turned to the congenial task of unhorsing his chief. He pushed the Schism Bill against the Nonconformists through the Houses of Parliament with all the conviction of one who was not himself a Christian. Oxford, whose wife and child attended chapel, sat glowering in the Lords and refused to vote. The Duke of Shrewsbury also abstained. And as Parliament was about to rise for the summer recess a counter-attack was launched against Bolingbroke, who was accused along with the Queen's favourite, Lady Masham, of corruption in connexion with the new Spanish treaty. The quarrel transferred itself from Westminster to the Cabinet Council. The invalid Queen, barely recovered from her latest illness, had been pressed from many sides to get rid of the Lord Treasurer. The case against him was personal rather than public. Though still capable of passion and intrigue, he had become sick, sodden, and lazy. 'He often', complained the Queen, 'came drunk. He behaved himself towards me with bad manners, indecency, and disrespect.' After a distasteful scene on 27 July, Oxford was summarily dismissed, much as Godolphin and Marlborough had been before him. But Bolingbroke was again disappointed. His dissipated life and dubious transactions militated against his promotion. Already the Queen had refused him an earldom; now she would not give him the vacant office of Lord Treasurer, of which the symbol was the White Staff. Yet for two days he was all-powerful; but he proved himself irresolute. He did not know whether at once to form a Jacobite Cabinet so as to call over the inflexible Pretender, if the Queen should die (but then she might not die), or to try to come to terms with the Whig Opposition and stake all on the Hanoverian Succession. The Whigs now, as in 1688, knew where they stood and had allies in the Whimsical Tories. The Duke of Marlborough, who had exiled himself abroad after his disgrace, had received a commission from the new Elector of Hanover to become commander-in-chief if the Queen should die, and was making ready to come home. If Bolingbroke had seriously attempted to plan for a Jacobite Restoration, the events of 1688 might well have repeated themselves; but no blood would have flowed, for once again the majority of the English people who cared did not want a Popish king.

Such was the position when the Duke of Shrewsbury took

control. He acted together with the Duke of Somerset, another moderate, whose wife now seems to have supplanted Lady Masham in the changeable affections of the Queen, and with the second Duke of Argyll, the most powerful magnate in Scotland who had distinguished himself by promoting the Act of Union and by fighting gallantly at Ramillies, Oudenarde, and Malplaquet. With them stood a number of younger statesmen and soldiers who had no Jacobite taint on their spiritual escutcheons. On 30 July a Privy Council met in Kensington Palace where Queen Anne now lay desperately ill. A large meeting gathered there, including Somerset and Argyll, who were not members of the Government. It was unanimously agreed that the Queen should be asked to nominate Shrewsbury as the new Lord Treasurer in place of Oxford. At one o'clock the Duke went into the Queen's bedchamber and received the White Staff from her dying hands. Whether she realized what she was doing is not certain.

A hundred and eleven years had passed since the Queen's great-grandfather, King James I, had left Scotland for England. He had known he was going into a prosperous land where he expected to be absolute. Now, after years of war against Spain, Holland, and France, the country was perhaps thrice as prosperous as it had been then; the Crowns of England and Scotland had at last united, as he had desired; and a British oversea Empire had come into being. But in spite of all the prerogative powers that the monarchy might still claim, absolutism was finished. It had vanished in the civil wars and was buried after the Glorious Revolution. In the reign of King Charles II political parties had been born and old stagers in the reign of Queen Anne were still deploring the 'detested names' of Whig and Tory. Also under King Charles II a modern Cabinet, though without a Prime Minister and usually presided over by the monarch, had begun to take shape and in the following reigns 'Inner Cabinets' had made major decisions. The House of Commons had risen to pre-eminence in the State and had forwarded Acts of Parliament that pared the powers of the throne. The spirit of puritanism, driven down at the Restoration, had gradually infected society and if in the Occasional Conformity Act of 1711 and the Schism Act of 1714 the principles of exclusive Anglicanism enjoyed their Indian summer, toleration and rationalism were coming into their own under their prophet, John Locke, and these Acts were in fact dead letters. Queen Anne was the last ruler to 'touch' her subjects to cure them of scrofula, 'the King's Evil'; she was the last sovereign to veto an act of Parliament; the last to preside constantly over her Cabinets; and the last who could hope, and indeed partly managed, to be the ultimate ruler of England 'above parties'. If the powers of the monarchy were to remain considerable until the reign of George III, the government had to use more subtle methods than those of the early Stuarts to maintain their authority.

So on Sunday, 1 August 1714, a phase in the history of England ended. Shrewsbury and his colleagues had completed every necessary military and civil preparation for the succession of King George I, who was thus able to make a leisurely entry into a sober and peaceable country whose language and politics he did not understand. On 2 August, John Arbuthnot, Tory author of *The History of John Bull*, who was also one of Queen Anne's doctors, wrote to Dean Swift:

My dear mistress's days were numbered even in my imagination, and could not exceed certain limits; but of that small number a great deal was cut off by the last troublesome scene of contention among her servants. I believe sleep was never more welcome to a weary traveller than death was to her.

BIBLIOGRAPHY

Bibliography

A Note on Further Reading

The second edition of the *Bibliography of British History, Stuart Period, 1603–1714*, edited by the late Godfrey Davies and revised by Mary Frear Keeler, was published in 1970. Although it contains a few omissions and does not in fact include several important books published after 1965, it is indispensable for the deep study of the subject. There are also *A Select Bibliography of British History, 1660–1760*, by C. L. Grose (1939); W. T. Morgan, *Bibliography of British History 1700–1715* (1937); W. C. Abbott, *Bibliography of Oliver Cromwell* (1929): this has to be supplemented by Paul H. Hardacre, 'Writings on Oliver Cromwell since 1929' in vol. XXX of the *Journal of Modern History* (1961). Recently Professor W. L. Sachse has published a bibliography which covers the reign of Charles II. A. T. Milne, *Writings on British History*, contains valuable bibliographical information; this has been published annually. Select bibliographies are in Godfrey Davies, *The Early Stuarts, 1603–1660* (2nd ed. 1959) and Sir George Clark, *The Later Stuarts, 1660–1714* (2nd ed. 1956). Ivan Roots, *The Great Rebellion* (1966, under revision) and G. E. Aylmers ed., *The Interregnum* (1972) contain useful bibliographies of the middle period.

For constitutional history the most up-to-date book is J. P. Kenyon, *The Stuart Constitution: Documents and Commentary* (1966); this supersedes earlier collections of constitutional documents and has a good bibliography. Professor Kenyon takes constitutional history in a broad sense, but Andrew Browning, *English Historical Documents 1660–1714* (1953) is more comprehensive in its scope. A similar volume to cover the period 1603–1660 is promised. A number of American historians have written about constitutional history during the period, including M. A. Judson, *The Crisis of the Constitution: an Essay in Constitutional and Political Thought in England 1603–1645* (1949); W. B. Mitchell, *The Rise of the Revolutionary Party in the English House of Commons 1603–1629* (1957); T. L. Moir, *The Addled Parliament of 1614* (1958); Clayton Roberts, *The Growth of Responsible Government in Stuart England* (1966); Robert E. Ruach,

The Parliament of 1624 (1972); F. D. Wormuth, *The Royal Pre-rogative 1603–1649* (1939); and Robert Zaller, *The Parliament of 1621* (1971). These books vary considerably in quality. W. A. Aiken and Basil Duke Henning, eds., *Conflict in Stuart England* is a collection of essays published in 1960 in honour of Wallace Notestein who inspired so much research into parliamentary history. Valuable books by British scholars are J. P. Kenyon, *The Popish Plot* (1972); Betty Kemp, *King and Commons, 1660–1832* (1957); J. R. Jones, *The First Whigs: the Politics of the Exclusion Crisis 1678–1683* (1961); C. Russell, *The Crisis of Parliaments* (1971); and David Underdown, *Pride's Purge* (1971). The essays in *The Interregnum: The Quest for Settlement 1646–1660* (ed. G. E. Aylmer, 1972) are illuminating. Three recent books on the revolution of 1688 are Maurice Ashley, *The Glorious Revolution of 1688* (1966), John Carswell, *The Descent on England* (1969) and J. R. Jones, *The Revolution of 1688 in England* (1972). The first has been described as straightforward, the last as subtle.

Detailed studies of the membership of parliament include D. Brunton and D. H. Pennington, *Membership of the Long Parliament* (1954), Mary Frear Keeler, *The Long Parliament, 1640–1641* (1954), W. M. Mitchell's and T. L. Moir's books (above) and Robert Walcott, *English Politics in the Early Eighteenth Century* (1956). Professor Walcott's views have been criticized by Professor J. H. Plumb and others. For law see W. S. Holdsworth, *A History of English Law* (1922–1964). An interesting recent book is Stuart E. Prail, *The Agitation for Law Reform during the Puritan Revolution, 1640–1660* (1966).

The best economic history of this period is Charles Wilson, *England's Apprenticeship, 1603–1763* (1965); J. H. Clapham, *Concise Economic History of Britain to 1850* (1949) is a short summary by a considerable economic historian. For agricultural history the best introduction is Lord Ernle, *English Farming Past and Present* (6th ed. 1961). There are also R. Trow-Smith, *English Husbandry* (1951) and various articles by G. E. Fussell. Though dealing with limited areas both W. G. Hoskins, *The Midland Peasant* (1957) and Joan Thirsk, *English Peasant Farming* (1957) throw much light on a difficult subject.

Books on industry include W. H. B. Court, *The Rise of the Midland Industries* (1938), Ralph Davis, *The Rise of the English Shipping Industry in the Seventeenth and Eighteenth Centuries* (1962), J. U. Nef, *The Rise of the British Coal Industry* (1932), A. P. Wadsworth and J. de L. Mann, *The Cotton Trade and Industrial Lancashire, 1660–1780*

(1931). For commerce W. R. Scott, *The Constitution and Finance of English, Scottish and Irish Joint Stock Companies to 1720* (1912) remains a useful introduction, but important new books include K. G. Davies, *The Royal African Company* (1957), R. W. K. Hinton, *The English Trade and the Commonwealth in the Seventeenth Century* (1939); B. E. Supple, *Commercial Crisis and Change in England, 1600–1642* (1959); and A. C. Wood, *A History of the Levant Company* (1935). For wage assessments see R. Keith Kelsall, *Wage Regulations and the Statute of Artificers* (1939). The policy and effectiveness of the navigation acts is examined by L. A. Harper, *The English Navigation Laws* (1939), but articles, among others by R. W. K. Hinton and O. A. Johnsen, supplement and modify this book. For banking see R. D. Richards, *Early History of Banking* (1929), J. H. Clapham, *The Bank of England: a History* (1944) and John Giuseppi, *The Bank of England: a History from its Foundation in 1694* (1966). Recent books on finance include Robert Ashton, *The Crown and the Money Market, 1603–1640* (1960), S. B. Baxter, *The Development of the Treasury, 1660–1702* (1957), and J. Keith Horsefield, *British Monetary Experiments* (1960). There are many studies of merchants and financiers including R. H. Tawney, *Business and Politics under James I* (1959), a study of Lionel Cranfield, Earl of Middlesex.

For social history G. M. Trevelyan, *Illustrated English Social History*, Volume II, *The Age of Shakespeare and the Stuart Period* (1950) is a bright introduction, while Wallace Notestein, *The English People on the Eve of Colonization, 1603–1630* (1954) is excellent for the first part of the century. For an original and sophisticated approach see Peter Laslett, *The World We Have Lost* (1965). This is based upon an examination into population and social structure derived from parish registers and other sources. The statistical methods used are expounded in E. A. Wrigley ed., *The Introduction to English Historical Demography* (1966). A less erudite book is Maurice Ashley, *Life in Stuart England* (revised 1967). Alice Clark, *Working Life of Women in the 17th Century* (1919), throws a vivid sidelight on the labouring classes. For the seamy side of life the recent masterpiece by K. V. Thomas, *Religion and the Decline of Magic* should be consulted. Social life is also dealt with in Charles Wilson's *England's Apprenticeship*.

Important studies of social and professional classes include Lawrence Stone, *The Crisis of the Aristocracy, 1558–1641* (1965) but account should be taken of D. C. Coleman's criticisms in *History* (1966); Mildred Campbell, *The English Yeoman* (1960); A. Simpson, *The Wealth of the Gentry, 1540–1660* (1961); G. E. Aylmer, *The*

King's Servants: The Civil Service of Charles I, 1625–1642 (1961); M. E. Finch, *The Wealth of Five Northamptonshire Families, 1540–1640* (1956).

Recent books on political theory and ideas include Joseph Frank, *The Levellers* (1955), W. H. Greenleaf, *Order, Empiricism and Politics* (1965), William Haller, *Liberty and Reformation in the Puritan Revolution* (1955), C. B. Macpherson, *The Political Theory of Possessive Individualism* (1962) – Professor Macpherson's arguments about the Levellers are not generally accepted – J. G. A. Pocock, *The Ancient Constitution and the Feudal Law* (1954), W. C. Schenck, *The Concern for Social Justice in the Puritan Revolution* (1954) and Perez Zagorin, *A History of Political Thought in the English Revolution* (1954). Professor Zagorin has also written a book entitled *The Court and Country: the Beginning of the English Revolution* (1969) in which he confutes Marxist views. For Professor Stone's latest book on the interminable subject of the origins of the civil war or 'English revolution' see *The Causes of the English Revolution, 1529–1642* (1972). Howard Shaw, *The Levellers* (1968) is a useful brief introduction to the subject. Peter Laslett's introductions to his editions of Filmer and Locke's political treatises are stimulating and of books on Hobbes there is literally no end.

For religion H. O. Wakeman, *A History of the Church of England* (1912) and J. R. H. Moorman, *A History of the Church of England* (1953) are useful summaries. R. G. Usher, *The Reconstruction of the Church of England* and R. S. Bosher, *The Making of the Restoration Settlement* (1954) are important, but both have been criticized. For nonconformity there are R. Tudor Jones, *Congregationalism in England, 1662–1962* (1962), S. B. Babbage, *Puritanism and Richard Bancroft* (1962), W. C. Braithwaite, *The Beginnings of Quakerism* (revised 1955), C. H. and Katherine George, *The Protestant Mind and the English Reformation, 1570–1640* (1961) and George Yule, *The Independents in the Civil War* (1964). For the Roman Catholics see Brian Magee, *The English Recusants* (1938) and Martin J. Havran, *The Catholics in Caroline England* (1962). For the Cambridge Platonists see the book by F. J. Powicke and for the general background W. K. Jordan, *The Development of Religious Toleration in England* (1938). Christopher Hill, *Economic Problems of the Church* (1956) and *Society and Puritanism* (1964) bear on religion from a secular point of view. Dr Hill has written other books on the intellectual history of the first half of the century and a general book entitled *The Age of Revolution*. Two of his latest books are *Anti-Christ in Seventeenth-Century England* (1971) (W. A. Lamont, *Godly Rule: Politics and*

Religion, 1603–1660 (1969) deals with a similar topic) and *The World Turned Upside Down* (1972), his most brilliant book. It should be remembered that all Dr Hill's books are written from a highly sophisticated Marxist standpoint.

The latest biographies of English monarchs are D. H. Willson and David Mathew on James I, Maurice Ashley on Charles II, F. C. Turner on James II, Nesca Robb and S. B. Baxter on William III (both good books with a different approach), Hester Chapman and Elizabeth Hamilton on Mary II and David Green on Queen Anne. There is no thoroughly researched book on Charles I, but John Bowle is writing one. Meanwhile Christopher Hibbert and D. R. Watson have both written excellent texts for two highly illustrated books on the martyred king. C. H. Firth's *Oliver Cromwell*, first published in 1901, cannot be bettered; see also his *Cromwell's Army*, reprinted in 1962 with an introduction by Professor Hardacre. As to biographies of statesmen and others, the following may be recommended: Menna Prestwich on Cranfield, C. V. Wedgwood on Thomas Wentworth, Earl of Strafford, Hugh Trevor-Roper on Laud, Harold Hulme on Eliot, Violet Rowe on Henry Vane the Younger, Pauline Gregg on John Lilburne, J. R. Powell on Robert Blake, B. H. G. Wormald on Clarendon, Sir Arthur Bryant on Samuel Pepys, Andrew Browning on Danby, K. H. D. Haley on Shaftesbury, Dorothy H. Somerville on Shrewsbury, J. H. Kenyon on Sunderland, Sir Tresham Lever on Godolphin, Sir Winston Churchill on Marlborough and (briefer) Ivor F. Burton, *The Captain-General* (1968), Angus MacInnes and Elizabeth Hamilton on Harley, H. T. Dickinson on Bolingbroke.

For literary history Dr C. V. Wedgwood's book in the Home University Library provides an excellent introduction (her *Poetry and Politics under the Stuarts* (1960) should also be read); R. P. McCutcheon deals with the eighteenth century in the same series. An up-to-date book is Boris Ford's *A Guide to English Literature*, vols. 3 and 4 (1961–4). More details will be found in the appropriate volumes of the *Cambridge History of English Literature*. Basil Willey, *The Seventeenth Century Background* (1950) and Sir Herbert Grierson, *Cross Currents in English Literature of the Seventeenth Century* (1929) are both illuminating. Sir Edward Chambers is still the most complete authority on Shakespeare, but A. L. Rowse and Peter Quennell have written the most recent biographies; there are many recent books on Milton; J. H. Hanford has written a good short book, *John Milton, Englishman* (1950). Another is Douglas Bush, *John Milton* (1965). For music, E. Walker, *A History of Music in England*

(1924) may be consulted. For education recent books include W. A. L. Vincent, *The State and School Education* (1950), *The Grammar Schools, their Continuing Tradition* (1969), and Mark H. Curtis, *Oxford and Cambridge in Transition* (1959). For science there are Herbert Butterfield, *Origins of Modern Science* (1949), G. N. Clark, *Science and Social Welfare in the Age of Newton* (1937), W. C. Dampier-Whetham, *A History of Science* (1929), and Richard S. Westfall, *Science and Religion in Seventeenth Century England* (1958). For the theatre Allardyce Nicoll and Bonamy Dobrée are the authorities, while for art M. Whinney and O. Millar, *English Art, 1625–1714* (1950) is indispensable. David Piper is the authority on portraiture.

For the rise of the British empire J. A. Williamson, *A Short History of British Expansion* (1953) makes a good introduction and so do the relevant chapters in the *Cambridge History of the British Empire*, vols. 1 and 4. There is no up-to-date book on India and the East India Company: S. A. Khan, *East India Trade in the Seventeenth Century* (1923) is slight. For Ireland there is Richard Bagwell, *Ireland under the Stuarts* (1936). H. F. Kearney deals with *Strafford in Ireland* (1959) rather severely. G. S. Pryde, *Scotland from 1603 to the Present Day* (1962) covers this period.

It is out of the question to deal here with articles recently published, but keen students should search through the *English Historical Review*, the *Economic History Review*, the *Historical Journal*, *History*, *History Today*, the *Journal of Modern History*, and *Past and Present*; the last has been particularly strong on the seventeenth century.

*   *   *

Two good books which have appeared while this reprint was going to press are *Cromwell Our Chief of Men* by Antonia Fraser and *The Origins of the English Civil War*, edited by Conrad Russell.

SELECT INDEX

MORE ABOUT PENGUINS
AND PELICANS

Penguinews, which appears every month, contains details of all the new books issued by Penguins as they are published. From time to time it is supplemented by *Penguins in Print*, which is a complete list of all books published by Penguins which are in print. (There are well over four thousand of these.)

A specimen copy of *Penguinews* will be sent to you free on request, and you can become a subscriber for the price of the postage – 30p for a year's issues (including the complete lists) if you live in the United Kingdom, or 60p if you live elsewhere. Just write to Dept EP, Penguin Books Ltd, Harmondsworth, Middlesex, enclosing a cheque or postal order, and your name will be added to the mailing list.

Some other books published by Penguins are described on the following pages.

Note: *Penguinews* and *Penguins in Print* are not available in the U.S.A. or Canada

HOBBES

Richard Peters

A PEREGRINE BOOK

In an age of intellectual exploration Thomas Hobbes can be ranked among the Drakes and Magellans of the mind. New ideas and discoveries in mathematics, astronomy, medicine, and mechanics set him off on a course of rational and analytical thinking. In philosophy and politics, as in his inquiries into human thought, senses, and nature, he charted whole new coastlines. Hobbes is often called the father of modern analytical philosophy: he can also claim to be the father of modern psychology.

This study by Richard Peters, which first appeared ten years ago in the Pelican Philosophy Series, is now re-issued in Peregrines as one of the best modern studies of an English thinker whose masterpiece, *Leviathan*, written against the seething intellectual and political background of the seventeenth century, can still be reckoned among the great books in philosophy.

'Dr Peters has surely provided the best critical presentation of the whole Hobbes; an exciting study of intellectual audacity, of breath-taking wrong-headedness, and of driving, all-pervading rationalism' – *Guardian*

THE PELICAN HISTORY OF ENGLAND

While each volume is complete in itself, the whole series has been planned to provide an intelligent and consecutive guide to the development of English society in all its aspects. The nine volumes are:

'As a portent in the broadening of popular culture the influence of this wonderful series has yet to receive full recognition and precise assessment. No venture could be more enterprising or show more confidence in the public's willingness to purchase thoughtful books . . .' – Listener